COLOR by Kristin

How to Design Your Own Beautiful Knits

KRISTIN NICHOLAS

Managing Editor
WENDY WILLIAMS

Editors
MICHELLE BREDESON
ERIN SLONAKER

Art Director
DIANE LAMPHRON

Technical Editor
CARLA SCOTT

Instructions Editor
PAT HARSTE

Model and Location Photography
JOHN GRUEN

Still Life Photography
JACK DEUTSCH

Stylist
JULIE HINES

Hair and Makeup
ELENA LYAKIR

Vice President, Publisher
TRISHA MALCOLM

Creative Director
JOE VIOR

Production Manager
DAVID JOINNIDES

President
ART JOINNIDES

sixth&spring
books

233 Spring Street
New York, NY
10013
sixthandspringbooks.com

Library of Congress Control Number:
2009928035

ISBN: 978-1-933027-83-8

Manufactured in China

3 5 7 9 10 8 6 4 2

First Edition

For my husband,
Mark Duprey,
who keeps life real and
colorful here on our farm.

Contents

A Life in Color

Color is irresistible to me. Rich reds, juicy oranges, spring-fresh greens, heavenly blues...they all find their way into my life and my work. My love affair with fiber and color began when I was a kid, and it hasn't let up.

My First Love: Sewing

You might not realize that my fascination with color started with fabric, not yarn. For years, sewing was my hobby of choice. I learned to sew when I was 9 years old and spent my afternoons after school at Abe's Fabric Store in downtown Dover, New Jersey, picking out fabrics. Abe's is gone now, as sadly so many fabric stores are, but my memories of the floor-to-ceiling bolts of fabric are imprinted deeply on my brain. I loved to pick out a dress or blouse pattern, then scour all the tables and walls stacked with printed, checked, striped, floral and solid fabrics looking for just the right one. I remember carefully choosing just the right shade of thread to match the fabric—and the buttons or zipper that would finish it off. When I got home, I would rip open the thin paper bag and spill the contents onto the sewing table, begging my mom to leave the supper cooking on the stove and come see what I was going to make. After I finished my homework, I would stay up late watching the Mets on the old black-and-white TV and create the garment I would wear to school the next day.

The picture of 70s style in one of my hand-sewn outfits.

Enter Knitting

It didn't stop there. In college I studied textile and clothing design. There I learned all about fibers, fabrics, textile labeling laws, thread count, fashion merchandising, economics (I was awful at that), textile chemistry, surface design, flat pattern making, and draping design. Along the way, I stumbled upon knitting. I had learned to knit when I was 9, but never got very far with it. During college, my mind was awakened to all the techniques and backstory that go into making a piece of cloth. Handknitting intrigued me. It was something that I could do without much equipment, and knitting was portable—great for someone like me who spent a lot of time on public transportation.

On one of my visits back home, my mom and I went to a craft and needlework store called The Craftique, which was full of yarns, stitchery kits, decoupage and basketry supplies, and crochet and knitting needles. I picked out a pattern for a yoke sweater. The shop owner helped me with needles and yarn choices; I left with several colors of green,

blue and silver Candide wool. Mom refreshed me on how to knit and purl. I persevered until I figured out what all the abbreviations meant, and I was off. Never in my wildest dreams did I think that that sweater would be the first of hundreds of colorful knitted projects.

I knit away like a madwoman, eager to be able to actually put the sweater on. I knit the body and the sleeves, joined them all together and started the colorwork yoke section. Before I knew it, I was done. I blocked the sweater, put it on, and felt more accomplished than I had in a very long time. Never mind that I had to shrug my shoulders in because I hadn't carried the yarn floats loosely enough—I wore that sweater to death.

Idea Board

This board hangs in my studio. When I need inspiration, I take a glance at the swatches, photos, postcards and ephemera I've saved over the years, and the ideas inevitably start to flow.

Northwest Adventure

The next year, I went to Corvallis, Oregon, to attend the university there on an exchange program. The Pacific Northwest was so unlike the heavily populated Northeast where I had lived my entire life. In Oregon I traveled, camped, backpacked and began to learn about how incredible the natural world is. I started to notice lilac, orange, fuchsia and mauve sunsets. They were unlike any I had ever seen. I was overwhelmed with the beauty of the pine green forests, the mossy olive green forest floor, the lush green ferns almost as tall as I was, and the grayish-purple peaks of the mountains.

While in Oregon, I immersed myself in textiles. I took as many weaving classes as I could and I learned how to felt raw wool. My friend Janice and I attended a handspinning class held at night at the home of a woman named Thelma. There was a store in Corvallis devoted to the fiber arts. I spent hours there talking to the owner, Charlotte. Besides fibers, yarns, and textile-making tools, the store sold many kinds of ethnic textiles. I totally splurged one day, spending the money I made washing dishes at the dining common on a mola made by the Kuna women of the San Blas Islands of Panama. My love affair with ethnic textiles began that year, and I haven't looked back.

It's funny how life takes you places you never thought you would go. After finishing the

The Jersey Girl, the Farmer and two of our first sheep.

KRISTIN NICHOLAS
Designer • Author

2 round st

Same cuff
as sock.

(there is some ...
under the cuff t...
make it tight.

t folds down over ribbing - a little rib
ck out below cuff.

rev st st chartreus
rev st st magenta

floral chart
background grey
motif squash

rev st st ridge magenta
looped edge chartreus

2x2 Rib in grey

magenta

grey

NASHUA
HANDKNITS
JULIA
Kristin Nicholas

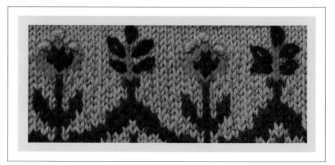

spinning class, I had a whole pile of handspun yarn—I had to do something with it. One of my professors suggested I pick up a book called *Knitting Without Tears* by Elizabeth Zimmermann and a Mon Tricot stitch dictionary. She told me I would be able to figure out how to design a sweater for myself from the handspun yarn with those two tools and some knitting needles. Off I went to make my first original sweater design.

While I was living in Oregon, I met a boy from a dairy farm in western Massachusetts. Mark was so different from anyone I had ever met. He loved the outdoors, hiking, exploring the mountains, and animals. He was studying sheep production, and he took me to the sheep barns on the university farms. I was smitten—with the boy, the sheep and their wool, and the way of life that farmers live.

My Career in Color

Several years later, after marrying "the boy" and starting a small flock of sheep, I was hired by a small yarn company in Massachusetts, where I was allowed to create my own title. I chose "Creative Director"—I thought it had a nice ring to it. For sixteen years, I designed yarn, colorways for yarn, handknitting patterns for sweaters, and advertising campaigns, and I desktop-published whatever needed to be done. I traveled the world in search of beautiful yarns for handknitters. I had fallen into my dream job.

Along the way, I discovered I had a real knack for working with color, although it was always there—something I just did. I didn't know that there was a call for it or that it could become a career. At the yarn company, I honed all my knitting and designing skills—I made it my personal goal to inspire knitters by giving them beautiful color palettes in natural fibers. But I also had to think of the bottom line. It was one big challenge.

When I introduced a new yarn, I always brought in a wide color range. I learned that even if some of the shades wouldn't sell as well as others, they would make the color card look complete and be more seductive to the shop owner. I always loved the odd shades (I can't get enough chartreuse or caramel), and I started to design knitting patterns that used many colors together. One of my bestselling designs was a yoke sweater that I colored in offbeat shades in our lovely mohair. We sold bag after bag of mohair, and lo and behold, our little company became known for its innovative colors. A few years later, I followed my knitting instincts and boldly introduced ethnically inspired booklets featuring instructions for socks, hats, and even little dolls. The booklets were packaged with enough yarn to make a little project. They, too, became a huge hit.

Farm Living

All this led me to where I am now, working with color and fibers and living a life I love. I live on a farm in western Massachusetts with my farmer, Mark, and our little girl, Julia. I have my own beautiful mohair/alpaca/wool blend yarn (named *Julia*), which is sold in the U.S. and Canada. We have (at this writing) more than three hundred sheep, twenty-five exotic egg-laying chickens, two Border Collies who help keep everything in line, and more cats than I'd

dare to count. I'm living life—making it up as I go along—and trying to bring all my interests together to make a living and keep being creative.

Our farmhouse is set into the side of a hill in a northerly Massachusetts town bordering Vermont. It was built in 1751; it's old and solid, and I wonder every day about the family who built it. I have filled it with the things I love—colorful ceramics, Persian rugs, ethnic textiles, yarn and fabric, and a library full of art, knitting, craft and animal husbandry books. I hand-painted the walls in wacky patterns and colors. I paint pictures to decorate the walls because I can't afford other people's art. Occasionally there's a lamb or two in the kitchen being nursed back to health. Outside, there's an abandoned apple orchard, fields where our sheep graze, and a spectacular hillside to hike where we can see for miles. I grow veggies and flowers and am surrounded by bountiful, colorful, glorious nature. It is at our farmhouse and the surrounding land that the photos in this book were shot.

I love living amongst nature and all its quirks. I am continually astounded by the colors I see. The shapes of leaves and blossoms, the way nature casually throws together drop-dead gorgeous combinations. Over the years, I have learned to pay attention just in case a serendipitous color or pattern moment occurs. I run for my camera to record it, hoping that the photo turns out as good as the nature in front of me. Later I grab some yarn or some paint and record the moment in a swatch or on canvas.

About This Book

I'm hoping that with this book I can bring part of my love of color and pattern to your knitting world. The projects mix them up with wild abandon, like the nature and ethnic textiles I find so inspiring. All of these projects are knit using the Fair Isle technique, an age-old method of knitting practiced by knitters the world over. Named for an island off the coast of Scotland, Fair Isle (stranded) knitting is made by knitting with only two colors in a row, following a chart. The projects here are made at a friendly gauge of 5 stitches per inch so that you'll actually be able to finish them.

I like to take my Fair Isle knitting to a different level. On top of my two-color patterns, I add embroidery, done after the knitting is complete, to further decorate the work. With a handful of easy embroidery stitches, it's not difficult to transform what looks to be a plain piece of two-color knitting into something fanciful.

I've spent a good thirty years knitting and designing and honing my skills. Knitting keeps me interested because I like to create new designs that are totally original to me. I'm hoping that you too will feel the passion to create your own designs and learn to decorate. By following my lead, you'll be on the road to learning about and exploring color. You'll be able to design your own Fair Isle patterns, and you'll learn to embellish your knits with embroidery on your own. And you'll put all of this knowledge to use knitting more than 25 colorful garments, accessories and home décor projects.

Most of all, I hope this book will help you find joy and creativity in colorful Fair Isle knitting! ■

RED
Geranium

RED-VIOLET
Magenta

RED-ORANGE
Harvest Spice

VIOLET
Purple Basil

CHAPTER I

The Joy of Color

John Ruskin once wrote, "I know well that happiness is in little things." For me, happiness is a little thing called color. Color is all around me and all around you.

I see fabulous combinations of color in the everyday scenes on our farm, color in packaging at the grocery store, color in my garden, color in the magazines that come in my mailbox, and color in the lovely yarns, paints and fabrics I use in my work. No matter what kind of project I undertake, whether knitting, crochet, embroidery, painting, sewing, or decorating, color is the driving force behind its creation.

Working with color is creative and fun. In fact, you can spend your entire life learning about color. When you are just beginning to experiment with color in your knitting, it can all be a little overwhelming. Just walking into a yarn store stocked to the ceiling with delicious yarns in fabulous colors can cause sensory overload and a feeling of bewilderment. This is a very normal reaction. Sorting out all the color options takes skill and practice.

As you work with color, you will begin to develop your own color comfort level. Each combination of colors will get easier to put together and more successful. You'll even begin to develop your own color style. Soon you'll be like me, obsessing about the perfect shade of periwinkle or fuchsia to combine with chartreuse or pumpkin to make the sweater of your dreams.

When first beginning to work with color, an artist's color wheel, available at your local craft store, is a very helpful tool. You can use a printed color wheel to help you build your own yarn color wheel from your stash of yarn as I have done here.

BLUE-VIOLET
Dried Lavender

BLUE
Bright Blue

BLUE-GREEN
Blue Thyme

GREEN
Spring Green

YELLOW-GREEN
Lady's Mantle

ORANGE
Persimmon

**YELLOW-
ORANGE**
Squash

YELLOW
Golden Honey

Using a Color Wheel

First up, let's talk about the color wheel, a tool that was developed by Sir Isaac Newton in 1699. The color wheel shows how colors relate to each other. I like to think of a color wheel as a rainbow in the round. You can build your own wheel out of yarn like I've done on the opposite page. The wheel is built around the three primary colors—red, blue and yellow—and all the other colors are made of combinations of these colors. Mix and match colors from the wheel to determine your own color schemes.

Colors that are close to each other on the wheel are called **analogous.** Knitting these colors together will create a piece of fabric that is calming and soothing. Analogous color combinations are the choice of most knitters because they are safe choices. Personally, I find combinations like this a bit boring.

Colors that are opposite each other on the wheel are called **complementary** or contrasting colors. Red and green, blue and orange, and yellow and violet are all complementary combinations. These colors when knit together make your work vibrate. They are exciting to look at and fun to knit and wear. I get a joyful feeling when I work with complementary color combinations.

The third classic color combination is the **tertiary** combination or triad. Draw an imaginary triangle with three equal sides on top of the wheel. The colors at each point of the triangle will form a tertiary combination. The primary colors—red, yellow and blue—form a tertiary combination, as do orange, purple and green. Tertiary combinations tend to be loud, jarring and quite lively.

Neutral-Free Zone

You'll probably notice that there's a lack of white and black in my designs. Generally, I don't work with black or white. I find that they make things stagnant. I'd rather use a very dark shade of brown or red instead of black—it makes a piece more interesting. In general, I don't use white because it gives a spare, minimalist feeling to patterns. I would much rather celebrate color in all its glory by combining many shades together. (I used this swatch to design the Little Shepherd's Scrap Yarn Scarf on page 58.)

The Importance of Swatching

Learning about the relationships between colors is important, but you won't really see or understand them until you swatch.

Not only are the colors themselves important; the value of the colors makes a world of difference. Simply put, value is the lightness or darkness of a color. In order for your pattern motif to stand out from the background of the fabric, the colors you use must be different in value. If the values are not different enough, there will be no differentiation, and the motifs will disappear. Using the color wheel will energize your colorwork—swatch to see how the effects come alive.

Here, you can see a swatch knit in an analogous combination of two shades of blue that have similar values. Notice how the lightness and darkness of the shades are not different enough for the pattern to stand out.

This swatch is knit in the same motif with two blues as the one at left, but one blue is a much darker value. In this swatch the flower design really stands out.

Next you can see a swatch in which I have worked the motif in orange—blue's complement. This swatch has a totally different feeling than the previous swatches knit in just blues.

I then worked a swatch like the one on the right above with two different values of blue, but I added a third complementary color in duplicate stitch to outline the motif. This addition breaks up the two very similar colors and makes it a more interesting and complex combination.

In this last example I morphed the complementary combination into something totally different by adding embroidery and duplicate stitch in several colors. You can see that by getting creative with a needle after you are done with knitting you can totally transform a piece of work into something new and fresh.

After only a few swatches, it is possible to learn a lot about color and what works best in combination.

Color Is All Around You

As you begin to open your eyes and explore more of what color has to offer, you'll find that the world around you can be your best teacher. Color is easily learned by just opening your eyes and letting it all sink in.

Nature is my favorite teacher. The beautiful color combinations found every day in nature are enough to keep me knitting swatches for years. Vivid purple iris against green foliage would make a fabulous swatch. Autumn leaves juxtaposed with a bright blue sky would vibrate in intensity when swatched.

A trip to a museum can fuel more swatches. Artists such as Matisse, Bonnard, Cézanne, Picasso and O'Keeffe became darlings of the art world because of the way they combined colors. Study their works, and you will begin to understand how they worked with color. And don't forget to look at paintings close up if you have the opportunity. You'll see that an artist's rendition of green may not be straight green but a combination of yellow, blue, and purple painted skillfully on a canvas. Translate that idea to a swatch and see what happens.

Closer to home, there is plenty of inspiration, too. Open a shelter magazine, and you'll see pages of color combinations to copy and glean ideas from. Develop a color file full of tear sheets from magazines. When your color well is dry, reach into it and see what swatches these images inspire. Do you have a favorite print on a chair or scarf? Why not choose yarn colors to emulate that favorite combination and turn it into a piece of knitwear?

The more you work with color, the more skilled you will become. Every colorful swatch you knit will be better and better. You'll be on your own path to becoming a great colorist. Your color confidence will increase, and you will feel more at ease with your own personal color choices. Keep at it! ■

Fair Isle Made Easy

Knitting as a textile craft has been practiced by many cultures throughout the world.
No one knows where or when two-color stranded knitting—what we generally call "Fair Isle"
knitting—first began. The stranded technique makes a fabric that is very thick due
to the use of two colors in every row, so it is easy to see why cultures in colder
climates embraced two-color knitting.

The term Fair Isle comes from an actual small island among the hundred Shetland Islands, which are off the coast of Scotland not far from Norway. On the real Fair Isle and other inhabited Shetland islands, knitters have practiced two-color knitting for hundreds of years. The nearby Scandinavian countries of Norway, Denmark and Sweden all celebrate two-color knitting in their folk costume.

In museums throughout the world, there are samples of this kind of knitting from all over the globe. The Metropolitan Museum of Art in New York City has a sock with Fair Isle stripes on it dating to between the eleventh and fourteenth centuries. Fair Isle knitting is practiced in Iran, Iraq and Egypt in the Middle East. Eastern European countries including Georgia, the Ukraine, Hungary, Serbia, Bulgaria, Macedonia, Anatolia, Albania and Greece all have two-color knitting traditions.

Across the Atlantic in the Southern Hemisphere, the Andean cultures of Peru and Bolivia have a rich knitting history of colorful hats, masks and arm- and legwarmers. Their incredibly intricate knit pieces all use Fair Isle knitting to create their fabulously patterned, finely stitched pieces of folk art, often featuring animal motifs including llamas, alpacas and birds.

As you can see, calling it "Fair Isle" knitting is actually a misnomer! Call it what you may—"Fair Isle," "two colored" or "stranded" knitting—just try it and you'll see why I am only one of thousands of knitters who are intrigued and fascinated by this challenging, beautiful knitting technique.

THE DREADED, ALTHOUGH MOST IMPORTANT, GAUGE

It's unavoidable and must be said first: You must do a gauge swatch before you start to knit. If you will be knitting in the round, you must work your gauge swatch in the round. Every knitter's tension varies when working in the round compared with back and forth knitting. Gauge will even vary on different days. We all have good and bad knitting days. Some nights when you are trying to relax from an awful day at the office by knitting, your gauge is so darn tight the knitting barely stretches. Then there are the weekend knitting hours when your knitting flows loosely off the needles.

To make a gauge swatch in the round, choose your preferred method of small-circumference working in the round, whether with double-pointed needles, a short circular needle, or the technique known as Magic Loop. Cast on more stitches than you think you'll need so that the swatch is roomy even when worked in the round. Always block the swatch before measuring the gauge, as this gives you the most accurate representation of how the work is knitting up and helps you to match the written instructions flawlessly.

Note that your gauge may even vary from colorwork pattern to colorwork pattern. I have devised a rather fun project (page 23) for which gauge won't matter. It's a draft dodger for your window or your door, made up of many swatches. Test out the colorwork pattern you will be working for whichever project in the book you chose by knitting up the swatch. Keep the funny little tube in your knitting bag and add to it with more gauge swatches over the course of many projects. Eventually you'll have a lovely little piece of knitting that when filled with dried beans and sewn together makes for a useful home item. Or make your gauge swatches a little wider and put them together for a skinny scarf for a little person in your life (page 26).

The How-to of Fair Isle Knitting

There are a lot of knitters out there who are terrified of knitting with two colors. Perhaps you are one of them. If you are, these instructions will help calm your nerves and take the mystery out of working with two colors. But don't fret, it's just knitting consecutive stitches with different strands of yarn. Still, there are tricks to getting it right. Let's start with the basics.

HOLDING BOTH YARNS

Every knitter will find the method of holding two yarns that works for them. It's definitely a matter of personal preference and comfort.

Let's start with how I knit with two colors: Normally, I am a continental knitter. I carry my yarn in my left hand and "pick" the stitches with the right needle. I also know how to knit the English or American way, commonly called "throwing the yarn," in which you manipulate the yarn with your right hand. When you have both these techniques under your belt, you can knit with two colors pretty quickly by holding a color in each hand. Simply follow your chart (more about charts soon) and "pick and throw" your way around.

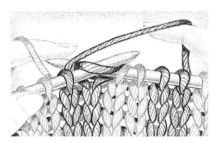

1. Hold the working yarn in your right hand and the non-working yarn in your left hand. Bring the working yarn over the top of the yarn in your left hand and knit with the right hand to the next color change.

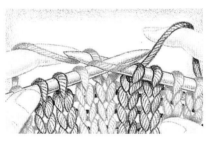

2. The yarn in your right hand is now the non-working yarn; the yarn in your left hand is the working yarn. Bring the working yarn under the non-working yarn and knit with the left hand to the next color change. Repeat steps 1 and 2.

If knitting with both hands is awkward or uncomfortable and you normally throw with your right, you can still knit Fair Isle, picking up each color as needed—it will just be a bit slower.

1. Drop the working yarn. Bring the new color (now the working yarn) over the top of the dropped yarn and work to the next color change.

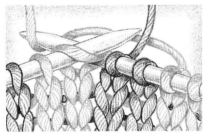

2. Drop the working yarn. Bring the new color under the dropped yarn and work to the next color change. Repeat steps 1 and 2.

It's really up to you to decide which method works best. Remember, there is no wrong way to knit. It's completely up to your personal sense of what works best for you.

HANDLING TWO COLORS AT ONCE

When working a Fair Isle chart, there will be one color you are knitting with and one yarn that is resting. To carry the color not being knit, just let it float at the back side of the work. When it's time to knit with the unused color again, pick it up and take a stitch with it. Make sure you don't pull this yarn too tightly across the back of the work, or it will pucker. Too loose is better than too tight. I separate my stitches on my right-hand needle, pulling them apart, then make a stitch with the new color. This guarantees that the floats will be nice and loose.

Maintaining Tension

When first learning to knit with the Fair Isle technique, you will be a bit timid and, most likely, tense. Tension and Fair Isle knitting don't mix, so take a deep breath and think loose—looser than you can imagine. I say this from experience. When I made my first Fair Isle yoke sweater, my floats were too tight. That sweater was always uncomfortable to wear.

When the stranded yarn is pulled too tight across the back of the work, it is impossible to loosen it by blocking. Stretching your floats every 5 to 10 stitches helps, too—it keeps everything even and loose as you go, when the yarn is still free to move. Just spread the last 5 to 10 stitches you worked apart slightly on the right-hand needle and keep knitting normally.

What should you do with those puckery, tight knits when they do happen? Throw them in the washing machine and felt them for potholders!

MANAGING LONG FLOATS

The "float" is the length of yarn that occurs on the backside of the fabric when the unused yarn spans several stitches. Floats can get snagged on rings, fingers, keys or other sharp objects, distorting the front of the fabric, so it is customary to catch them into the back of the knitted work as you go. The general rule most knitters follow is that if the unused yarn isn't being knit with for six stitches or more, it should be caught in the back of the work. As with most techniques in knitting, there are a few ways you can do it.

Twisting

I prefer to twist the two yarns. It is easy and makes a neat backside to the fabric. The fabric remains flexible, soft and "knit-like." Here's how you do it:

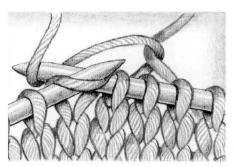

Twist the working yarn and the carried yarn around each other once. Then continue knitting with the same color as before.

Weaving

Other knitters I know like to weave the yarn into the back of the work. This results in a very neat backside. The only downside of this technique is that the fabric becomes thicker and stiffer.

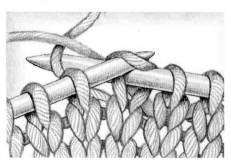

1. Hold working yarn in right hand and yarn to be woven in your left. To weave yarn above a knit stitch, bring it over right needle. Knit stitch with working yarn, bringing it under woven yarn.

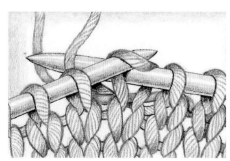

2. The woven yarn will go under the next knit stitch. With the working yarn, knit the stitch, bringing the yarn over the woven yarn. Repeat steps 1 and 2 to the next color change.

If you have the time and energy, teach yourself both the twisting and weaving techniques and use the one that seems most appropriate for what you are working on. The twisting technique does result in lots of untwisting of yarn balls; as long as you keep untwisting them every few rows, they won't become too cumbersome. The weaving technique is a little trickier to learn; use it for thick, sturdy fabrics such as on a coat, winter mittens, or potholders.

JOINING A NEW COLOR

To join a new color, simply drop the first color of yarn, pick up your second color of yarn, and begin knitting with it, leaving a tail of about 4 inches. I don't do anything fancy except this: As you are working your project, there may be a bit of a hole where you joined the second color. When you are done, tighten up the hole by gently tugging on the tail of the added color. Then, using a blunt tapestry needle, weave the new color through the backs of the stitches, making sure it doesn't show on the front side of the work. Clip the tail, leaving about ½" loose. Leaving a tail will keep the end from working itself to the outside of the fabric during wear and washing.

This isn't the only way to join a new color of yarn. Some knitters prefer to knot the second color with the first color. Others weave in the tail immediately (see Weaving, above). It's personal preference!

Working in the Round

Almost all of the projects in this book are knit in the round on circular or double-pointed needles. Fair Isle knitting is much easier to work in the round. When knitting in the round, you will always be knitting on the right side of the work, so you only have to knit. This also means that when reading a chart, you will always be reading the chart from right to left as you knit—no need to switch on every row. Circular knitting makes efficient use of a knitter's time and skills in Fair Isle knitting.

If you choose to work Fair Isle back and forth on straight needles, knitting from charts is more of a challenge. Work the chart from right to left on the right side of the fabric. Work the chart from left to right on the wrong side of the fabric.

I admit to finding working colorwork (or any) charts backward difficult. This is my excuse for falling onto the "circular knitting" bandwagon. My purl stitches are always slightly off in tension, so circular knitting is a better choice for me. And then there is my addiction to color and pattern and the ease of doing it in the round. All these quirky things have led me to become a circular groupie. Try it and you'll never look back.

WORKING ON DOUBLE-POINTED NEEDLES

When I first learned to knit, I watched with fascination as my Aunt Addie crafted beautiful Norwegian mittens for her children using wool yarn on double-pointed needles. When I began knitting in earnest during my college days, I bought myself some double-pointed needles, as the pattern I was following instructed. I quickly learned that knitting with double-pointed needles wasn't too hard.

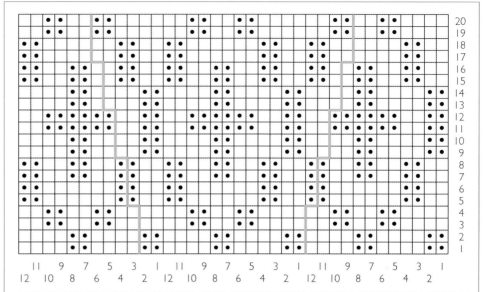

Increasing for Sleeves

Increasing in a Fair Isle color pattern at the underarm of a sleeve is a bit tricky at first. In all of the patterns in this book, I added a decorative two-stitch alternating color stripe at the underarm, which identifies the underarm in a decorative way and acts as a guide to where the increases should be made. Following the written instructions, increase in the color that will be next on the chart. I use an m1 or a simple backward loop cast-on for my increase because it is easy and it disappears into the work nicely. As with all knitting, there are many different ways to increase, and each knitter has a preference.

If you can't easily tell from looking at the chart which color would be above the increase, make three photocopies of the chart and tape them together. Draw increase lines, as on the chart above, to follow their path.

The ugly part was the holes that developed between each needle. I quickly learned to make the first two stitches I knit on each double-pointed needle a little tighter than I thought they should be, and the holes would disappear. Times have changed, and you can now purchase circular needles that are only 12 inches around, which works nicely for sleeves. I still prefer my double points, though, as my hands are large and I feel too confined on those little things.

GETTING STARTED IN THE ROUND

To knit in the round on double-pointed needles, cast the required number of stitches onto three needle. Make sure your cast-on is loose. Divide the stitches evenly onto three needles, taking care not to twist. Draw them into a triangular shape and work the first stitch, which will join the cast-on stitches into a circle. That's it. Knit until the needle is empty, and then use the empty needle to knit from the next needle full of stitches. The same principle applies when working on a circular needle—cast on loosely, then orient the work so that you're about to knit the very first stitch cast on, being careful not to twist the cast-on edge stitches. That's it!

It's very useful—almost crucial—to place a marker to mark the beginning of the round, lest you lose your place midway. When working on double-pointed needles, place the marker one stitch in from the beginning of the round and one stitch before the end of the round. When working on circular needles, place a marker between the first and last stitches and slip it each round.

No Twisted Edges

I'm a bit impatient and find messing about with joining the cast-on stitches perfectly without twisting a bit tedious. To make my knitting more enjoyable, I usually work a couple of rows back and forth on my double-pointed needles. (On the wrong side, I switch the knits and the purls so that the edge pattern will be correct.) When I do join my stitches in the round, I am positive that they won't be twisted.

How to Follow a Fair Isle Chart

A graphed chart is a road map to building your knitted fabric. But how do you read a chart? A knitting chart is made
up of little boxes with symbols or colors in them. Each box represents a stitch. Start reading the chart at the bottom right corner.
Each horizontal row represents the repeat you will follow when knitting a row or round of knitting.
After a complete round is done, move up to the second row of boxes on the chart (or round 2) and follow its symbols.
Soon, you will see the chart becoming fabric before your eyes. It really is quite a magical process.
As you continue to knit, you'll notice that the pattern repeat becomes almost automatic.
You will memorize it and have to refer to the chart less and less.

ALL ABOUT CHARTS

Sometimes you will knit from a chart and the pattern repeat will be an exact multiple of the number of stitches needed for the project. For instance: A hat is knit circularly on 60 stitches and the colorwork chart repeat is 5 stitches wide.

Begin by knitting Round 1, working stitches 1 to 5 (from right to left, remember). Keep repeating them around the work until you have finished the round. Then begin Round 2 and repeat it until the end of the round.

Occasionally, a pattern repeat will not be an exact multiple of the stitches needed for the pattern. The goal is to have the pattern centered within the fabric, making it a balanced design. For instance, if you were to cast on 66 stitches and you chose a pattern with a stitch repeat of 12 stitches, the pattern would not fit perfectly. To center the pattern, divide 66 by 12 to get 5 complete repeats with 6 stitches left over. In order for the pattern to be centered, you need to split the 6 remaining stitches in half—6 divided by 2 is 3. This means that you will need to work the last 3 stitches and the first 3 stitches of the pattern repeat on either side of the work.

The lower chart shows how this is done. The repeated section is clearly outlined by the box, and the stitches on either side are the ones that help to center the pattern.

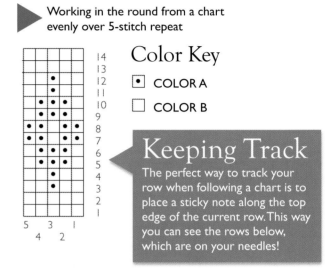

Working in the round from a chart evenly over 5-stitch repeat

Color Key

⊡ COLOR A

☐ COLOR B

Keeping Track

The perfect way to track your row when following a chart is to place a sticky note along the top edge of the current row. This way you can see the rows below, which are on your needles!

Large chart showing repeat box over 12-stitch repeat and 20 rounds. The stitches outside the red repeat box on the right and left sides will make the pattern be centered.

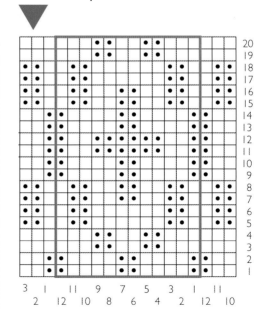

Centering a Pattern Repeat

Sometimes you will want to center a pattern repeat with an even amount of space above and below. You'll need to determine how many times the repeat can fit in whole, then split the remainder at the top and bottom. To do that, work a gauge swatch to determine your row gauge. Suppose your knitting needs to be 14 inches long and your row gauge is 6 stitches per inch. Determine the number of rows in the 14-inch piece: 14 inches times 6 rows = 84 rows. If your pattern chart is 20 rows long, you will be able to get 4 complete repeats of the pattern into the 84 rows with 4 left over. To make the pattern fit perfectly, work Rows 19 and 20, then work Rows 1 to 20 4 times for 80 rows, then work Rows 1 and 2.

Fair Isle Magic: The Steek

First of all, what is a steek? Briefly, a steek is an extra set of stitches knit into a garment which will become a seam later on. A steek makes it possible to knit sweaters (or anything for that matter) in the round that later need to be seamed or have a zipper or edging added to them without ever having to switch to knitting flat. One big tube can be strategically cut to make the front and back of a sweater, as long as you prep the knitting by adding steeks. I knit my steeks in alternate colors (knit 1 dark, knit 1 light) so that the yarns are caught into the fabric, making a sturdy steek. On the next round, I swap the colors—a little check fabric develops.

Steeks are tucked in where they are needed—sometimes continuous with the knitting (as for an armhole—A) and sometimes after binding off a few stitches (as for a neck—B).

Next, set your machine to a medium zig-zag stitch. You'll now stabilize the two center stitches of the steek separately. Find the two center stitches and stitch down them one at a time (D). It is important to keep the knit fabric flat and neat while stitching. Do not pull on it as you sew, or it will distort and ripple.

Now, take a deep breath, and using a sharp pair of scissors, cut between the two center rows of stitches (E). Be careful not to snip the sewing machine stitches (although probably nothing much will happen if you do). Be careful when you come to the end of the armhole steek so you don't inadvertently clip the main part of your sweater!

That's all there is to it. The opening for the sleeve or the neck is now present, and the pattern will give you more directions on picking up for the edging or sewing on the other parts.

Before you begin cutting into the steek, you need to block it and then stabilize it. There are different methods for stabilizing—some people crochet along the inner edge. I use my trusty old Bernina sewing machine to stitch my steeks before cutting them, which ensures that nothing comes apart in the process. In these photos, I have used white thread so you can see the seams, but matching thread is a good idea. Set the machine to a straight stitch and sew between the stitches on the outside of the steek stitches (C). I call this "stitching in the ditch"—the machine stitching will actually disappear. Do this on both sides of the steek.

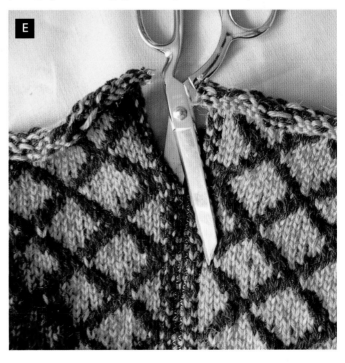

The Miracle of Duplicate Stitch

Duplicate stitch is an easy embroidery technique used to actually "duplicate" a knitted stitch. I use duplicate stitch to embellish my Fair Isle patterns with additional colors—the sky's the limit! Once you learn duplicate stitch, you'll find it is one of those life-changing techniques you will use often in your knitting. You simply stitch atop existing stitches, following them exactly—they cover the old stitches and no one's the wiser.
Just like when you were learning to carry a second color, think loose. The stitched color should float above the work, almost giving a raised look to the fabric. Don't pull the stitching thread too tight or it will disappear. Here's how you do it.

Cut a length of yarn in the color you will be stitching, and thread it into a blunt tapestry needle. I find that a sharp needle tends to split the yarn as I'm stitching, which slows me down and has messy results. On the back, directly behind where the duplicate stitch is to begin, take two small stitches into a small bit of the yarn (I usually split the yarn here). By doing this, nothing shows through on the right side.

Next, come up to the front of the stitch through the bottom opening of the stitch you want to cover.

Follow the legs of the stitch to where they loop through the stitch above it.

Go back down through the bottom. At the same time, poke the needle through the next stitch opening.

Repeat until design is complete.

Stitch loosely so that the fabric isn't distorted, and don't worry if the stitches aren't covered perfectly—I personally think the fabric looks more interesting if a little of the original knitted color shows through.

Bring the needle to the backside and weave the needle through the back of the stitches to end off. I clip the thread, leaving about ¾ to 1"; I prefer leaving a longer tail so that it won't pop through to the right side with wear.

Those are the main issues you'll need to deal with when Fair Isle knitting. It may sound like a lot to take in, but don't be intimidated. Once you start working in Fair Isle, it will make more sense, and the more you do it, the better you'll get. Trust me!

PRACTICE PROJECT

Chill Stopper

When you are first beginning to work with color, small knitted items with no shaping are perfect learning projects. This window or door snake is a fun and quick project. It's worked in a long tube that is filled with dried beans, then sewn closed at both ends.

FINISHED MEASUREMENTS
Approx 34"/86.5cm long x 6"/15cm circumference

YARN
Nashua Handknits *Julia* (wool/mohair/alpaca), 1¾oz/50g, 93yd/85m
A Gourd NHJ1784—1 skein
B Velvet Moss NHJ6086—1 skein
C Squash NHJ0120—1 skein
D Lady's Mantle NHJ3961—1 skein
E Berry Berry NHJ0124—1 skein
F Steel Gray NHJ0122—1 skein
G Dried Lavender NHJ8126—1 skein
H Coleus NHJ4345—1 skein
I Dried Wheat NHJ0128—1 skein

NEEDLES
One set (4) each sizes 5 and 7 (3.75 and 4.5mm) double-pointed needles (dpns) *or size needed to obtain correct gauge*

Stitches
STOCKINETTE STITCH
Knit every round.

REVERSE STOCKINETTE STITCH RIDGE
Rnd 1 Knit.
Rnds 2 and 3 Purl.
Work rnds 1–3 for rev St st ridge.

NOTIONS
◆ Stitch marker
◆ Tapestry needle
◆ 1½lb/350g of small dried beans

GAUGE
20 sts and 22 rnds = 4"/10cm in St st over chart pats using larger dpns. *Be sure to obtain correct gauge.*

DOOR/WINDOW SNAKE
With smaller dpns and A, cast on 30 sts. Divide sts evenly between 3 dpns. Join, taking care not to twist sts on needle, pm for beg of rnds.
Reverse stockinette stitch ridge
Rnds 1–3 Work rnds 1–3 of rev St st ridge. Break A. Change to B.

Beg chart I
NOTE All one-color rnds are worked on smaller dpns and all two-color rnds are worked on larger dpns.
Cont in St st on all sts as foll:
Rnd 1 Work 5-st pat rep 6 times. Cont to foll chart in this manner through rnd 10. Break yarns. Change to smaller dpns and D.
Reverse stockinette stitch ridge
Rnds 1–3 Work rnds 1–3 of rev St st ridge. Break D. Change to C.

Beg chart II
NOTE All rnds are worked on larger dpns.
Cont in St st on all sts as foll:
Use A for first color, E for second color and F for third color.

CHART I
MULTIPLE OF 5 sts

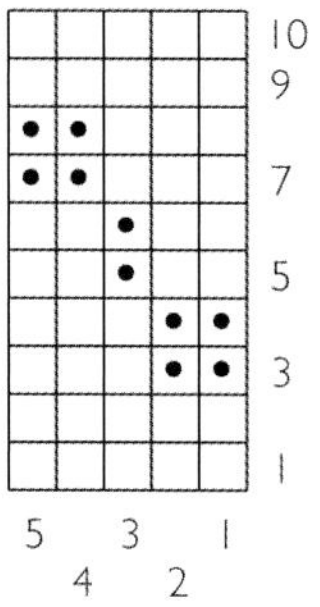

Color Key
☐ **B** Velvet Moss
▣ **C** Squash

CHART II
MULTIPLE OF 5 sts

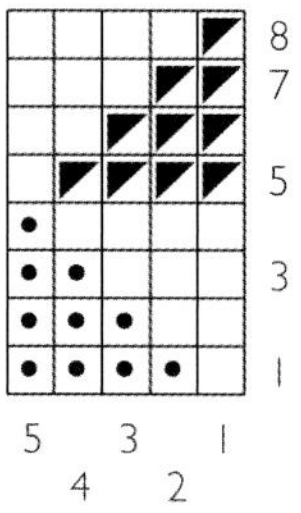

Color Key
☐ First Color
▣ Second Color
◪ Third Color

CHART III
MULTIPLE OF 5 sts

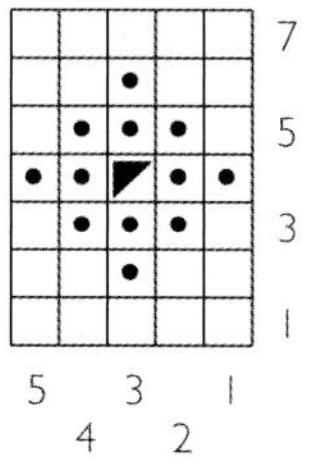

Color Key
☐ **A** Gourd
◪ **C** Squash
▣ **H** Coleus

Rnds 1–8 Work 5-st pat rep 6 times. Cont to foll chart in this manner through rnd 8. Break yarns. Change to D.
Use D for first color, F for second color and G for third color.
Rnds 9–16 Work 5-st pat rep 6 times. Cont to foll chart in this manner through rnd 8. Break yarns. Change to C.
Use C for first color, G for second color and E for third color.
Rnds 17–24 Work 5-st pat rep 6 times. Cont to foll chart in this manner through rnd 8. Break yarns. Change to B.
Reverse stockinette stitch ridge
Rnds 1–3 Work rnds 1–3 of rev St st ridge. Break B. Change to A.

Beg chart III
NOTE All one-color rnds are worked on smaller dpns and all two-color rnds are worked on larger dpns.
Cont in St st on all sts as foll:
Rnd 1 Work 5-st pat rep 6 times. Cont to foll chart in this manner through rnd 7. Break yarns. Change to smaller dpns and F.
Reverse stockinette stitch ridge
Rnds 1–3 Work rnds 1–3 of rev St st ridge. Break F. Change to I.

Beg chart IV
NOTE All one-color rnds are worked on smaller dpns and all two-color rnds are worked on larger dpns. Cont in St st on all sts as foll:
Rnd 1 Work 5-st pat rep 6 times. Cont to foll chart in this manner through rnd 9. Break yarns. Change to smaller dpns and A.
Reverse stockinette stitch ridge
Rnds 1–3 Work rnds 1–3 of rev St st ridge. Break A. Change to H.

Beg chart V
NOTE All one-color rnds are worked on smaller dpns and all two-color rnds are worked on larger dpns.
Cont in St st on all sts as foll:

Rnd 1 Work 5-st pat rep 6 times. Cont to foll chart in this manner through rnd 8. Break yarns. Change to smaller dpns and I.
Reverse stockinette stitch ridge
Rnds 1–3 Work rnds 1–3 of rev St st ridge. Break I. Change to G.

Beg chart VI
NOTE All rnds are worked on larger dpns. Cont in St st on all sts as foll:
Rnd 1 Work 5-st pat rep 6 times. Cont to foll chart in this manner through rnd 6. Break yarns. Change to smaller dpns and H.
Reverse stockinette stitch ridge
Rnds 1–3 Work rnds 1–3 of rev St st ridge. Break I. Change to C.

Beg chart VII
NOTE All one-color rnds are worked on smaller dpns and all two-color rnds are worked on larger dpns. Cont in St st on all sts as foll:
Rnd 1 Work 5-st pat rep 6 times. Cont to foll chart in this manner through rnd 12. Break yarns. Change to smaller dpns and G.
Reverse stockinette stitch ridge
Rnds 1–3 Work rnds 1-3 of rev St st ridge. Break G. Change to E.

Beg chart VIII
NOTE All rnds are worked on larger dpns.
Cont in St st on all sts as foll:
Rnd 1 Work 5-st pat rep 6 times. Cont to foll chart in this manner through rnd 5. Rep rnds 1–5 once more, then rnds 1–3 once. Break yarns. Change to smaller dpns and H.
Reverse stockinette stitch ridge
Rnds 1–3 Work rnds 1–3 of rev St st ridge. Break H. Change to A.

Notes
1. For chart pats, all one-color rnds are worked on smaller dpns and all two-color rnds are worked on larger dpns.
2. All rev St st ridges are worked on smaller dpns.

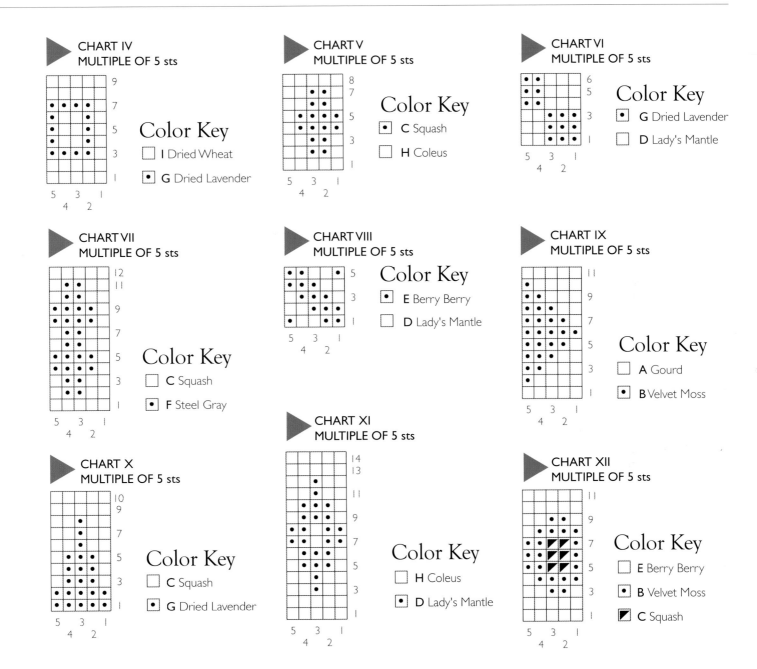

CHART IV
MULTIPLE OF 5 sts

Color Key

☐ **I** Dried Wheat

⊡ **G** Dried Lavender

CHART V
MULTIPLE OF 5 sts

Color Key

⊡ **C** Squash

☐ **H** Coleus

CHART VI
MULTIPLE OF 5 sts

Color Key

⊡ **G** Dried Lavender

☐ **D** Lady's Mantle

CHART VII
MULTIPLE OF 5 sts

Color Key

☐ **C** Squash

⊡ **F** Steel Gray

CHART VIII
MULTIPLE OF 5 sts

Color Key

⊡ **E** Berry Berry

☐ **D** Lady's Mantle

CHART IX
MULTIPLE OF 5 sts

Color Key

☐ **A** Gourd

⊡ **B** Velvet Moss

CHART X
MULTIPLE OF 5 sts

Color Key

☐ **C** Squash

⊡ **G** Dried Lavender

CHART XI
MULTIPLE OF 5 sts

Color Key

☐ **H** Coleus

⊡ **D** Lady's Mantle

CHART XII
MULTIPLE OF 5 sts

Color Key

☐ **E** Berry Berry

⊡ **B** Velvet Moss

◪ **C** Squash

Beg chart IX
NOTE All one-color rnds are worked on smaller dpns and all
two-color rnds are worked on larger dpns. Cont in St st
on all sts as foll:
Rnd I Work 5-st pat rep 6 times. Cont to foll chart in this
manner through rnd 11. Break yarns. Change to smaller
dpns and F.
Reverse stockinette stitch ridge
Rnds 1–3 Work rnds 1–3 of rev St st ridge. Break F.
Change to C.

Beg chart X
NOTE All one-color rnds are worked on smaller dpns
and all two-color rnds are worked on larger dpns. Cont in
St st on all sts as foll:
Rnd I Work 5-st pat rep 6 times. Cont to foll chart in this manner
through rnd 10. Break yarns. Change to smaller dpns and I.
Reverse stockinette stitch ridge
Rnds 1–3 Work rnds 1–3 of rev St st ridge. Break I.
Change to H.

Beg chart XI

NOTE All one-color rnds are worked on smaller dpns and all two-color rnds are worked on larger dpns. Cont in St st on all sts as foll:

Rnd 1 Work 5-st pat rep 6 times. Cont to foll chart in this manner through rnd 14. Break yarns. Change to smaller dpns and I.

Reverse stockinette stitch ridge

Rnds 1–3 Work rnds 1–3 of rev St st ridge. Break I. Change to E.

Beg chart XII

NOTE All one-color rnds are worked on smaller dpns and all two-color rnds are worked on larger dpns. Cont in St st on all sts as foll:

Rnd 1 Work 5-st pat rep 6 times. Cont to foll chart in this manner through rnd 11. Break yarns. Change to smaller dpns and F.

Reverse stockinette stitch ridge

Rnds 1–3 Work rnds 1–3 of rev St st ridge. Bind knitwise using F.

FINISHING

Steam-block to even out colorwork. Sew bottom edge closed. Fill tube with beans. Sew top edge closed. ■

KEEP PRACTICING

Child's Sampler Scarf

This little scarf is a great project to keep handy in your knitting basket as you explore color. It's similar to the Chill Stopper window/door snake, but you get to choose your own patterns! Add to the scarf when you want to try out new color ideas or patterns.

FINISHED MEASUREMENTS

Approx 34"/86.5cm long x 4"/10cm wide

PICKING YARN COLORS

You'll want a nice array of contrasting colors. The *Julia* colors featured here are:
Harvest Spice NHJ0178, Lady's Mantle NHJ3961, Purple Basil NHJ3158, Blue Thyme NHJ4936, Steel Gray NHJ0122, Pretty Pink NHJ8141, Gourd NHJ1784, Golden Honey NHJ2163, Rock Henna NHJ2230, Lupine NHJ5178, Sage NHJ0115, Dried Lavender NHJ8126, Anemone NHJ9235, Berry Berry NHJ0124, Deep Blue Sea NHJ6396 and Bright Blue NHJ4037.

CHOOSING CHARTS

You'll be working with 40 sts and this number can be divided by 2, 4, 5, 8, 10 and 20. Go to the Colorwork Chart Glossary (page 148) to choose about a dozen charts that have any of these stitch multiples.

CASTING ON

With smaller dpns and first color, cast on 40 sts. Cont to follow the same instructions as for the window/door snake, beg and ending with Reverse Stockinette Stitch Ridges, and using them to separate your chart pats. When knitting is completed, steam or block to even out colorwork. Sew the ends of the tube closed. ■

At the Farmhouse

Outside our farmhouse windows it is gray, white and black all winter long. No wonder I crave color in my knitting and interiors!

It may grow on you...

Don't rip out unpleasing combinations. Keep them to refer to later to remind yourself that, no, you didn't like it. And you never know—in a few years that awful combination may start to look good.

CHAPTER 3

Designing Fair Isle Knits

Years ago, I would look for colorful patterns in knitting stitch dictionaries, which I would follow explicitly. Back then, charting wasn't popular. Most of the patterns were written out in a long and tedious format ("knit 3 in Color A Blue, knit 4 in Color B Yellow"). You can imagine how long those instructions were! Then there was a shift, and it became popular to give knitting instructions in chart form. When I felt confident enough in my knitting skills, I began designing my own Fair Isle stitch patterns.

I found the chart form friendly to my visual style of learning and doing. Now, graph paper is always in my knitting bag in case I feel the urge to work out a new stranded color design.

I usually decide on a concept for my colorwork design in my mind before putting it to graph paper. I may find inspiration in the pages of a magazine or on a colorful package from the grocery store. I take a piece of graph paper and start filling in the boxes to see where the pattern will take me. You'll notice that when you are beginning to design charts, geometric objects such as triangles, diamonds, and squares are easy to begin with. Let me show you how easy this is to do and then you can have a go at it, too.

TAKE IT EASY: FIRST DESIGNS

It helps to have some parameters when designing a stitch pattern. Let's take a mitten that will be knit in a stitch gauge of about 5 stitches per inch. A mitten isn't very big, so it's a nice project to start your design adventures with. An average-size mitten for a woman could have a total of 36 stitches around (18 for the front, 18 for the back). With that in mind, you're going to have to design a relatively small pattern in order for it to fit on your mitten. For this little "workshop," below, we'll design a small 6-stitch pattern that could be used on a 36-stitch mitten all the way up the piece.

Let's chart a diamond pattern with a 6-stitch repeat. **Chart 1** shows a small diamond. The diamonds are placed on a contrasting background color, and the center of the diamond is in the background color.

CHART 1

The diamonds will be floating on the background with two rounds of background color behind them. The solid orange line around the chart shows the pattern repeat.

Chart 2 shows how the pattern will look over 18 stitches and 12 rounds. The diamonds are stacked on top of each other.

CHART 2

Chart 3 shows how the diamonds can be staggered. To do this, the second row of diamonds is moved over 3 squares, giving a different look to the diamond pattern.

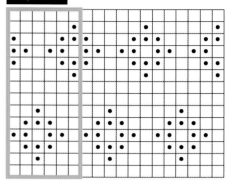

CHART 3

In **Chart 4**, I repeated Chart 3 but changed the background color to form stripes, and the diamond color was also changed.

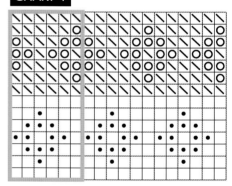

CHART 4

In **Chart 5**, the diamonds are closer together to form a tighter staggered pattern. This pattern could also be knit with different colors of diamonds.

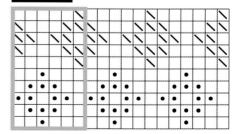

CHART 5

In **Chart 6**, I moved the diamonds even closer together to make a very tight design.

CHART 6

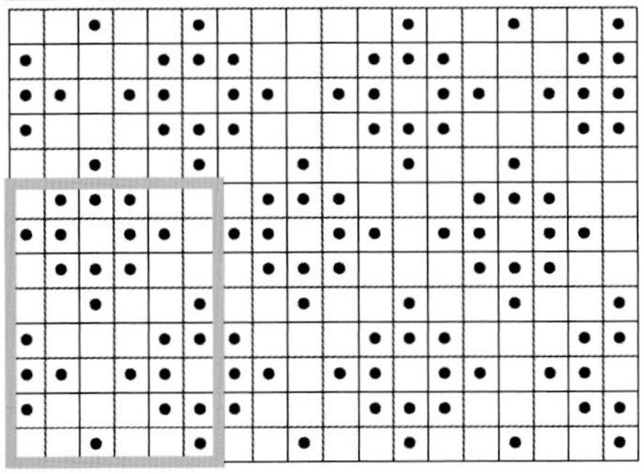

Because the diamond motif overlaps at the small points on the diamonds, this pattern would be better worked in only two colors. This fabric would be the thickest of all of the samples, because it has colorwork in every single row.

These charts serve to show how versatile even a small stitch pattern can be, and how the chart form allows for some clever manipulation and many different looks.

TAKING IT UP A NOTCH: ADDING COMPLEXITY

Now that you know how to design a pattern with a small, very simple stitch repeat, let's tackle one that's a little more challenging.

For this larger, more complex pattern, I chose a repeat of 20 stitches. **Chart 7** shows 2 diamonds, one inside the other. They are stacked with one row in between. To connect the motifs into one larger scheme, I added zigzags 3 stitches wide on the outside of the larger diamond. Little diamonds fill in the open spaces, resulting in an intricate, but easy to follow, diamond-themed pattern.

Chart 8 again shows two diamonds (one inside the other) stacked upon each other. Instead of zigzags around the diamonds, I drew a larger diamond in the open space. This pattern gives a looser look, and the background color of the fabric will dominate. In the upper part of the chart, I showed you how the chart could be decorated with duplicate stitch to bring other colors to make the pattern more colorful and intricate. That wasn't so hard, was it?

CHART 7

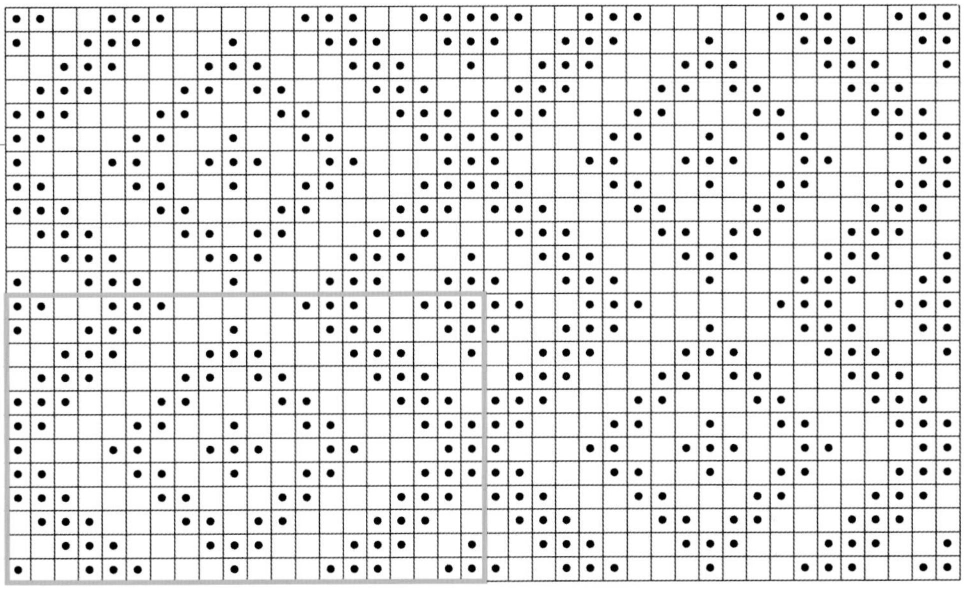

CHART 8

Cuffed Mittens and Socks
page 130

Felted Laptop Cozy
page 79

PERFECT SYMMETRY

Say you want to create a motif that is symmetrical in all directions. Let's start with a basic 20 stitch by 20 row graph.

In **Step 1**, I have identified the center stitch of the pattern. Although the chart has 20 stitches, I want there to be an exact center to the design. Twenty divided by 2 = 10. I have moved the center point over to be stitch 9. Stitch 1 will act as the "transition stitch" and Row 1 will be the "transition row."

The motif we will draw is going to end up being 19 stitches wide. The transition stitch will be the blank point between each motif. Using small dots, I drew a design in the top left quadrant of the block of boxes. It has a geometric feeling to it and reminds me of a snowflake.

STEP 1

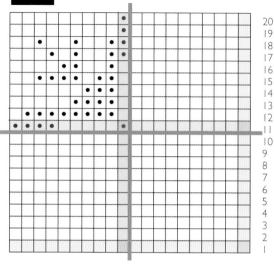

STEP 2

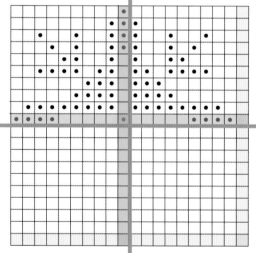

In **Step 2**, I flipped the motif so that it is a mirror image of the left quadrant. The motif was flipped across the center stitch, but I did not repeat the center stitch. You can see how the pattern is starting to build.

In **Step 3**, I flipped both of these quadrants over the horizontal axis, again not including the center stitch. This almost completes the design.

At this point in my design process, I need to visualize how the stitch repeat is going to look in multiples. The motif needs to be tied together at both the transition row and stitch. By repeating the motif, it is easier to visualize the finished pattern. During this step, I also think about the actual knitting of the motif. I consider the number of long floats on the back of the fabric. This particular design could go many ways—I chose to tie the snowflake motif together with diagonal lines. There is only one row in the pattern that will require a lot of

STEP 3

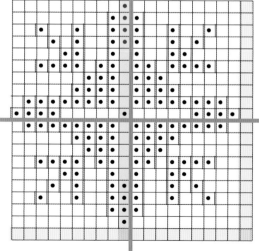

STEP 4

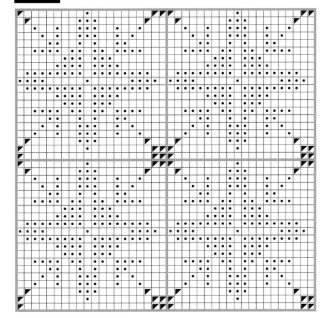

weaving of the floats (Row 1). Although I drew the transition stitches in a bolder dot, I plan to knit this entire design in just two colors.

Knitting is based on stitches and rows, and most Fair Isle patterns tend to be very geometric. But that needn't be. Now we'll look at how we can create an organic or rounded motif using the same 20-stitch block of stitches.

Swatch It

I knit all my swatches in the round on double-pointed needles, adding a steek to cut later (see page 21). I try to make them large enough to get an overall feeling for the pattern. When finished, I sew and cut the steek, steam the swatch and then decide if I want to use it for a project.

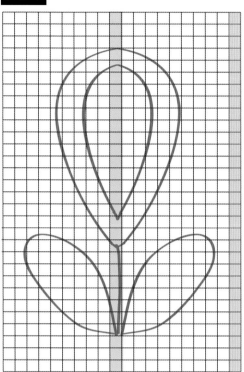

GOING ORGANIC: FLOWER DESIGNS

Flowers are one of my favorite things, and most knitters have knit a flower or two in their lives. Most flowers are round with some pointy bits.

To chart a flower, I start by drawing a flower shape on my graph paper as shown in **Step 1**. Don't worry too much about the grid of the graph paper at this point—just rough out the shape where you want it. Again, I have marked the center stitch and the transition stitch, which I will leave open.

Then in **Step 2**, I fill in outlines on the graph, keeping the flower symmetrical. My plan is to knit the flower in one color and the stem in another color, so I have to watch the placement of the leaves to

STEP 2

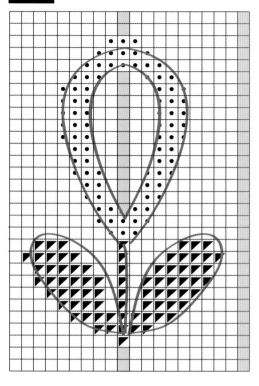

STEP 3

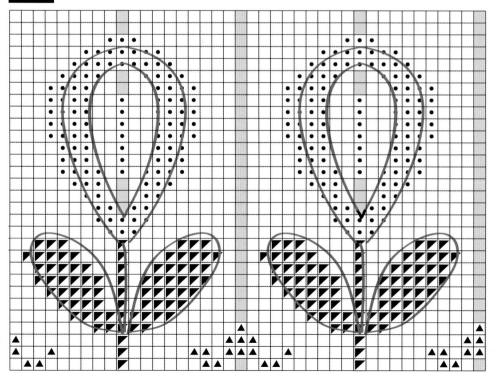

prevent having three colors in a single row.

In **Step 3**, I repeat the motif. I add some thickness to the outside edge of the flower, and I add a center vertical dark row of stitches to make the knitting more pleasurable—fewer floats to worry about, more of a rhythm! At the lower edge, I add a little design between the leaves so there won't be too many rows of long floats.

In the finished swatch, you can see that after knitting, the pattern was ripe for more decoration. Using embroidery stitches and duplicate stitch, I was able to make the design even more organic and intricate.

As you can see, building a colorwork pattern isn't difficult. It just takes a little practice. But designing on paper means you can play with it until you hit on the design that sings for you. Designing your own colorwork patterns will give your knitting complete originality. And there's nothing more satisfying than producing something that is all yours! ■

Grow Your Own Garden

I've used flower motifs in many of the designs in this book. Some are part of the colorwork patterns, some are added later in duplicate stitch and others are embroidered.

Projects & Patterns

Bloomsbury Gauntlets

These romantic gloves may look like only an expert knitter could make them, but look again. After the sculpted edging and Fair Isle border, it's all easy knitting working with only one color at a time. The embroidery takes a bit of extra effort, but it puts the gloves over the top.

Magic Multiple for Edging: 7 sts
Color Chart Multiple:
4, 6, 8 or 12 sts

SIZES
Woman's Small (Large).
Shown in size Small.

FINISHED MEASUREMENTS
Hand circumference: 6¾ (8½)"/
17 (21.5)cm
Length of cuff: 4½"/11.5cm

YARN
Nashua Handknits *Julia*
(wool/mohair/alpaca), 1¾oz/50g,
93yd/85m
A Magenta NHJ2083—2 skeins
B Velvet Moss NHJ6086—1 skein
C Coleus NHJ4345—1 skein
D Lady's Mantle NHJ3961—1 skein
E Deep Blue Sea NHJ6396—1 skein

NEEDLES
One set (4) each sizes 5 and 7 (3.75
and 4.5mm) double-pointed needles
(dpns) *or size needed to obtain correct
gauge*

NOTIONS
◆ Stitch marker
◆ Stitch holders
◆ Tapestry needle

GAUGE
20 sts and 22 rnds = 4"/10cm in
St st over chart pat using larger dpns.
20 sts and 24 = 4"/10cm in St
st on smaller dpns.
Be sure to obtain correct gauge.

Notes
1. Right and left gloves are made exactly the same.
2. All one-color rnds are worked on smaller dpns and all two-color rnds are worked on larger dpns.

Abbreviations
M1 Make 1
k2tog Knit 2 stitches together

Stitches
SCULPTED EDGING
(multiple of 7 sts)
Row 1 (WS) *K4, [k3, turn] 4 times, k3; rep from * to end.
Work row 1 for sculpted edging.

REVERSE STOCKINETTE STITCH RIDGE
Rnd 1 Knit.
Rnds 2 and 3 Purl.
Work rnds 1–3 for rev St st ridge.

STOCKINETTE STITCH
Knit every round.

GLOVES (make 2)
Cuff
With larger dpn and A, cast on 49 sts. Using 2 dpns, work row 1 of sculpted edging. Divide sts evenly on 3 dpns. Turn work to RS. Join and pm taking care not to twist sts on needles. Purl next rnd. Break A. Change to B.
Reverse stockinette stitch ridges
Rnds 1–3 Work rnds 1–3 of rev St st ridge. Break B. Change to C.
Rnds 4–6 Work rnds 1–3 of rev St st ridge, dec 1 st on last rnd—48 sts. Break C. Change to D.

Beg chart pat
NOTE All one-color rnds are worked on smaller dpns and all two-color rnds are worked on larger dpns. Cont in St st on all sts as foll:
Rnd 1 Work 12-st pat rep 4 times. Cont to foll chart in this manner through rnd 17. Break yarns. Change to smaller dpns and C.

Reverse stockinette stitch ridges
Rnds 1–3 Work rnds 1–3 of rev St st ridge. Break C. Change to E.
Rnds 4–6 Work rnds 1–3 of rev St st ridge, dec 14 (6) sts evenly spaced around first rnd—34 (42) sts. Break E. Change to A and smaller dpns.

Hand
Cont in St st, work even for 3 (5) rnds.
Shape thumb gusset
Next (inc) rnd K17 (21), pm, M1, pm, k17 (21)—35 (43) sts. Knit next rnd.
Next (inc) rnd K to first marker, sl marker, M1, k to next marker, M1, sl marker, k to end—37 (45) sts. Knit next rnd. Rep last 2 rnds 5 (6) times more—47 (57) sts; 13 (15) sts between markers.
Next rnd K to first marker, drop marker, place next 13 (15) sts on holder for thumb, drop next marker, k to end—34 (42) sts. Work even in St st until hand measures 3½ (4)"/9 (10)cm from beg of thumb gusset. Break A. Change to C.

Reverse stockinette stitch ridge
Rnds 1–3 Work rnds 1–3 of rev St st ridge. Break C. Place first 17 (21) sts on one holder and last 17 (21) sts on a 2nd holder.

Thumb

Place sts from thumb gusset holder on 2 smaller dpns. With RS facing, join C at beg of thumb sts.

Reverse stockinette stitch ridge

Rnd 1 K across thumb sts, then pick up and k 1 st at base of hand—14 (16) sts. Divide sts between 3 dpns, then pm for beg of rnds.

Rnds 2 and 3 Purl Work rnds 1–3 of rev St st ridge. Break C. Change to B. Work even in St st until thumb measures 1¾ (2)"/4.5 (5)cm.

Shape top

Next (dec) rnd [K2tog] 7 (8) times—7 (8) sts. Cut yarn leaving a 6"/15.5cm tail. Thread tail in tapestry needle, then thread through rem sts. Pull tog tightly and secure end on WS.

Pinkie

Place first 4 (5) sts from first holder and last 4 (5) sts from 2nd holder on 2 smaller dpns. Join B to 2nd dpn, leaving a 10"/25.5cm tail.

Next rnd K across sts, then cast on 1 st—9 (11) sts. Divide sts evenly between 3 dpns. Join and pm for beg of rnds. Cont to work even in St st for 2 (2¼)"/5 (5.5)cm.

Shape top

Next (dec) rnd [K2tog] 4 (5) times, k1—5 (6) sts. Finish same as thumb.

Ring finger

Place next 5 sts from first holder to a smaller dpn and next 4 (6) sts from 2nd holder to a 2nd smaller dpn. Join E to 2nd dpn, leaving a 10"/25.5cm tail.

Next rnd K 4 (6), pick up and k 1 st at base of pinkie, k5, then cast on 1 st—11 (13) sts. Divide sts evenly between 3 dpns. Join and pm for beg of rnds. Cont to work even in St st for 2½ (2¾)"/6.5 (7)cm.

Shape top

Next (dec) rnd [K2tog] 5 (6) times, k1—6 (7) sts. Finish same as thumb.

Middle finger

Place next 4 (6) sts from first holder to a smaller dpn and next 5 sts from 2nd holder to a 2nd smaller dpn. Join B to 2nd dpn, leaving a 10"/25.5cm tail.

Next rnd K5, pick up and k 1 st at base of ring finger, k 4 (6), then cast on 1 st—11 (13) sts. Divide sts evenly between 3 dpns. Join and pm for beg of rnds. Cont to work even in St st for 2¾ (3)"/7 (7.5)cm.

Shape top

Next (dec) rnd [K2tog] 5 (6) times, k1—6 (7) sts. Finish same as thumb.

Index finger

Divide rem sts from holders evenly on 2 smaller dpns—8 (10) sts. Join E, leaving a 10"/25.5cm tail.

Next rnd K across, then pick up and k 2 sts at base of middle finger—10 (12) sts. Divide sts as evenly between 3 dpns. Join and pm for beg of rnds. Cont to work even in St st for 2½ (2¾)"/6.5 (7)cm.

Shape top

Next (dec) rnd [K2tog] 5 (6) times—5 (6) sts. Finish same as thumb.

FINISHING

Use yarn tails to close up holes between fingers. Weave in ends.

◆ **Cuff embellishments**

Spiderweb embroidery

Using A, embroider a 1"/2.5cm-diameter spiderweb (see page 171) in center of each motif.

French knot embroidery

Using a double strand of E in tapestry needle, work a French knot (see page 171) in center of each spiderweb. Using a double strand of D, work evenly spaced French knots between each pair of rev St st ridges.

◆ **Back of hand embellishments**

NOTE Make sure you make a right and left hand when placing embroidery. The embroidery is done on the back of each hand.

Spiderweb embroidery

Referring to photo, embroider a ⅝"/1.5cm-diameter spiderweb flower center using B for bottom flower and E for top flower.

Lazy daisy stitch embroidery

Using tapestry needle and D, embroider 11½"/1.3cm lazy daisy stitch petals (see page 171) around bottom flower centers, then 10 petals around top flower centers.

Fern stitch stitch embroidery

Using C, embroider 3 or 4 1"/2.5cm to 1¼"/3cm-long fern stitch stems (see page 171) around each flower as shown.

French knot embroidery

Using a double strand of A in tapestry needle, work a French knot in center of each flower. ■

► CHART FOR GLOVES
MULTIPLE OF 12 sts

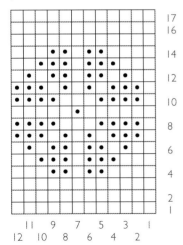

Color Key

☐ **D** Lady's Mantle

⊡ **C** Coleus

Color Combos

This simple design lends itself to complementary colors. Try turquoise gloves with orange cuffs for fun!

Over-the-Top Shawl

I love big patterned shawls and have many in my wardrobe. They are so easy to throw over a plain sweater or jacket to create a statement. And they look just as nice draped over the arm of a sofa or chair when you're not wearing them.

Magic Multiple for Edging: 5 sts
Colorwork Chart Multiple:
5, 10, 12 or 24 sts

SIZE
One size fits most.

FINISHED MEASUREMENTS
Approx 25" x 72"/63.5cm x 183cm (excluding fringe)

YARN
Nashua Handknits *Julia* (wool/mohair/alpaca), 1¾oz/50g, 93yd/85m
A Rock Henna NHJ2230—2 skeins
B Blue Thyme NHJ4936—1 skein
C Golden Honey NHJ2163—1 skein
D Geranium NHJ6085—2 skeins
E Lady's Mantle NHJ3961—2 skeins
F Deep Blue Sea NHJ6396—7 skeins
G Autumn Brown NHJ0123—6 skeins

NEEDLES
Size 5 and 7 (3.75 and 4.5mm) circular needles, 32"/81cm long *or size needed to obtain correct gauge*

NOTIONS
◆ Stitch markers
◆ Tapestry needle

GAUGE
20 sts and 22 rnds = 4"/10cm in St st over chart pats using larger circular needle.
20 sts and 24 rnds = 4"/10cm in rev St st ridge using smaller circular needle.
Be sure to obtain correct gauge.

Stitches

BOBBLE EDGING
(multiple of 5 sts)
Rnd 1 (RS) *P3, work [k1, p1] twice in next st, turn; p4, turn; k4, turn; p4, turn; pass the 2nd st over the first, the 3rd st over the first, the 4th st over the first st (bobble made), sl this st to RH needle, p1; rep from *, end p1.
Work rnd 1 for bobble edging.

BOBBLE EDGING BIND-OFF
(multiple of 5 sts)
Rnd 1 (RS) *Bind off 3 sts purlwise, work [k1, p1] twice in next st; turn; p4; turn; k4; turn; p4; turn; pass the 2nd st over the first, the 3rd st over the first, the 4th st over the first st (bobble made), bind off this st purlwise, bind off next st purlwise; rep from *, end bind off last st purlwise.
Work rnd 1 for bobble edging bind-off.

REVERSE STOCKINETTE STITCH RIDGE
Rnd 1 Knit.
Rnds 2 and 3 Purl.
Work rnds 1–3 for rev St st ridge.

STOCKINETTE STITCH
Knit every round.

SHAWL
With smaller needle and A, cast on 381 sts. Join taking care not to twist sts on needle, pm for beg of rnds.

Bobble edging
Rnd 1 K10 (steek sts), pm, work rnd 1 of bobble edging over next 361 sts, pm, k10 (steek sts).
Rnds 2 and 4 K10 (steek sts), sl marker, k to next marker, sl marker, k10 (steek sts).
Rnds 3 and 5 K10 (steek sts), sl marker, p to next marker, sl marker, k10 (steek sts). Break A. Change to B.

Reverse stockinette stitch ridges
Rnds 1–3 Keeping 10 steek sts at beg and end of rnds in St st, work rnds 1–3 of rev St st ridge over rem sts. Break B. Change to C.
Rnds 4–6 Keeping 10 steek sts at beg and end of rnds in St st, work rnds 1–3 of rev St st ridge over rem sts. Break C. Change to D.

Beg chart I
NOTE All one-color rnds are worked on smaller needle and all two-color rnds are worked on larger needle. Cont in St st on all sts as foll:
Rnd 1 Work first 10 steek sts, sl marker, work 5-st pat rep 72 times, then work st 1 once more, sl marker, work last 10 steek sts. Cont to foll charts in this manner through rnd 12. Break yarns. Change to smaller needle and F.

Reverse stockinette stitch ridges
Rnds 1–3 Keeping 10 steek sts at beg and end of rnds in St st, work rnds 1–3 of rev St st ridge over rem sts. Break F. Change to A.
Rnds 4–6 Keeping 10 steek sts at beg and end of rnds in St st, work rnds 1–3 of rev St st ridge over rem sts. Break A. Change to D.

Beg chart II
NOTE All one-color rnds are worked on smaller needle and all two-color rnds are worked on larger needle.
Cont in St st on all sts as foll:
Rnd 1 Work first 10 steek sts, sl marker, work 24-st pat rep 15 times, then work st 1 once more, sl marker, work last 10 steek sts. Cont to foll charts in this manner through rnd 29. Repeat rnds 1–29 2 times. Break yarns. Change to smaller

On the Fringe

The fringe on this shawl is made by a clever technique. The shawl is knit in the round with a steek at the center. The fabric is cut up the center of the steek without any reinforcing of the stitches. The steek stitches are then unraveled up to the beginning of the shawl pattern. As every four rounds are unraveled, an overhand knot is tied to stop the fabric from unraveling further and to create fringe.

Notes

1. The shawl is worked in the round forming a tube, with steek sts at beginning and end of rounds.

2. After knitting is completed, the shawl is cut open and the steek sts will be unraveled to form a fringe at each short edge.

3. All one-color rnds are worked on smaller needle and all two-color rnds are worked on larger needle.

CHART I   MULTIPLE OF 5 sts

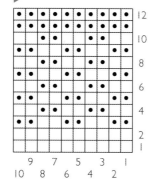
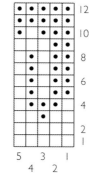
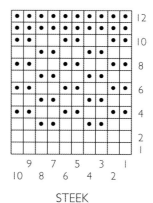

STEEK   STEEK

Color Key

☐ **D** Geranium

⊡ **E** Lady's Mantle

CHART III   MULTIPLE OF 5 sts

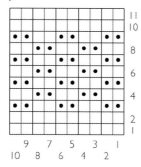
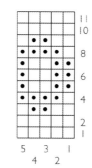
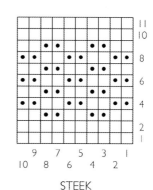

STEEK   STEEK

Color Key

☐ **A** Rock Henna

⊡ **C** Golden Honey

CHART II   MULTIPLE OF 24 sts

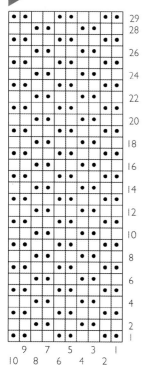
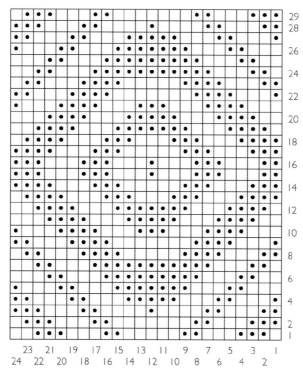
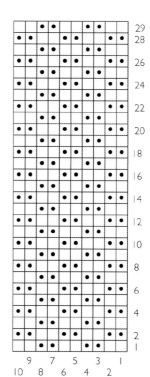

STEEK   STEEK

Color Key

☐ **G** Autumn Brown

⊡ **F** Deep Blue Sea

needle and D.

Reverse stockinette stitch ridges

Rnds 1–3 Keeping 10 steek sts at beg and end of rnds in St st, work rnds 1–3 of rev St st ridge over rem sts. Break D. Change to E.

Rnds 4–6 Keeping 10 steek sts at beg and end of rnds in St st, work rnds 1–3 of rev St st ridge over rem sts. Break E. Change to A.

Beg chart III

NOTE All one-color rnds are worked on smaller needle and all two-color rnds are worked on larger needle. Cont in St st on all sts as foll:

Rnd 1 Work first 10 steek sts, sl marker, work 5-st pat rep 72 times, then work st 1 once more, sl marker, work last 10 steek sts. Cont to foll charts in this manner through rnd 11. Break yarns. Change to smaller needle and B.

Reverse stockinette stitch ridges

Rnds 1–3 Keeping 10 steek sts at beg and end of rnds in St st, work rnds 1–3 of rev St st ridge over rem sts. Break B. Change to D.

Rnds 4–6 Keeping 10 steek sts at beg and end of rnds in St st, work rnds 1–3 of rev St st ridge over rem sts. Break D. Change to E.

Bobble edging

Rnds 1 and 3 K 10 steek sts, sl marker, k to next marker, sl marker, k 10 steek sts.

Rnds 2 and 4 K 10 steek sts, sl marker, p to next marker, sl marker, k 10 steek sts.

Rnd 5 Bind off first 10 steek sts knitwise, drop marker, work rnd 1 of bobble edging bind-off over next 361 sts, drop marker, bind off last 10 steek sts knitwise.

FINISHING

Cut the steek to form the fringe by cutting the shawl in the center ditch between the two groups of 10 steek sts; do not cut near the chart pat areas.

Fringe

Using a knitting needle or tapestry needle and beginning at the bound-off edge, carefully unravel 4 rnds of sts from the 10 steek sts at each end of the shawl.

Tie each set of 4 unraveled ends in an overhand knot, positioning the knot against the chart pat section. Cont in this manner until all unraveled tails have been knotted. Trim fringe to make even. Steam-block center section of shawl to even out colorwork. ■

Mix It Up

For several designs in this book I've included alternative colorways you can substitute. And don't be afraid to try out your own color combinations!

More Colors to Try

Spring Green NHJ5185; Velvet Moss NHJ6086; Rock Henna NHJ2230; Anemone NHJ9235; Persimmon NHJ0121; Purple Basil NHJ3158; Geranium NHJ6085

Many Hearts Baby Afghan

This patchwork baby afghan is a perfect project for a group of knitting friends to make for an expectant mama. Each person can make one heart. After a group sewing bee to join all the blocks, the blanket can be passed around for each member to add a stripe or two. Don't forget to embellish the patches—the chain- and cross-stitch embroidery makes this project really special.

FINISHED MEASUREMENTS
Approx 40" × 40"/101.5cm × 101.5cm

YARN
Nashua Handknits *Julia* (wool/mohair/alpaca), 1¾oz/50g, 93yd/85m

A Magenta NHJ208 —2 skeins
B Spring Green NHJ5185—2 skeins
C Lady's Mantle NHJ3961—2 skeins
D Persimmon NHJ0121—2 skeins
E Pretty Pink NHJ8141—3 skeins
F Bright Blue NHJ4037—2 skeins
G Golden Honey NHJ2163—2 skeins
H Geranium NHJ6085—3 skeins
I Midnight Blue NHJ6416—3 skeins

NEEDLES
For heart squares
Size 7 (4.5mm) straight needles *or size needed to obtain correct gauge*
For striped border
Size 5 (3.75mm) circular needle, 40"/101cm long *or size needed to obtain correct gauge*

NOTIONS
◆ Stitch markers
◆ Tapestry needle

GAUGE
20 sts and 22 rows = 4"/10cm in St st over chart pats using size 7 (4.5mm) needles.
20 sts and 40 rnds = 4"/10cm in garter st using size 5 (3.75mm) circular needle.
Be sure to obtain correct gauge.

Notes
1. Squares are worked back and forth in St st, then sewn together.
2. Heart motif is worked in intarsia technique using a separate strand of color for each color section.
3. Striped border is worked in the round in garter st.

Stitches
STOCKINETTE STITCH
Row 1 (RS) Knit.
Row 2 Purl.
Rep rows 1 and 2 for St st.

GARTER STITCH
Rnd 1 Knit.
Rnd 2 Purl.
Rep rnds 1 and 2 for garter st.

HEART SQUARES
With straight needles and background color, cast on 33 sts.

Beg chart pat
Working in St st, beg chart on row 1 and work to row 35. Bind off all sts purlwise. Square should measure 6½" × 6½"/16.5cm × 16.5cm. Make 1 square each in color combinations as foll:

SQUARE 1
Colors for chart
◆ Background color— **A** Magenta
◆ Heart color— **B** Spring Green
Colors for embroidery
◆ Outer chain-stitch— **I** Midnight Blue
◆ Inner chain-stitch— **D** Persimmon

SQUARE 2
Colors for chart
◆ Background color— **C** Lady's Mantle
◆ Heart color— **D** Persimmon
Colors for embroidery
◆ Outer chain-stitch— **H** Geranium
◆ Inner chain-stitch— **A** Magenta

SQUARE 3
Colors for chart
◆ Background color— **E** Pretty Pink
◆ Heart color— **F** Bright Blue
Colors for embroidery
◆ Outer chain-stitch— **B** Spring Green
◆ Inner chain-stitch— **I** Midnight Blue

SQUARE 4
Colors for chart
◆ Background color—**G** Golden Honey
◆ Heart color—**E** Pretty Pink
Colors for embroidery
◆ Outer chain-stitch—**F** Bright Blue
◆ Inner chain-stitch—**B** Spring Green

SQUARE 5
Colors for chart
◆ Background color—**H** Geranium
◆ Heart color—**C** Lady's Mantle
Colors for embroidery
◆ Outer chain-stitch—**I** Midnight Blue
◆ Inner chain-stitch— **D** Persimmon

SQUARE 6
Colors for chart
◆ Background color—**B** Spring Green
◆ Heart color—**I** Midnight Blue
Colors for embroidery
◆ Outer chain-stitch—**E** Pretty Pink
◆ Inner chain-stitch—**G** Golden Honey

SQUARE 7
Colors for chart
◆ Background color—**F** Bright Blue
◆ Heart color—**H** Geranium
Colors for embroidery
◆ Outer chain-stitch—**G** Golden Honey
◆ Inner chain-stitch—**D** Persimmon

SQUARE 8
Colors for chart
◆ Background color—**D** Persimmon
◆ Heart color—**I** Midnight Blue
Colors for embroidery
◆ Outer chain-stitch—**A** Magenta
◆ Inner chain-stitch—**B** Spring Green

SQUARE 9
Colors for chart
◆ Background color—**I** Midnight Blue
◆ Heart color—**E** Pretty Pink
Colors for embroidery
◆ Outer chain-stitch—**C** Lady's Mantle
◆ Inner chain-stitch—**G** Golden Honey

At the Farmhouse
Our kittens love to curl up in the sunniest, softest places—especially on top of my knitting projects!

FINISHING

Steam-block squares to measurements and to even out colorwork. Referring to diagram for assembling, arrange squares as shown. Sew squares together using mattress stitch (see page 170).

Striped border

Rnd 1 With RS facing, circular needle and H, pick up and k 94 sts evenly spaced across bottom edge of assembled squares, pm, pick up and k 1 st in corner, pm, pick up and k 83 sts evenly spaced across side edge, pm, pick up and k 1 st in corner, pm, pick up and k 94 sts evenly spaced across top edge, pm, pick up and k 1 st in corner, pm, pick up and k 83 sts evenly spaced across side edge, pm, pick up and k 1 st in corner, pm for beg of rnds—358 sts.

Rnd 2 *P to next marker, sl marker, k1, sl marker; rep from * 3 times more.

Rnd (inc) 3 *K to next marker, inc 1 using backward loop method, sl marker, k1, sl marker, inc 1; rep from * 3 times more—8 sts increased. Rep rnds 2 and 3 twice more, then rnd 2 once—8 rnds completed (4 garter st ridges). Break H. Change to B.

Rnds 9, 11, 13, 15 *K to next marker, inc 1 using backward loop method, sl marker, k1, sl marker, inc 1; rep from * 3 times more.

Rnds 10, 12, 14, 16 *P to next marker, sl marker, k1, sl marker; rep from * 3 times more. Break F. Rep rnds 9–16 for each remaining stripe and cont in color sequence as foll: I, E, G, F, D, A, C, H, B, I and E. Bind off loosely knitwise using E (13 stripes from beg). Steam or handwash afghan to even out sts.

Chain-stitch embroidery

Working in chain stitch (see page 171), using tapestry needle and colors listed for each square, outline outer edge of heart with outer color, then inner edge of heart with inner color.

Cross-stitch embroidery

Working in cross stitch (see page 171) and using tapestry needle, embroider a vertical line of cross stitches over vertical seams as foll: I over seam between squares 1 and 2; I over seam between squares 2 and 3; F over seam between squares 4 and 5; F over seam between squares 5 and 6; I over seam between squares 7 and 8; H over seam between squares 8 and 9. Embroider a horizontal line of cross stitches over horizontal seams as foll: B over seam between squares 1 and 4; D over seam between squares 2 and 5; H between squares 3 and 6; H over seam between squares 4 and 7; B over seam between squares 5 and 8; D over seam between squares 6 and 9. ■

CHART FOR HEART SQUARE

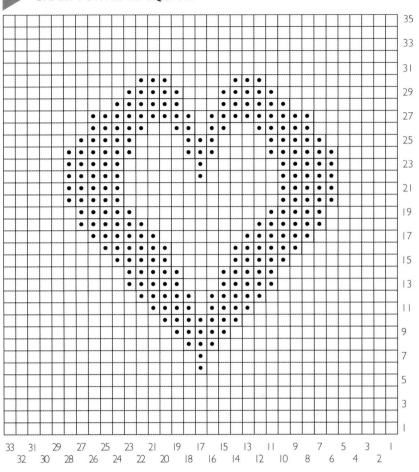

ASSEMBLY DIAGRAM

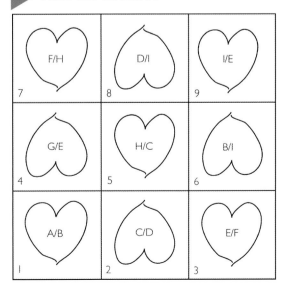

Color Key

☐ Background Color

⊡ Heart Color

47

Family of Slipper Socks

Years ago, I went to Greece on a yarn buying trip. I saw plenty of yarn and visited several textile mills, but what I remember most are the open-air markets. You could buy beautiful handcrafted things, including pottery, rugs and fabulous knitted socks. My favorite purchases were a few pairs of very finely knit antique, moth-eaten socks. My Americanized version, these slipper socks, are knit at a much quicker, friendlier knitting gauge. Sized for all ages, they make great gifts for everyone on your list.

Magic Multiple for Edging:
You could choose any of the decorative bind-offs and adjust the stitch number to fit those multiples.
Colorwork Chart Multiple: See "Basic Slipper Socks," below.

SIZES
Infant (Child's Small, Child's Medium, Child's Large, Woman's Small, Woman's Average, Woman's Large/Man's Small, Man's Average). Shown in sizes Child's Small, Child's Medium, Woman's Average, and Man's Average.

FINISHED MEASUREMENTS
Length: 4 (5½, 6½, 7, 8, 9, 10, 11)"/10 (14, 16.5, 17.5, 20.5, 23, 25.5, 28)cm
Circumference around foot:
4¾ (5½, 6½, 7¼, 8, 8¾, 9½, 10)"/12 (14, 16.5, 18.5, 20.5, 22, 24, 25.5)cm

YARN
Nashua Handknits *Julia* (wool/mohair/alpaca), 1¾oz/50g, 93yd/85m
One skein each of 3 to 4 colors.
For colors used for slipper socks shown, see individual instructions that follow basic slipper socks.

NEEDLES
For toe
One set (4) each sizes 5 and 7 (3.75 and 4.5mm) double-pointed needles (dpns) *or size needed to obtain correct gauge*
For back of foot
One pair size 5 (3.75mm) needles *or size needed to obtain correct gauge*

NOTIONS
◆ Stitch marker
◆ Tapestry needle

GAUGE
20 sts and 22 rnds = 4"/10cm in St st over chart pat using larger dpns.
20 sts and 40 rows = 4"/10cm in garter st using size 5 (3.75mm) needles.
Be sure to obtain correct gauge.

Notes
1. Slipper socks will stretch as they are worn, so it is best to choose a slightly smaller size.
2. Slipper sock begins at the back of the foot and is worked back and forth in a 2-row striped garter st using straight needles.
3. The toe is worked in the round in St st using dpns.

Abbreviations
k2tog Knit 2 stitches together
p2tog tbl Purl 2 stitches together through back loops

BASIC SLIPPER SOCKS
Back of foot
Beg at back seam, with straight needles and first color, cast on 24 (28, 32, 36, 40, 44, 48, 50) sts. Working back and forth in garter st, work a 2-row stripe pat using 2 or 3 colors, until piece measures 2 (2¾, 3¼, 3½, 4, 4¾, 5¼, 6)"/5 (7, 8, 9, 10, 12, 13.5, 15)cm from beg, end with a WS row.

Toe
Arrange sts on 3 larger dpns. First and third needle will hold side sts and second needle will hold bottom of foot sts. Divide sts as foll:
◆ Infant—6 (12) 6
◆ Child's Small—7 (14) 7
◆ Child's Medium—8 (16) 8
◆ Child's Large—9 (18) 9
◆ Woman's Small—10 (20) 10
◆ Woman's Average—11 (22) 11
◆ Woman's Large/Man's Small—12 (24) 12
◆ Man's Average—12 (25) 13

Chart pat
Choose a chart pat that has a st rep (or multiple of sts) that will fit into the number of sts you are working on (see page 148). You will be working for 6 (11, 12, 14, 17, 20, 24, 27) rnds, so you should also choose a design that can be centered between where the back of foot ends and the toe shaping begs. If necessary, you can add or subtract a rnd so design is perfectly centered.
◆ Infant: 24 sts—choose a 2, 4, or 6 st rep.
◆ Child's Small: 28 sts—choose a 2 or 4 st rep.
◆ Child's Medium: 32 sts—choose a 2, 4 or 8 st rep.
◆ Child's Large: 36 sts—choose a 2, 4 or 12 st rep.
◆ Woman's Small: 40 sts—choose a 2, 4, 5 or 8 st rep.
◆ Woman's Average: 44 sts—choose a 2 or 4 st rep.
◆ Woman's Large/Man's Small: 48 sts—choose a 2, 4, 6, 8 or 12 st rep.
◆ Man's Average: 50 sts—choose a 2, 5 or 10 st rep.

Beg chart pat
Cont in St st as foll:
Rnd 1 (RS) Beg chart with second needle (bottom of foot). When rnd 1 is completed, join and pm for beg of rnds. Cont to foll chart for 5 (10, 11, 13, 16, 19, 23, 26) rnds more.

Shape toe
You can work the toe in St st, garter st or a combination of St st and 2-row garter st ridges in colors as desired. If working in garter st, work decs on the knit rnd (not the purl rnd). Work your first dec rnd with however many sts you have been working on, then cont to dec every other rnd as foll:
50 sts [K2tog, k23] twice—48 sts. Work next rnd even.
48 sts [K2tog, k10] 4 times—44 sts. Work next rnd even.
44 sts [K2tog, k9] 4 times—40 sts. Work next rnd even.
40 sts [K2tog, k8] 4 times—36 sts. Work next rnd even.
36 sts [K2tog, k7] 4 times—32 sts. Work next rnd even.
32 sts [K2tog, k6] 4 times—28 sts. Work next rnd even.
28 sts [K2tog, k5] 4 times—24 sts. Work next rnd even.
24 sts [K2tog, k4] 4 times—20 sts. Work next rnd even.

Cont to dec every rnd as foll:
20 sts [K2tog, k3] 4 times—16 sts.
16 sts [K2tog, k2] 4 times—12 sts.
12 sts [K2tog, k1] 4 times—8 sts.
8 sts [K2tog] 4 times—4 sts. Cut yarn, leaving a 6"/15.5cm tail. Thread tail in tapestry needle, then thread through rem sts. Pull tog tightly and secure end.

FINISHING
Sew back of foot seam.

Top edging
With RS facing, larger dpn and desired color, pick up and k 1 st in back seam, pick up and k 1 st in each garter st ridge to center front of foot, pick up and k 2 sts at center front of foot, pick up and k 1 st in each garter st ridge to end. Join

Stitches
GARTER STITCH
Knit every row.

GARTER STITCH
(in the round)
Rnd 1 Knit.
Rnd 2 Purl.
Rep rnds 1 and 2 for garter st.

STOCKINETTE STITCH
Knit every round.

and pm for beg of rnds. Purl next rnd. Knit next rnd. Bind off all sts purlwise. Steam or wash to block.

CHILD'S SMALL SLIPPER SOCKS
Yarn
A Anemone NHJ9235—1 skein
B Spring Green NHJ5185—1 skein
C Pretty Pink NHJ8141—1 skein

Back of foot
Foll basic slipper sock instructions for Child's Small, cast on using A. Working back and forth in garter st, work a 2-row stripe pat using A and B to given measurement.

Beg chart pat
Divide sts on 3 dpns. Cont in St st as foll:
Rnd 1 (RS) Beg chart with second needle (bottom of foot). When rnd 1 is completed, join and pm for beg of rnds. Cont to foll chart in this manner through rnd 4. Rep rnds 1–4 once more, then rnds 1–3 once—11 rnds completed. Change to A.

Shape toe
Work your first dec rnd as foll:
28 sts [K2tog, k5] 4 times—24 sts. Purl next rnd (garter st ridge made). Break A. Change to C. Cont in St st, cont to dec foll basic instructions. Cut yarn, leaving a 6"/15.5cm tail. Thread tail in tapestry needle, then thread through rem sts. Pull tog tightly and secure end. Finish same as for basic slipper socks, using A for top edging.

CHILD'S LARGE SLIPPER SOCKS
Yarn
A Rock Henna NHJ2230—1 skein
B Golden Honey NHJ2163—1 skein
C Pretty Pink NHJ8141—1 skein
D Blue Thyme NHJ4936—1 skein

Back of foot
Foll basic slipper sock instructions for Child's Large, cast on using A. Working back and forth in garter st, work a 2-row stripe pat in color sequence as foll: *A, B, C, B; rep from * to given measurement.

Beg chart pat
Divide sts on 3 dpns. Cont in St st as foll:
Rnd 1 (RS) Beg chart with second needle (bottom of foot). When rnd 1 is completed, join and pm for beg of rnds. Cont to foll chart in this manner through rnd 12. Change to A.

Shape toe
Work your first dec rnd as foll:

▶ CHART FOR CHILD'S LARGE
MULTIPLE OF 9 sts

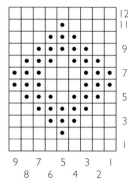

Color Key

☐ **C** Pretty Pink

⊡ **B** Golden Honey

▶ CHART FOR EMBROIDERY AND
DUPLICATE STITCH (CHILD'S LARGE)

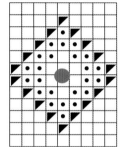

Color Key

◧ **C** Blue Thyme duplicate stitch

⬤ **A** Rock Henna French knot

▶ CHART FOR CHILD'S SMALL
MULTIPLE OF 4 sts

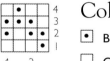

Color Key

⊡ **B** Spring Green

☐ **C** Pretty Pink

▶ CHART FOR MAN'S AVERAGE
MULTIPLE OF 10 sts

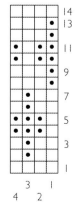

Color Key

⊡ **C** Deep Blue Sea

☐ **B** Lady's Mantle

◩ **A** Rock Henna

▶ CHART FOR WOMAN'S AVERAGE
MULTIPLE OF 4 sts

Color Key

☐ **C** Golden Honey

⊡ **A** Geranium

36 sts [K2tog, k7] 4 times—32 sts. Purl next rnd (first garter st ridge made). Break A. Change to B.
32 sts [K2tog, k8] 4 times—28 sts. Purl next rnd (second garter st ridge made). Break B. Change to D. Cont in St st, cont to dec foll basic instructions. Cut yarn, leaving a 6"/15.5cm tail. Thread tail in tapestry needle, then thread through rem sts. Pull tog tightly and secure end.

Duplicate stitch embroidery
Using tapestry needle and C, embroider duplicate stitches (see page 22) around outer edge of motif as shown on chart.

French knot embroidery
Using a double strand of A in tapestry needle, work a French knot (see page 171) in center of each motif as shown on chart. Finish same as for basic slipper socks, using C for top edging.

WOMAN'S AVERAGE SLIPPER SOCK
Yarn
A Geranium NHJ6085—1 skein
B Blue Thyme NHJ4936—1 skein
C Golden Honey NHJ2163—1 skein

Back of foot
Foll basic slipper sock instructions for Woman's Average, cast on using A. Working back and forth in garter st, work a 2-row stripe pat using A and B to given measurement.

Beg chart pat
Divide sts on 3 dpns. Cont in St st as foll:
Rnd 1 (RS) Beg chart with second needle (bottom of foot). When rnd 1 is completed, join and pm for beg of rnds. Cont to foll chart in this manner through rnd 13. Rep rnds 2–7 once more, then rnd 14 once—20 rnds completed. Change to B.

Shape toe
Work your first dec rnd as foll:
44 sts [K2tog, k9] 4 times—40 sts. Purl next rnd (first garter st ridge made). Break B. Change to A.
40 sts [K2tog, k8] 4 times—36 sts. Purl next rnd (second garter st ridge made). Break A. Change to B. Cont in St st, cont to dec foll basic instructions. Cut yarn, leaving a 6"/15.5cm tail. Thread tail in tapestry needle, then thread through rem sts. Pull tog tightly and secure end. Finish same as for basic slipper socks, using A for top edging.

MAN'S AVERAGE SLIPPER SOCK
Yarn
A Rock Henna NHJ2230—1 skein
B Lady's Mantle NHJ3961—1 skein
C Deep Blue Sea NHJ6396—1 skein

Back of foot
Foll basic slipper sock instructions for Man's Average, cast on using A. Working back and forth in garter st, work a 2-row stripe pat using A and B to given measurement.

Beg chart pat
Divide sts on 3 dpns. Cont in St st as foll:
Rnd 1 (RS) Beg chart with second needle (bottom of foot). When rnd 1 is completed, join and pm for beg of rnds. Cont to foll chart in this manner through rnd 13. Rep rnds 1–13 once more, then rnd 1 once—27 rnds completed. Change to A.

Shape toe
Work your first dec rnd as foll:
50 sts [K2tog, 23] 4 times—48 sts. Purl next rnd. Break A. Change to C.
48 sts [K2tog, k10] 4 times—44 sts. Purl next rnd. Break C. Change to A.
44 sts [K2tog, k9] 4 times—40 sts. Purl next rnd. Break A. Change to C.
40 sts [K2tog, k8] 4 times—36 sts. Purl next rnd. Break C. Change to A.
36 sts [K2tog, k7] 4 times—32 sts. Purl next rnd.
32 sts [K2tog, k6] 4 times—28 sts. Purl next rnd.
28 sts [K2tog, k5] 4 times—24 sts. Purl next rnd.
24 sts [K2tog, k4] 4 times—20 sts. Purl next rnd.
Cont in garter st, dec every rnd as foll:
20 sts [K2tog, k3] 4 times—16 sts.
16 sts [P2tog tbl, p2] 4 times—12 sts.
12 sts [K2tog, k1] 4 times—8 sts.
8 sts [P2tog tbl] 4 times—4 sts. Cut yarn, leaving a 6"/15.5cm tail. Thread tail in tapestry needle, then thread through rem sts. Pull tog tightly and secure end. Finish same as for basic slipper socks, using C for top edging. ■

At the Farmhouse
I have a clothesline in my kitchen where I hang swatches, small projects and my daughter's art. Looking at it makes me happy!

Child's Zip-Up Cardigan

I've been making zippered cardigans for my daughter, Julia, for many years. I make them too big and then hope she will be able to wear them for a few seasons. To make this cardigan for a boy, change the colors and choose a less "girly" edging.

Magic Multiple for Edging: 5 sts
Colorwork Chart Multiple:
Border 5 or 10 sts; *body* 5 or 15 sts

SIZES
Child's X-Small (Small, Medium, Large, X-Large). Shown in size Large.

FINISHED MEASUREMENTS
Chest (closed): 22 (26, 30, 34, 38)"/56 (66, 76, 86.5, 96.5)cm
Length: 13 (14, 16, 18, 19)"/33 (35.5, 40.5, 45.5, 48)cm
Upper arm: 11 (12, 13, 14, 15)"/28 (30.5, 33, 35.5, 38)cm

YARN
Nashua Handknits *Julia* (wool/mohair/alpaca), 1¾oz/50g, 93yd/85m
A Magenta NHJ2083—4 (4, 5, 5, 6) skeins
B Espresso NHJ0118—4 (4, 5, 5, 6) skeins
C Lady's Mantle NHJ3961—1 (1, 1, 1, 2) skeins
D Blue Thyme NHJ4936—1 skein

NEEDLES
For sweater body and border
Size 5 and 7 (3.75 and 4.5mm) circular needles, 24"/60cm long *or size needed to obtain correct gauge*
For sleeves
One set (4) each sizes 5 and 7 (3.75 and 4.5mm) double-pointed needles (dpns) *or size needed to obtain correct gauge*

NOTIONS
◆ Stitch markers
◆ Tapestry needle
◆ Matching sewing thread
◆ Sewing needle
◆ Sewing machine
◆ One 11 (12, 14, 16, 17)"/28 (30.5, 35.5, 40.5, 43)cm brown heavy-duty separating zipper (see Resources on page 169)

GAUGE
20 sts and 22 rnds = 4"/10cm in St st over chart pats using larger circular needle.
Be sure to obtain correct gauge.

Notes
1. The body of the sweater is worked in the round to the shoulders with steeked sections for front opening, armholes and front neck. During finishing, the steeks are secured with machine stitching, then cut open. See page 21 for securing a steek.
2. Each sleeve is worked in the round, then sewn into the cut armhole openings.
3. Use smaller circular needle or dpns for garter st ridge rnds.
4. When working chart pats, use smaller circular needle or dpns for all one-color rnds and larger circular needle or dpns for all two-color rnds.

BODY
With smaller circular needle and A, cast on 182 (214, 246, 278, 310) sts. Do not join.
Next row (WS) P3, pm, work row 1 of picot edging to last 3 sts, pm, p3—116 (136, 156, 176, 196) sts. Turn work to RS. Break A. Change to B.
Next rnd (RS) With B, k to end, slipping markers. Join sts to work in the round and establish the steek as foll:
Next rnd With B, k3 (steek), sl marker, purl to next marker, sl marker, k3 (steek)—6 sts for steek established and first garter st ridge completed. Cont working first and last 3 sts in St st for steek. Break B. Change to C. Cont to work rnds 1 and 2 of garter st ridge in color sequence as foll: C, B and D, inc 1 st in center of last rnd—117 (137, 157, 177, 197) sts. Break D. Change to C.

Beg chart I

NOTE All one-color rnds are worked on smaller needle and all two-color rnds are worked on larger needle.
Cont in St st on all sts as foll:

Rnd 1 K3 foll steek chart, sl marker, work 10-st pat rep 11 (13, 15, 17, 19) times, then work st 1 once more, sl marker, k3 foll steek chart. Cont to foll charts in this manner through rnd 18. Break yarns. Change to smaller needle and C. Cont to work first and last 3 sts in St st for steek, work rnds 1 and 2 of garter st ridge. Break C. Change to D. Work rnds 1 and 2 of two-color garter st. Break yarns. Change to C. Work rnds 1 and 2 of garter st ridge. Break C.

Beg chart II

NOTE Work all rnds on larger needle.
Cont in St st on all sts as foll:

◆ **For X-Small size only**
Rnd 1 K3 foll steek chart, sl marker, work sts 13–15, work 15-st rep 7 times, then work sts 1–3 once more, sl marker, k3 foll steek chart.

◆ **For Small size only**
Rnd 1 K3 foll steek chart, sl marker, work sts 10–15, work 15-st rep 8 times, then work sts 1–5 once more, sl marker, k3 foll steek chart.

◆ **For Medium size only**
Rnd 1 K3 foll steek chart, sl marker, work st 15, work 15-st rep 10 times, sl marker, k3 foll steek chart.

◆ **For Large size only**
Rnd 1 K3 foll steek chart, sl marker, work sts 13–15, work 15-st rep 11 times, work sts 1–3 once more, sl marker, k3 foll steek chart.

◆ **For X-Large size only**
Rnd 1 K3 foll steek chart, sl marker, work sts 10–15, work 15-st rep 12 times, work sts 1–5 once more, sl marker, k3 foll steek chart.

◆ **For all sizes**
Cont to foll charts in this manner through rnd 11, then rep rnds 1–11 to the end. AT THE SAME TIME, when piece measures 7½ (8, 9½, 11, 11½)"/19 (20.5, 24, 28, 29)cm from beg, establish steek sts each side for armhole openings as foll:

Establish armhole steeks

Next rnd K3 steek sts, sl marker, work 26 (31, 36, 41, 46) sts for right front, pm, using the backward loop cast-on method cast on 6 sts as foll: [1 st with B, 1 st with A] 3 times, pm, work 53 (63, 73, 83, 93) sts for back, pm, using the backward loop cast-on method cast on 6 sts as foll: [1 st with B, 1 st with A] 3 times, pm, work 26 (31, 36, 41, 46) sts for left front, k3 steek sts—129 (149, 169, 189, 209) sts.
You will now be working chart II on 26 (31, 36, 41, 46) sts for each front and 53 (63, 73, 83, 93) sts for back as established, AT THE SAME TIME, you will be working steek chart (beg on rnd 2) on 6 sts each side of body and 6 sts at center front as

established. Work even until armhole steek section measures 3½ (4, 4½, 5)"/9 (10, 11.5, 12.5)cm from beg.

Shape front neck

Next rnd Bind off first 3 steek sts, bind off next 10 (11, 12, 13, 14) sts for right front neck edge, work to last 10 (11, 12, 13, 14) sts before last steeks sts, bind off next 10 (11, 12, 13, 14) sts for left front neck edge, then bind off last 3 steek sts.

Establish front neck steek

Next rnd Using backward loop cast-on method and alternating A and B, cast on 3 sts for neck steek, work foll chart to end of rnd, cast on 3 sts alternating B and A for neck steek.
Next (dec) rnd K 3 steek sts alternating colors, ssk, work foll chart to last 2 sts before next neck steek sts, k2tog, k 3 steek sts alternating colors—1 st dec from each side of front neck edge. Work next rnd even. Rep last 2 rnds 3 times more. Work even in established pats until armhole steek section measures 5½ (6, 6½, 7, 7½)"/14 (15, 16.5, 17.5, 19)cm from beg. Bind off all sts knitwise.

SLEEVES

With smaller circular needle and A, cast on 40 (48, 56, 56, 56) sts. Do not join.
Next row (WS) Work row 1 of picot edging—25 (30, 35, 35, 35) sts. Turn work to RS. Divide sts evenly on 3 smaller dpns. Join and pm, taking care not to twist sts on needles. Break A. Change to B. Work rnds 1 and 2 of garter st ridge in color sequence as foll: B, C, B and D. Break D. Change to B.

Beg chart I

NOTE All one-color rnds are worked on smaller dpns and all two-color rnds are worked on larger dpns.
Cont in St st on all sts as foll:

Rnd 1 K, inc 5 (0, 5, 5, 5) sts evenly spaced around—30 (30, 45, 45, 45) sts.
Rnd 2 Work 15-st rep 2 (2, 3, 3) times. Cont to work chart in this manner through rnd 18. Break B. Change to smaller dpns and C. Work rnds 1 and 2 of garter st ridge, inc 2 (inc 2, dec 1, dec 1, dec 1) sts evenly spaced around—32 (32, 44, 44, 44) sts. Break C. Change to D. Work rnds 1 and 2 of two-color garter st. Break yarns. Change to C.
Work rnds 1 and 2 of garter st ridge, inc 0 (0, 3, 3, 3) sts evenly spaced around last rnd, dropping marker—32 (32, 47, 47, 47) sts. Break C.

Beg chart II

NOTE Work all rnds on larger dpns. Cont in St st on all sts as foll:
Rnd 1 K1 with A, pm, work 15-st rep 2 (2, 3, 3, 3) times, pm, k1 with B.
Rnd 2 K1 with B, pm, work 15-st rep 2 (2, 3, 3, 3) times,

pm, k1 with A.

Work chart through rnd 11, then rep rnds 1–11 to the end. AT THE SAME TIME, cont to alternate colors used for the 2 sts between st markers to create a checkerboard pat (faux "sleeve seam"). Beg shaping sleeve after 0 (0, 2, 2, 0) rnds.

Shape sleeve

Next (inc) rnd K1 with A, sl marker, M1 incorporating inc in chart pat, work 15-st rep 2 (2, 3, 3, 3) times, M1 incorporating inc in chart pat, sl marker; k1 with B. Cont to inc 1 st after first marker and 1 st before 2nd marker every other rnd 10 (9, 0, 0, 2) times more, then every 4th rnd 0 (4, 8, 11, 11) times—54 (60, 65, 71, 75) sts. Work even until piece measures 10 (11½, 13, 14, 15)"/25.5 (29, 33, 35.5, 38)cm from beg. Bind off all sts knitwise.

FINISHING

Securing and cutting the steeks

See page 21 before you begin. It is important to keep the knit fabric flat and neat while stitching. Do not pull on it as you sew or it will distort and ripple. Set sewing machine to straight stitch. On each side of front steek section, sew between the steek st and the chart pat st; this is called "stitching in the ditch." Now, set sewing machine to a medium zigzag stitch. Stitch the two center steek sts as foll: locate the 3rd steek st and sew a row of machine sts on top of the knit sts, then rep along top of the 4th steek st. Using sharp scissors, cut through the center of the two zigzag rows of stitching from the bound-off edge to the beg of the steek section, taking care not to snip the sewing machine stitches. Secure and cut front neck steek and armhole steeks in the same manner. Sew shoulder seams.

Fronts and neck border

With RS facing, smaller circular needle and D, pick up and k 61 (65, 68, 71, 74) sts along right front edge, pm, pick up and k 1 st in corner, pm, pick up and k 58 (61, 64, 67, 70) sts along neck edge, pm, pick up and k 1 st in corner, pm, pick up and k 61 (65, 68 71, 74) sts along left front edge—182 (193, 202, 211, 220) sts. Do not join. Knit next row. Break D. Change to B. Miter neck corners as foll:

Next (inc) row (RS) K to marker; *inc 1 st using the backward loop cast-on method, sl marker, k corner st, inc 1 st, sl marker; rep from * once more, k to end. Knit next row. Break B. Change to C. Rep last 2 rows. Break C. Change to B. Rep last 2 rows. Break B. Change to A. Rep inc row. Bind off all sts loosely knitwise. Sew sleeves into armholes. Weave in ends. Steam or block to even out colorwork. Sew in zipper using sewing needle and thread.

French knot embroidery

Refer to photo. Using a double strand of D in tapestry needle, work 2 French knots (see page 171) at base of each flower of chart 1. ■

Stitches

PICOT EDGING (multiple of 8 sts; decs to 5 sts)
Row 1 (WS) *K2, (k2, sl 2nd st on RH needle over first st to bind off 1 st, [k1, bind off 1 st] twice), k2; rep from * to end. Work row 1 for picot edging.

GARTER STITCH RIDGE
Rnd 1 Knit.
Rnd 2 Purl.
Work rnds 1 and 2 for garter st ridge.

STOCKINETTE STITCH
Knit every round.

TWO-COLOR GARTER STITCH
(multiple of 4 sts)
Rnd 1 *K2 with D, k2 with B; rep from * around.
Rnd 2 *Bring D to front and p2, bring D to back, bring B to front and p2, bring B to back; rep from * around. Work rnds 1 and 2 for two-color garter st.

GARTER STITCH
Knit every row.

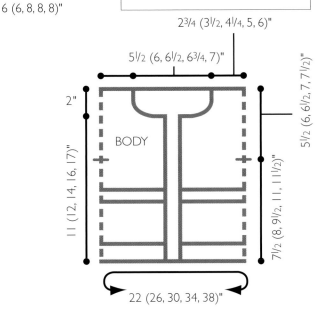

11 (12, 13, 14, 15)"

SLEEVE

10 (12, 13, 14, 15)"

6 (6, 8, 8, 8)"

2³/4 (3¹/2, 4¹/4, 5, 6)"

5¹/2 (6, 6¹/2, 6³/4, 7)"

2"

BODY

5¹/2 (6, 6¹/2, 7, 7¹/2)"

11 (12, 14, 16, 17)"

7¹/2 (8, 9¹/2, 11, 11¹/2)"

22 (26, 30, 34, 38)"

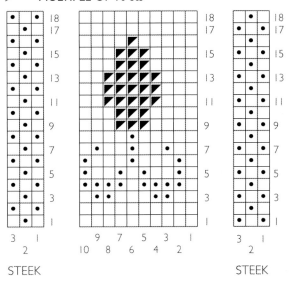

▶ CHART I
MULTIPLE OF 10 sts

STEEK   STEEK

Color Key

☐ B Espresso

⊡ C Lady's Mantle

◪ A Magenta

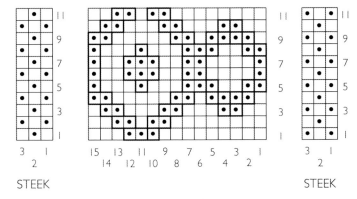

▶ CHART II
MULTIPLE OF 15 sts

STEEK   STEEK

Color Key

☐ A Magenta

⊡ B Espresso

Little Shepherd's Scrap Yarn Scarf

This is the ultimate stash-buster scarf, made by knitting stripes of different colors in sections.
Pull out all your odds and ends of yarn in similar weights and get to it. It's an easy technique, but
I urge you to try out the technique in a swatch—it will make more sense to you.
Make one for everyone in your flock!

FINISHED MEASUREMENTS
Approx 65"/165cm long x 5½"/14cm
wide

YARN
Nashua Handknits *Julia*
(wool/mohair/alpaca), 1¾oz/50g,
93yd/85m
A Blue Thyme NHJ4936—1 skein
B Golden Honey NHJ2163—1 skein
C Lady's Mantle NHJ3961—1 skein
D Pretty Pink NHJ8141—1 skein
E Magenta NHJ2083—1 skein
F Velvet Moss NHJ6086—1 skein
G Espresso NHJ0118—1 skein
H Persimmon NHJ0121—1 skein
I Squash NHJ0120—1 skein
J Geranium NHJ6085—1 skein
K Harvest Spice NHJ0178—1 skein
or approx 7oz/200g (400yd/366m) of
assorted colors of scrap yarn

NEEDLES
For scarf
Size 9 (5.5mm) circular needle,
32"/81cm long *or size needed to obtain
correct gauge*

For swatch
One pair size 9 (5.5mm) needles
or size needed to obtain correct gauge

NOTIONS
◆ Tapestry needle

GAUGE
16 sts and 30 rows = 4"/10cm in
Reverse Stockinette Stitch Ridge using
size 9 (5.5mm) circular needle.
Be sure to obtain correct gauge.

Stitches
GARTER STITCH
Knit every row.

**REVERSE STOCKINETTE
STITCH RIDGE**
Odd number ridges (#1, #3,
#5, #7 and #9)
Row 1 (RS) Knit.
Row 2 Knit.
Row 3 Purl.
Even number ridges (#2, #4,
#6, #8 and #10)
Row 1 (WS) Purl.
Row 2 Purl.
Row 3 Knit.

MAKE A SWATCH FOR GAUGE AND TECHNIQUE
To understand this technique, it is necessary to make a
swatch (see photo on page 13). Both the swatch and scarf
begin and end with 5 rows of garter st. The bright,
staggered colorblock pattern is made by working short
rows. With straight needles and A, cast on 30 sts. Work in
garter st for 5 rows.

Reverse Stockinette Stitch Ridge #1
Rows 1–3 (RS) K15 with B, turn; k15 with B, turn; p15 with B
(you have ended in the middle of the row). K15 with C, turn;
k15 with C, turn; p15 with C (you have ended at the end of
the row)—3 rows completed with 2 colors.

Reverse Stockinette Stitch Ridge #2

Rows 1–3 (WS) P10 with D, turn; p10 with D, turn; k10 with D (you have ended one-third of the way into the row); p10 with E, turn; p10 with E, turn; k10 with E (you are two-thirds of the way into the row); p10 with F, turn; p10 with F, turn; k10 with F (you have ended at the end of the row)—3 rows completed with 3 colors. Cont as established (working RS ridges and WS ridges), varying the number of sts you work in each colorblock across each 3-row Reverse Stockinette Stitch Ridge. Try not to have same or similar colors too close together for best results. Measure for gauge and adjust needle size if necessary.

SCARF

With circular needle and A, cast on 260 sts. Do not join. Work back and forth in garter st for 5 rows.
Working in colors as desired, cont in same technique as swatch, staggering colors across each Reverse Stockinette Stitch Ridge as foll:

Reverse Stockinette Stitch Ridge #1
Work blocks of 60, 50, 50, 50, and 50 sts.

Reverse Stockinette Stitch Ridge #2
Work blocks of 85, 50, 50, 50, and 25 sts.

Reverse Stockinette Stitch Ridge #3
Work blocks of 25, 50, 50, 75, and 60 sts.

Reverse Stockinette Stitch Ridge #4
Work blocks of 70, 80, 40, 30, and 40 sts.

Reverse Stockinette Stitch Ridge #5
Work blocks of 40, 60, 75, 50, and 35 sts.
Beg with a WS ridge, cont to stagger colorblocks as desired for 5 more ridges, or rep Reverse Stockinette Stitch Ridges #2–#5 once more, then #1 once. Change to E and work in garter st for 5 rows. Bind off all sts loosely knitwise.

FINISHING
Weave in ends and sew the side edges of the colorblock changes tog to close openings. ◼

At the Farmhouse

In the springtime, when the grass grows at warp speed, we graze our sheep close to the house to trim the lawn. Sheep are amazing mowing machines!

Mad for Plaid Mittens

When I design knitwear, I think about how an edging will tie in with the colorwork pattern. Sometimes magic happens, as with these mittens. The checked border made by alternating corrugated rib columns is echoed in the mini check pattern in the body of the mitten.

Magic Multiple for Edging: 4 sts
Colorwork Chart Multiple: 4 sts

SIZES
Child's Small (Child's Medium, Woman's Small, Woman's Medium, Woman's Large/Man's Small). Shown in size Woman's Small.

FINISHED MEASUREMENTS
Hand circumference: 5½ (6½, 7¼, 8, 8¾)"/14 (16.5, 18.5, 20.5, 22)cm
Length of cuff: 2 (2¾, 3, 3¼, 3½)"/5 (7, 7.5, 8, 9)cm

YARN
Nashua Handknits *Julia* (wool/mohair/alpaca), 1¾oz/50g, 93yd/85m
A Deep Blue Sea NHJ6396—1 (1, 1, 2, 2) skeins
B Lady's Mantle NHJ3961—1 skein
C Harvest Spice NHJ0178—1 skein
D Magenta NHJ2083—1 skein

NEEDLES
One set (4) each sizes 5 and 7 (3.75 and 4.5mm) double-pointed needles (dpns) *or size needed to obtain correct gauge*

NOTIONS
◆ Stitch marker
◆ Stitch holders
◆ Tapestry needle

GAUGE
20 sts and 22 rnds = 4"/10cm in St st over chart pat using larger dpns.
Be sure to obtain correct gauge.

> ## Note
> Right and left mittens are made exactly the same.
>
> ## Abbreviations
> **M1** Make 1
> **k2tog** Knit 2 stitches together

MITTENS (make 2)
Cuff
With smaller dpn and A, cast on 28 (32, 36, 40, 44) sts. Divide sts evenly on 3 dpns. Join and pm, taking care not to twist sts on needles. Purl next rnd. Break A. Change to B. Work rnds 1–7 of 2 x 2 checked corrugated rib, then rep rnd 2 until piece measures 2 (2¾, 3, 3¼, 3½)"/5 (7, 7.5, 8, 9)cm from beg. Break yarns.

Hand
Change to larger dpns. Cont in St st as foll:
Beg chart I
Rnd 1 Work 4-st pat rep 7 (8, 9, 10, 11) times. Cont to foll chart I in this manner through rnd 3. Cont chart I and beg chart II as foll:

CHART I
MULTIPLE OF 4 sts

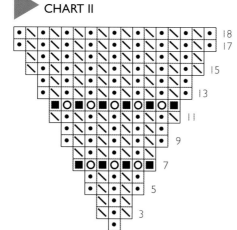

CHART II

Color Key

⊠ **D** Magenta

⊡ **A** Deep Blue Sea

■ **B** Lady's Mantle

◉ **C** Harvest Spice

Stitches

2 X 2 TWO-COLOR CORRUGATED CHECKED RIB
(multiple of 4 sts)
Rnd 1 (RS) *K2 with B, k2 with C; rep from * around.
Rnds 2 and 3 *K2 with B, p2 with C; rep from * around.
Rnd 4 *K2 with C, k2 with B; rep from * around.
Rnds 5 and 6 *P2 with C, k2 with B; rep from * around.
Rnd 7 Rep rnd 1.
Rnd 8 Rep rnd 2.
Work rnds 1–7 once, then rep rnd 8 for corrugated rib.

STOCKINETTE STITCH
Knit every round.

More Colors to Try

Berry Berry NHJ0124;
Golden Honey NHJ2163;
Purple Basil NHJ3158;
Velvet Moss NHJ6086

Shape thumb gusset

Rnd (inc) 4 K14 (16, 18, 20, 22), pm, M1 with A (st 1 of rnd 1 of chart II), pm, k 14 (16, 18, 20, 22)—29 (33, 37, 41, 45) sts.
Rnd 5 Work even (rnd 2 of chart II). Cont to rep rnds 1–5 of chart I for hand, AT SAME TIME, cont to work rnd 3 of chart II as foll:
Rnd (inc) 1 K to first marker; sl marker; M1 with D, k1 with A, M1 with D, sl marker; k to end—31 (35, 39, 43, 47) sts.
Rnd 2 Work even (rnd 4 of chart II). Cont to inc for thumb gusset every other round (foll chart II) until there are 9 (11, 13, 15, 17) sts between gusset markers—37 (43, 49, 55, 61) sts.
Next rnd Work chart I to first marker, drop marker, place next 9 (11, 13, 15, 17) sts on holder for thumb, drop next marker, work chart I to end—28 (32, 36, 40, 44) sts. Work even until hand measures 4 (4 1/2, 5, 6, 6 1/2)"/10 (11.5, 12.5, 15, 16.5)cm from end of thumb gusset. Break yarns, except for A. Change to smaller dpns. With A, cont in St st as foll:

Shape top

Next (dec) rnd *K2, k2tog; rep from * around—21 (24, 27, 30, 33) sts. Knit next rnd.
Next (dec) rnd *K1, k2tog; rep from * around—14 (16, 18, 20, 22) sts. Knit next rnd.
Next (dec) rnd *K2tog; rep from * around—7 (8, 9, 10, 11) sts.
Next (dec) rnd *K2tog; rep from * around, end k 1 (0, 1, 0, 1)—4 (4, 5, 5, 6) sts. Cut yarn, leaving a 6"/15.5cm tail. Thread tail in tapestry needle, then thread through rem sts. Pull tog tightly and secure end on WS.

Thumb

Place sts from thumb gusset holder on 2 larger dpns. With RS facing, join color in progress at beg of thumb sts to cont in vertical stripe pat as established.

Next rnd K across thumb sts, then pick up and k 1 st at base of hand—10 (12, 14, 16, 18) sts. Divide sts between 3 dpns, then pm for beg of rnds. Work even in vertical stripe pat until thumb measures 1 (1 1/4, 1 1/2, 1 3/4, 2)"/2.5 (3, 4, 4.5, 5)cm. Break D. Change to smaller dpns. With A, cont in St st as foll:

Shape top

Next (dec) rnd *K2tog; rep from * around—5 (6, 7, 8, 9) sts.
Next (dec) rnd *K2tog; rep from * around, end k 1 (0, 1, 0, 1)—3 (3, 4, 4, 5) sts. Cut yarn, leaving a 6"/15.5cm tail. Thread tail in tapestry needle, then thread through rem sts. Pull tog tightly and secure end on WS.

FINISHING

Use yarn tail at base of thumb to close up gap between thumb and hand. Weave in ends. ■

First-Timers

If you are just beginning to experiment with Fair Isle knitting, these checked mittens are a good choice for a first project.

On-the-Go Knitter's Tote

What knitter isn't a "bag lady" of some sort? I've got bags of yarn, bags for every ongoing project, and now fabric bags for my groceries. This colorful knitted bag is the perfect size to carry your knitting projects and a magazine or two.

Magic Multiple for Edging: 8 sts
Colorwork Chart Multiple: 4, 5, 10 or 20 sts

FINISHED MEASUREMENTS
Approx 16"/40.5cm wide × 14"/35.5cm high × 4"/10cm deep (excluding handles)

YARN
Nashua Handknits *Julia* (wool/mohair/alpaca), 1¾oz/50g, 93yd/85m
A Velvet Moss NHJ6086—3 skeins
B Dried Wheat NHJ1028—3 skeins
C Coleus NHJ4345—3 skeins
D Harvest Spice NHJ0178—1 skein
E Blue Thyme NHJ 4936—1 skein
F Geranium NHJ6085—1 skein
G Magenta NHJ2083—1 skein
H Gourd NHJ1784—1 skein

NEEDLES
Size 5 and 7 (3.75 and 4.5mm) circular needles, 24"/61cm long *or size to obtain correct gauge*

NOTIONS
◆ Stitch markers
◆ Tapestry needle
◆ 20"/51cm Plain Sew-On Leather Handles (see Resources on page 169)
◆ 1yd/1m of 45"/114.5cm-wide medium-weight lining fabric
◆ 3¾" × 15¾"/9.5cm × 40cm piece of mat board
◆ Matching sewing thread
◆ Sewing needle
◆ Sewing machine (optional)

GAUGE
20 sts and 22 rnds = 4"/10cm in St st over chart pat using larger circular needle.
20 sts and 40 rows = 4"/10cm in garter st using smaller circular needle.
Be sure to obtain correct gauge.

BAG
Base
With smaller circular needle and A, cast on 80 sts. Work back and forth in garter st for 40 rows (20 ridges).

Sides
Next rnd K 80 sts, pick up and k 20 sts (1 st in each ridge) across first short side, pick up and k 80 sts across cast-on edge, pick up and k 20 sts across opposite short edge—200 sts. Join and pm for beg of rnds.
Next rnd Purl. Cont to work around in garter st for 4 rnds more. Break A. Change to larger circular needle and cont in St st on all sts as foll:

Beg chart pat
Rnd 1 Work 20-st pat rep 5 times. Cont to foll chart in this manner through rnd 40, then rep rnds 1–40 until sides measure 12"/30.5cm from beg. Break yarns. Change to smaller needle and A.

Border
Work around in garter st for 4 rnds. Break A. Change to D. Work rnds 1–6 of undulating edge st. Break D. Change to A. Work around in garter st for 4 rnds. Bind off all sts knitwise.

FINISHING
Steam-block sides to even out colorwork.

Duplicate stitch embroidery
Using tapestry needle and E, embroider duplicate stitches (see page 22) foll chart for duplicate stitch embroidery.

Chain stitch and duplicate stitch embroidery
Working in chain stitch (see page 171) and referring to chart for chain stitch and duplicate stitch embroidery, use tapestry needle and G to outline inner edge of a whole diamond motif near bottom of bag, then embroider a duplicate stitch in center of motif. Working in the same manner, cont to embellish every other diamond motif around. To finish the first rnd of whole diamonds, embellish remaining diamond motifs using H. For second rnd of whole diamonds, alternate D and F. For third rnd of whole diamonds, alternate G and H,

> ### Notes
> 1. Bottom of bag is worked back and forth in garter st.
> 2. Sides of bag are worked in the round.

Color Cues

I've been accused of designing projects that are too bright. For this tote, I decided to go more neutral than usual, but here is a more vibrant color scheme for you fellow color lovers.

staggering the color sequence of the first rnd of whole motifs so same colors do not align. For half diamond motifs at bottom of bag, alternate D and F, staggering the color sequence of the second rnd of whole diamonds so same colors do not align.

Mat board liner

Cut two 4¾" × 17¾"/12cm × 45cm pieces from lining fabric. With RS facing and using a ½"/1.3cm seam allowance, sew around three sides, leaving one short edge open. Clip corners; turn RS out. Insert mat board. Fold open edge ½"/1.3cm to WS and whipstitch opening closed. Set aside.

Lining

Measure width of bag, then add 1"/2.5cm to measurement for seam allowance. Cut out two pieces of lining fabric to width measurement × 17"/43cm length. Pin pieces together, RS facing. Using a ½"/1.3cm seam allowance, sew around three sides, leaving top edge open. Clip corners, then press seams open. Insert mat board liner into bottom of lining, making sure top edges of lining remain even. Form the excess fabric at the bottom of each side into a point. Fold each point up to meet side seam; pin. Remove mat board liner. Tack each point securely to side seam. Insert lining into bag, then insert mat board liner into bottom of lining. Fold top edge of lining over to WS, so folded edge is ½"/1.3cm from top edge of bag. Slipstitch lining in place. Sew on leather handles. ◼

More Colors to Try

Maine Coast Blue NHJ4726; Magenta NHJ2083; Velvet Moss NHJ6086; Lupine NHJ5178; Sunflower NHJ1054; Spring Green NHJ5185

BEFORE

AFTER

Brighten It Up

It's amazing how the embroidery transformed the rather plain knitted bag into a brighter and more upbeat design.

CHART FOR SHOPPING BAG
MULTIPLE OF 20 sts

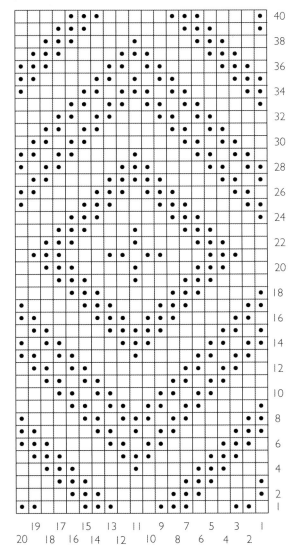

19 17 15 13 11 9 7 5 3 1
20 18 16 14 12 10 8 6 4 2

CHART FOR DUPLICATE STITCH AND EMBROIDERY

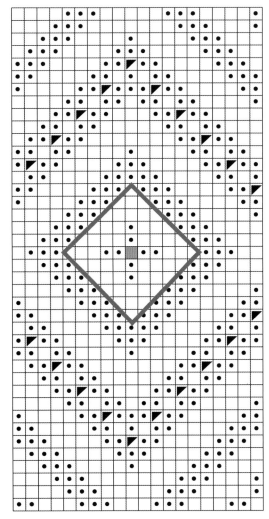

At the Farmhouse

I love decorating the walls of my house with different paint techniques, including colorwashing, stamping and handpainting.

Color Key

☐ **B** Dried Wheat

▣ **C** Coleus

Color Key & Stitch Key

◣ Duplicate stitch using **E** Blue Thyme

▨ Duplicate stitch

▬▬▬▬ Chain stitch

Java Jacket

I started making coffee with a French press many years ago after visiting Paris.
Using it reminds me of sitting outside a café imbibing my favorite brew. The only disadvantage to using a French press is that the coffee can get cold quickly in our old farmhouse. Once again, it's knitting to the rescue! Now my pot looks stylish and the brew stays warm.

Magic Multiple for Edging:
Garter stitch edging. You could add a fancy bind-off like the bobbled bind-off or the picot edge.
Colorwork Chart Multiple:
4, 6, 8, 12 or 24 sts

SIZE

Fits medium-size French press coffeepot.

YARN

Nashua Handknits *Julia* (wool/mohair/alpaca), 1³/₄oz/50g, 93yd/85m
A Lupine NHJ5178—1 skein
B Persimmon NHJ0121—1 skein
C Coleus NHJ4345—1 skein
D Magenta NHJ2083—1 skein
E Lady's Mantle NHJ3961—1 skein

NEEDLES

One pair each size 5 and 7 (3.75 and 4.5mm) needles *or size needed to obtain correct gauge*

NOTIONS
◆ Stitch markers
◆ Tapestry needle
◆ Two size 4 sew-on snaps
◆ Sewing threads to match A and D
◆ Sewing needle

GAUGE

20 sts and 22 rows = 4"/10cm in St st over chart pat using larger needles.
20 sts and 40 rows = 4"/10cm in garter st using smaller needles.
Be sure to obtain the correct gauge.

Notes
1. Coffee cozy is worked back and forth in garter st and St st.
2. Work chart following color key, then add duplicate stitches in colors listed after work is completed.

COFFEEPOT COZY

With smaller needles and A, cast on 50 sts.
Bottom border
Work in garter st for 6 rows. Break A. Change to larger needles and B. Cont in St st on all sts as foll:
Beg chart
Row 1 (RS) K1 using A (selvage st), pm, work 24-st rep twice, pm, k1 using A (selvage st). Keeping 1 selvage st each side in A, cont to foll chart in this manner through row 27. Break yarns. Change to smaller needles and D. Purl next row.
Top border
Work in garter st for 6 rows. Bind off all sts knitwise.
Side borders
With RS facing and E, pick up and k 25 sts evenly spaced across side edge. Work in garter st for 10 rows. Bind off all sts knitwise. Rep on opposite side edge.
Right closing tab
With RS of right side border facing and D, skip first 6 sts, pick up and k 1 st in each of next 13 sts. Cont in garter st for 13 rows. Bind off all sts knitwise.
Left closing tab
With RS of left side border facing and A, skip first 6 sts, pick up and k 1 st in each of next 13 sts. Cont in garter st for 13 rows. Bind off all sts knitwise.

FINISHING

Steam-block to even out colorwork.
Duplicate stitch embroidery
Using tapestry needle, embroider duplicate stitches (see page 22) foll color key and chart.
French knot embroidery
Using a double strand of A in tapestry needle, work five French knots (see page 171) evenly spaced across color B of row 25 of chart (see photo on page 70 for placement). Sew snaps on closing tabs using sewing needle and matching threads. ■

CHART FOR JAVA JACKET
MULTIPLE OF 24 sts

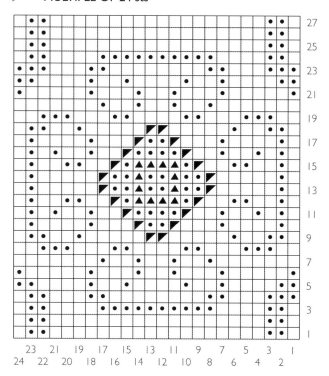

27
25
23
21
19
17
15
13
11
9
7
5
3
1

23 21 19 17 15 13 11 9 7 5 3 1
24 22 20 18 16 14 12 10 8 6 4 2

Stitches
GARTER STITCH
Knit every row.

STOCKINETTE STITCH
Row 1 (RS) Knit.
Row 2 Purl.
Rep rows 1 and 2 for St st.

Color Key

☐ ◪ ▲ **B** Persimmon

⊡ **C** Coleus

Duplicate Stitch Key

◪ **A** Lupine

▲ **E** Lady's Mantle

Mix It Up
If you want to add some variety, you can reverse the colors for the duplicate stitch pattern on the other side of the warmer.

Round and Round
This is one of only two projects in this book that are knit back and forth. If you are a diehard in the round knitter, add a 6-stitch steek to the edges of the rectangle and work it in the round. It's a bit tricky to sew and cut such a little piece of knitting, but it is possible. You may have to sew a bit, cut a bit, then sew some more and cut again.

Best Friends Pullovers

Julia's Sweater (on the left) has a shaped and bobbled border, a floral bottom panel and allover pattern on most of the sweater. A different motif is used on the sleeves. Bridget's pullover mixes it up a bit more—with many different stripes stacked atop each other.

Magic Multiple for Edging:
Julia's Sweater uses a bobbled pointed edging, which begins with more stitches than it ends with. See page 142 for how to adapt an edging that starts and ends with a different number of sts.
Colorwork Chart Multiple:
4, 5, 10 or 20 sts.

JULIA'S SWEATER

SIZES
Child's Small (Medium, Large, X-Large). Shown in size X-Large.

FINISHED MEASUREMENTS
Chest: 24 (28, 32, 36)"/61 (71, 81, 91.5)cm
Length: 14 (16, 18½, 21)"/35.5 (40.5, 47, 53.5)cm
Upper arm: 11 (12, 13, 14)"/28(30.5, 33, 35.5)cm

YARN
Nashua Handknits *Julia* (wool/mohair/alpaca), 1¾oz/50g, 93yd/85m
A Magenta NHJ2083—2 (2, 2, 3) skeins
B Squash NHJ0120—1 skein
C Blue Thyme NHJ4936—3 (3, 3, 4) skeins
D Coleus NHJ4345—2 (2, 3, 3) skeins
E Velvet Moss NHJ6086—1 skein
F Lady's Mantle NHJ3961—2 (2, 3, 3) skeins

NEEDLES
For sweater body
Size 5 and 7 (3.75 and 4.5mm) circular needles, 24"/60cm long *or size needed to obtain correct gauge*
For sleeves and neckband
One set (4) each sizes 5 and 7 (3.75 and 4.5mm) double-pointed needles (dpns) *or size needed to obtain correct gauge*

NOTIONS
◆ Stitch markers
◆ Tapestry needle
◆ Matching sewing thread
◆ Sewing machine

GAUGE
20 sts and 22 rnds = 4"/10cm in St st over chart pats using larger circular needle.
Be sure to obtain correct gauge.

Notes
1. The body of the sweater is worked in the round to the shoulders with steeked sections for the armholes and front neck. During finishing, the steeks are secured with machine stitching, then cut open. See page 21 for securing a steek.
2. Each sleeve is worked in the round, then sewn into the cut armhole openings.
3. Use smaller circular needle or dpns for garter st rnds.
4. When working chart pats, use smaller circular needle or dpns for all one-color rnds and larger circular needle or dpns for all two-color rnds.

BODY
With smaller circular needle and A, cast on 187 (220, 242, 275) sts. Join taking care not to twist sts on needle, pm for beg of rnds. Work rnd 1–4 of pointed bobble edging—119 (140, 154, 175) sts. Cont in garter st, working 2 rnds each in color sequence as foll: B, C and D. Break D. Change to A.
Next (inc rnd) K inc 1 (0, 6, 5) sts evenly spaced around—120 (140, 160, 180) sts.
Next rnd P 60 (70, 80, 90) sts, pm (for armhole steek placement), p to end. Break A. Change to E.

Beg chart 1
NOTE All one-color rnds are worked on smaller needle and all two-color rnds are worked on larger needle. Cont in St st on all sts as foll:
Rnd 1 Work 20-st pat rep 6 (7, 8, 9) times. Cont to foll chart in this manner through rnd 23. Break yarns. Change to

▶ CHART I
MULTIPLE OF 20 sts

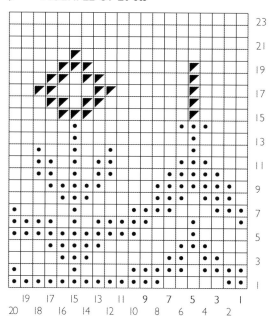

23
21
19
17
15
13
11
9
7
5
3
1

19 17 15 13 11 9 7 5 3 1
20 18 16 14 12 10 8 6 4 2

Color Key

- [•] **E** Velvet Moss
- [ ] **F** Lady's Mantle
- [◢] **A** Magenta

▶ CHART I
MULTIPLE OF 20 sts

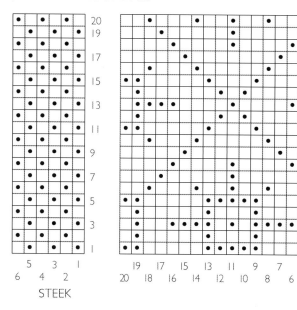

20
19
17
15
13
11
9
7
5
3
1

5 3 1
6 4 2
STEEK

20
19
17
15
13
11
9
7
5
3
1

19 17 15 13 11 9 7 5 3 1
20 18 16 14 12 10 8 6 4 2

Color Key

- [•] **D** Coleus
- [ ] **C** Blue Thyme

Stitches

POINTED BOBBLE EDGING
(multiple of 11 sts; decs to a multiple of 7 sts)
Rnd 1 *P5, work [k1, p1] twice in next st, turn; p4, turn; k4, turn; p4, turn; pass the 2nd st over the first, the 3rd st over the first, the 4th st over the first st (bobble made), sl this st to RH needle, p5; rep from * around.
Rnd 2 *P4, sl2, k1, p2sso, p4; rep from * around.
Rnd 3 *K3, sl2, k1, p2sso, k3; rep from * around.
Rnd 4 Purl.
Work rnds 1–4 for pointed bobble edging.

GARTER STITCH
Rnd 1 Knit.
Rnd 2 Purl.
Rep rnds 1 and 2 for garter st.

STOCKINETTE STITCH
Knit every round.

Abbreviations

p2sso Pass 2 slipped stitches over the k1
k2tog Knit 2 stitches together
ssk Slip, slip, knit these 2 stitches together
M1 Make 1

▶ CHART III
MULTIPLE OF 5 sts

5
3
1

5 3 1
4 2

Color Key

- [ ] **F** Lady's Mantle
- [•] **A** Magenta

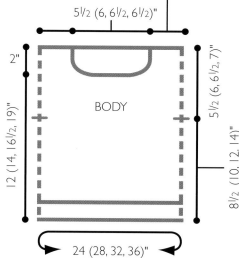

3¼ (4, 4¾, 5¾)"
5½ (6, 6½, 6½)"
2"
12 (14, 16½, 19)"
BODY
5½ (6, 6½, 7)"
8½ (10, 12, 14)"
24 (28, 32, 36)"

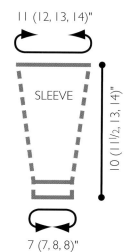

11 (12, 13, 14)"
SLEEVE
10 (11½, 13, 14)"
7 (7, 8, 8)"

smaller needle and D. Cont in garter st, working 2 rnds each in color sequence as foll: D, B and E. Break E. Change to larger needle and D.

Beg chart II

NOTE All rnds are worked on larger needle.
Cont in St st on all sts as foll:
Rnd 1 Work 20-st pat rep 6 (7, 8, 9) times. Cont to foll chart in this manner through rnd 20, then rep rnds 1–20 to the end. AT THE SAME TIME, when piece measures 8½ (10, 12, 14)"/21.5 (25.5, 30.5, 35.5)cm from beg, establish steek sts each side for armhole openings as foll:

Establish armhole steeks

Next rnd Work chart II as established to next marker, sl marker, using the backward loop cast-on method, cast on 6 sts as foll: [1 st with C, 1 st with D] 3 times, pm; work chart II as established to next marker, sl marker, using the backward loop cast-on method cast on 6 sts as foll: [1 st with C, 1 st with D] 3 times, pm for new beg of rnd—132 (152, 172, 192) sts. You will now be working chart II on 60 (70, 80, 90) sts on front and back, and working steek chart (beg on rnd 2) on 6 sts each side of body. Work even until armhole steek section measures 3½ (4, 4½, 5)"/9 (10, 11.5, 12.5)cm from beg.

Shape front neck

Next rnd Work chart II as established across first 20 (24, 28, 33) sts, bind off center 20 (22, 24, 24) sts, work as established to end of rnd—20 (24, 28, 33) sts each side of front neck bound-off sts, 60 (70, 80, 90) sts on back and 6-st steek sections each side.

Establish front neck steek

Next rnd Work chart II as established across first 20 (24, 28, 33) sts, pm, using the backward loop cast-on method, cast on 6 sts as foll: [1 st with C, 1 st with D] 3 times, pm, work as established to end of rnd—138 (158, 178, 198) sts.
Next (dec) rnd Work chart II as established to 2 sts before next marker, k2tog, sl marker, work 6-st steek section at center front neck beg on rnd 2 of steek chart, sl marker, ssk, work as established to end of rnd—1 st dec from each side of front neck. Work next rnd even. Rep last 2 rnds 3 times more—16 (20, 24, 29) sts each side of front neck bound-off sts. Work even in established pats until armhole steek section measures 5½ (6, 6½, 7)"/14 (15, 16.5, 17.5)cm. Bind off all sts knitwise.

SLEEVES

With smaller dpn and A, cast on 30 (32, 34, 36) sts. Divide sts evenly on 3 dpns. Join and pm, taking care not to twist sts on needles. Purl next rnd. Break A. Change to E. Cont in garter st, working 2 rnds each in color sequence as foll: E, B and C. Break C. Change to D.

Next (inc) rnd K inc 7 (5, 8, 6) sts evenly spaced around—37 (37, 42, 42) sts. Purl next rnd, dropping marker. Break D. Change to F.

Beg chart III

NOTE All one-color rnds are worked on smaller dpns and all two-color rnds are worked on larger dpns. Cont in St st on all sts as foll:
Rnd 1 K1 with F, pm, work 5-st pat rep 7 (7, 8, 8) times, pm, k1 with A.
Rnd 2 K1 with A, sl marker, work 5-st rep 7 (7, 8, 8) times, sl marker, k1 with F. Work chart through rnd 5, then rep rnds 1–5 to the end. AT THE SAME TIME, cont to alternate colors used for the 2 sts between st markers to create a checkerboard pat (faux "sleeve seam"). Work 3 rnds more.

Shape sleeve

Next (inc) rnd K1 with A, sl marker, M1 incorporating inc in chart pat, work rnd 1 of chart II working 5-st rep 7 (7, 8, 8) times, M1 incorporating inc in chart pat, sl marker, k1 with F. Cont to inc 1 st after first marker and 1 st before 2nd marker every 4th rnd 4 (7, 5, 6) times more, then every 6th round 4 (4, 6, 7) times—55 (61, 66, 70) sts. Work even as established until piece measures 10 (11½, 13, 14)"/25.5 (29, 33, 35.5)cm from beg. Bind off all sts knitwise.

FINISHING

Securing and cutting the steeks

See page 21 before you begin. It is important to keep the knit fabric flat and neat while stitching. Do not pull on it as you sew or it will distort and ripple. Set sewing machine to straight stitch. On each side of an armhole steek section, sew between the steek st and the chart pat st; this is called "stitching in the ditch." Now, set sewing machine to a medium zigzag stitch. Stitch the two center steek sts as foll: locate the 3rd steek st and sew a row of machine sts on top of the knit sts, then rep along top of the 4th steek st. Using sharp scissors, cut through the center of the two zigzag rows of stitching from the bound-off edge to the beg of the steek section, taking care not to snip the sewing machine stitches. Rep for second armhole. Secure and cut front neck steek in the same manner. Sew shoulder seams.

Neckband

With RS facing, smaller dpns, A and beg at left shoulder seam, pick up and k 82 (84, 86, 90) sts evenly spaced around neck edge. Join and pm for beg of rnds. Purl next rnd. Break A. Change to C. Cont in garter st, working 2 rnds each in color sequence as foll: C, B and F. Break F. Change to A. Knit next rnd. Bind off all sts loosely purlwise. Sew sleeves into armholes. Weave in ends. Steam or block to even out colorwork.

Duplicate stitch embroidery

Refer to photo. Using tapestry needle and D, embroider duplicate stitches (see page 22) to fill in center of each flower of chart I. Using B, embroider duplicate stitches around center D-st of square motif around bottom of chart II.

French knot embroidery

Refer to photo. Using a double strand of B in tapestry needle, work 3 French knots (see page 171) at top of each flower of chart I.

Lazy daisy stitch embroidery

Refer to photo. Using tapestry needle and D, embroider 5 lazy daisy stitches (see page 171) along each stem of chart I, with 2 on each side of stem and one at top. ■

Magic Multiple for Edging: Bridget's Sweater has a simple garter stitch edging.
Colorwork Chart Multiple: 4, 5, 10 or 20 sts.

BRIDGET'S SWEATER

SIZES

Child's Small (Medium, Large, X-Large). Shown in size Large.

FINISHED MEASUREMENTS

Chest: 24 (28, 32, 36)"/61 (71, 81, 91.5)cm
Length: 14 (16, 17, 19)"/35.5 (40.5, 43, 48)cm
Upper arm: 11 (12, 13, 14)"/28 (30.5, 33, 35.5)cm

YARN

Nashua Handknits *Julia* (wool/mohair/alpaca), 1¾oz/50g, 93yd/85m
A Anemone NHJ9235—1 (2, 2, 3) skeins
B Squash NHJ0120—1 skein
C Lady's Mantle NHJ3961— 2 (2, 2, 3) skeins
D Geranium NHJ6085—1 (1, 1, 2) skeins
E Golden Honey NHJ2163—2 (2, 2, 3) skeins
F Rock Henna NHJ2230—2 (2, 2, 3) skeins
G Espresso NHJ0118—1 skein

NEEDLES

For sweater body
Size 5 and 7 (3.75 and 4.5mm) circular needles, 24"/60cm long *or size needed to obtain correct gauge*

For sleeves and neckband
One set (4) each sizes 5 and 7 (3.75 and 4.5mm) double-pointed needles (dpns) *or size needed to obtain correct gauge*

NOTIONS

◆ Stitch markers
◆ Tapestry needle
◆ Matching sewing thread
◆ Sewing machine

GAUGE

20 sts and 22 rnds = 4"/10cm in St st over chart pats using larger circular needle.
Be sure to obtain correct gauge.

Notes

1. The body of the sweater is worked in the round to the shoulders with steeked sections for the armholes and front neck. During finishing, the steeks are secured with machine stitching, then cut open. See page 21 for securing a steek.
2. Each sleeve is worked in the round, then sewn into the cut armhole openings.
3. Use smaller circular needle or dpns for garter st rnds.
4. When working chart pats, use smaller circular needle or dpns for all one-color rnds and larger circular needle or dpns for all two-color rnds.

Abbreviations

k2tog Knit 2 stitches together
ssk Slip, slip, knit these 2 stitches together
M1 Make 1

BODY

With smaller circular needle and A, cast on 108 (126, 144, 162) sts. Join taking care not to twist sts on needle, pm for beg of rnds. Purl next rnd. Cont in garter st, working 2 rnds each in color sequence as foll: B, C, D. Break D. Change to E.

Next (inc rnd) K inc 12 (14, 16, 18) sts evenly spaced around—120 (140, 160, 180) sts.

Next rnd P 60 (70, 80, 90) sts, pm (for armhole steek placement), p to end.

Beg chart I

NOTE All one-color rnds are worked on smaller needle and all two-color rnds are worked on larger needle. Cont in St st on all sts as foll:

Rnd 1 Work 5-st pat rep 24 (28, 32, 36) times. Cont to foll chart in this manner through rnd 6. Break yarns. Change to smaller needle and G. Cont in garter st, working 2 rnds each in color sequence as foll: G, B and A. Break A. Change larger needle and C.

Beg chart II

NOTE All rnds are worked on larger needle. Cont in St st on all sts as foll:

Rnd 1 Work 20-st pat rep 6 (7, 8, 9) times. Cont to foll chart in this manner through rnd 21. Break yarns. Change to smaller needle and A. Cont in garter st, working 2 rnds each in color sequence as foll: A, F and E. Break E. Change larger needle and G.

Beg chart III

NOTE All rnds are worked on larger needle. Cont in St st on all sts as foll:

Rnd 1 Work 5-st pat rep 24 (28, 32, 36) times. Cont to foll chart in this manner through rnd 5.

◆ **For Small size only**
Rep rnds 1 and 2 once more.

◆ **For Medium and Large sizes only**
Rep rnds 1–5 once more.

◆ **For X-Large size only**
Rep rnds 1–5 once more, then rnds 1 and 2.

◆ **For all sizes**
Break yarns. Change to smaller needle and E. Cont in garter st, working 2 rnds each in color sequence as foll: E, F and C. Break C. Change larger needle and E.

Beg chart IV

NOTE All rnds are worked on larger needle. Cont in St st on all sts as foll:

Rnd 1 Work 10-st pat rep 12 (14, 16, 18) times. Cont to foll chart in this manner through rnd 16, then rep rnds 1–16 to the end. AT THE SAME TIME, when piece measures 8½ (10, 12, 14)"/21.5 (25.5, 30.5, 35.5)cm from beg, establish steek sts each side for armhole openings as foll:

Establish armhole steeks

Next rnd Work chart IV as established to next marker, sl marker, using the backward loop cast-on method, cast on 6 sts as foll: [1 st with E, 1 st with A] 3 times, pm; work chart IV as established to next marker, sl marker, using the backward loop cast-on method cast on 6 sts as foll: [1 st with E, 1 st with A] 3 times, pm for new beg of rnd—132 (152, 172, 192) sts. You will now be working chart IV on 60 (70, 80, 90) sts on front and back, and working steek chart (beg on rnd 2) on 6 sts each side of body. Work even until armhole steek section measures 3½ (4, 4½, 5)"/9 (10, 11.5, 12.5)cm from beg.

Shape front neck

Next rnd Work chart IV as established across first 20 (24, 28, 33) sts, bind off center 20 (22, 24, 24) sts, work as established to end of rnd—20 (24, 28, 33) sts each side of front neck bound-off sts, 60 (70, 80, 90) sts on back and 6-st steek sections each side.

Establish front neck steek

Next rnd Work chart IV as established across first 20 (24, 28, 33) sts, pm, using the backward loop cast-on method, cast on 6 sts as foll: [1 st with A, 1 st with E] 3 times, pm, work as established to end of rnd—138 (158, 178, 198) sts.

Next (dec) rnd Work chart IV as established to 2 sts before next marker, k2tog, sl marker, work 6-st steek section at center front neck beg on rnd 2 of steek chart, sl marker, ssk, work as established to end of rnd—1 st dec from each side of front neck. Work next rnd even. Rep last 2 rnds 3 times more—16 (20, 24, 29) sts each side of front neck bound-off sts. Work even in established pats until armhole steek section measures 5½ (6, 6½, 7)"/14 (15, 16.5, 17.5)cm. Bind off all sts knitwise.

SLEEVES

With smaller dpn and E, cast on 30 (32, 34, 36) sts. Divide sts evenly on 3 dpns. Join and pm, taking care not to twist sts on needles. Purl next rnd. Break E. Change to D. Cont in garter st, working 2 rnds each in color sequence as foll: D, G and B. Break B. Change to A.

Next (inc) rnd K inc 7 (5, 7, 5) sts evenly spaced around—37 (37, 42, 42) sts. Purl next rnd, dropping marker. Break A. Change to F.

Beg chart V

NOTE All one-color rnds are worked on smaller dpns and all two-color rnds are worked on larger dpns. Cont in St st on all sts as foll:

Rnd 1 K1 with F, pm, work 5-st pat rep 7 (7, 8, 8) times, pm, k1 with C.

Rnd 2 K1 with C, sl marker, work 5-st rep 7 (7, 8, 8) times, sl marker, k1 with F. Work chart through rnd 5, then rep rnds 1–5 to the end. AT THE SAME TIME, cont to alternate colors

used for the 2 sts between st markers to create a checkerboard pat (faux "sleeve seam"). Work 3 rnds more.

Shape sleeve

Next (inc) rnd K1 with C, sl marker, M1 incorporating inc in chart pat, work rnd 1 of chart V working 5-st rep 7 (7, 8, 8) times, M1 incorporating inc in chart pat, sl marker, k1 with F. Cont to inc 1 st after first marker and 1 st before 2nd marker every 4th rnd 4 (7, 5, 6) times more, then every 6th round 4 (4, 6, 7) times—55 (61, 66, 70) sts. Work even as established until piece measures 10 (11½, 13, 14)"/25.5 (29, 33, 35.5)cm from beg. Bind off all sts knitwise.

FINISHING

Securing and cutting the steeks

See page 21 before you begin. It is important to keep the knit fabric flat and neat while stitching. Do not pull on it as you sew or it will distort and ripple. Set sewing machine to straight stitch. On each side of an armhole steek section, sew between the steek st and the chart pat st; this is called "stitching in the ditch." Now, set sewing machine to a medium zigzag stitch. Stitch the two center steek sts as foll: locate the 3rd steek st and sew a row of machine sts on top of the knit sts, then rep along top of the 4th steek st. Using sharp scissors, cut through the center of the two zigzag rows of stitching from the bound-off edge to the beg of the steek section, taking care not to snip the sewing machine stitches. Rep for second armhole. Secure and cut front neck steek in the same manner. Sew shoulder seams.

Neckband

With RS facing, smaller dpns, B and beg at left shoulder seam, pick up and k 82 (84, 86, 90) sts evenly spaced around neck edge. Join and pm for beg of rnds. Purl next rnd. Break B. Change to G. Cont in garter st, working 2 rnds each in color sequence as foll: G, D and E. Break E. Change to F. Knit next rnd. Bind off all sts loosely purlwise. Sew sleeves into armholes. Weave in ends. Steam or block to even out colorwork.

Chain stitch embroidery

Working in chain stitch (see page 171), using tapestry needle and A, outline inner edge of center circle on each X motif of chart II.

French knot embroidery

Using a double strand of G in tapestry needle, work a French knot (see page 171) in center of each motif of chart II.

Cross stitch and straight stitch embroidery

Using tapestry needle and D, embroider a cross stitch (see page 171) in center of a small cross motif on chart IV, then embroider a short vertical straight stitch over the intersection of the cross stitch. Work a cross stitch with a vertical straight stitch in center of each rem cross motif. ■

BRIDGET'S SWEATER

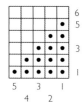

CHART I
MULTIPLE OF 5 sts

Color Key
- [•] **E** Golden Honey
- [ ] **F** Rock Henna

6
5
3
1
5 3 1
4 2

CHART III
MULTIPLE OF 5 sts

Color Key
- [•] **G** Espresso
- [ ] **B** Squash

5
3
1
5 3 1
4 2

CHART V
MULTIPLE OF 5 sts

Color Key
- [ ] **C** Lady's Mantle
- [•] **F** Rock Henna

6
5
3
1
5 3 1
4 2

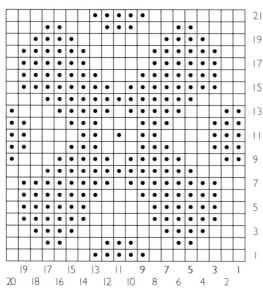

CHART II
MULTIPLE OF 20 sts

21
19
17
15
13
11
9
7
5
3
1

19 17 15 13 11 9 7 5 3 1
20 18 16 14 12 10 8 6 4 2

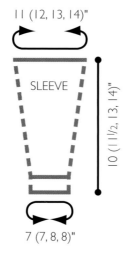

SLEEVE

11 (12, 13, 14)"

10 (11½, 13, 14)"

7 (7, 8, 8)"

Color Key
- [ ] **C** Lady's Mantle
- [•] **D** Geranium

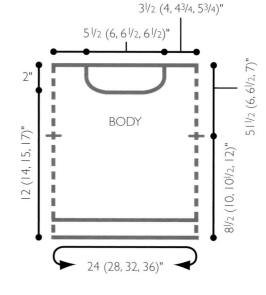

3½ (4, 4¾, 5¾)"

5½ (6, 6½, 6½)"

2"

BODY

12 (14, 15, 17)"

5½ (6, 6½, 7)"

8½ (10, 10½, 12)"

24 (28, 32, 36)"

CHART IV
MULTIPLE OF 10 sts

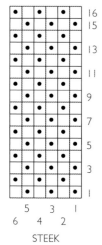

16
15
13
11
9
7
5
3
1

5 3 1
6 4 2

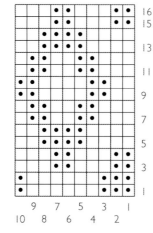

16
15
13
11
9
7
5
3
1

9 7 5 3 1
10 8 6 4 2

STEEK

Stitches
GARTER STITCH
Rnd 1 Knit.
Rnd 2 Purl.
Rep rnds 1 and 2 for
garter st.

STOCKINETTE STITCH
Knit every round.

Color Key
- [•] **E** Golden Honey
- [ ] **A** Anemone

Felted Laptop Cozy

I guess you could say that if there is an object that can be wrapped in wool, I'm going to do it. I love my laptop and the portability it gives my writing, but I find most commercially produced laptop sleeves too bland for my taste. This felted Fair Isle design is both practical and fun to carry. I sewed on snaps to close it, but hook-and-loop closures would work just as well.

Magic Multiple for Edging:
There is no edging on this project.
Colorwork Chart Multiple:
4, 5, 10 or 20 sts

SIZES
To fit 11 (13, 15)"/28 (33, 38)cm notebook computer.

FINISHED MEASUREMENTS
Approx 10¾ (12¾, 14¾)"/27.5 (32.5, 37.5)cm wide × 10"/25.5cm high × 1¼"/3cm deep (after felting)

YARN
Nashua Handknits *Julia* (wool/mohair/alpaca), 1¾oz/50g, 93yd/85m
A Rock Henna NHJ2230—2 skeins
B Deep Blue Sea NHJ6396—3 skeins
C Magenta NHJ2083—1 skein
D Lady's Mantle NHJ3961—3 skeins

NEEDLES
Size 7 and 8 (4.5 and 5mm) circular needles, 24"/61cm long *or size needed to obtain correct gauge*

NOTIONS
◆ Stitch marker
◆ Tapestry needle
◆ Two black size 10 sew-on snaps
◆ Sewing thread to match B
◆ Sewing needle

GAUGE
20 sts and 26 rnds = 4"/10cm in St st over chart pat using larger circular needle (before felting).
16 sts and 32 rows = 4"/10cm in garter st using smaller circular needle (before felting).
Be sure to obtain correct gauge.

Notes
1. Bottom and flap of case are worked back and forth in garter st.
2. Sides of case are worked in the round in St st.

Stitches
GARTER STITCH
Knit every row.

GARTER STITCH (in the round)
Rnd 1 Knit.
Rnd 2 Purl.
Rep rnds 1 and 2 for garter st.

STOCKINETTE STITCH
Knit every round.

LAPTOP SLEEVE
Base
With smaller circular needle and A, cast on 56 (64, 72) sts. Work back and forth in garter st for 16 rows (8 ridges).
Sides
Next rnd K 56 (64, 72) sts, pick up and k 8 sts (1 st in each ridge) across first short side, pick up and k 56 (64, 72) sts across cast-on edge, pick up and k 8 sts across opposite short edge—128 (144, 160) sts. Join and pm for beg of rnds.
Next rnd Purl.
Next 4 rnds Work in garter st. Break A. Change to B.
Next 6 rnds Work in garter st. Break B. Change to C.
Next 6 rnds Work in garter st. Break C. Change to A.
Next 5 rnds Work in garter st.

CHART FOR LAPTOP SLEEVE
MULTIPLE OF 20 sts

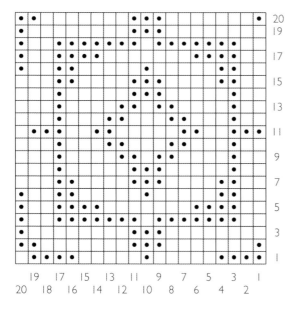

19 17 15 13 11 9 7 5 3 1
20 18 16 14 12 10 8 6 4 2

Color Key

• **B** Deep Blue Sea

☐ **D** Lady's Mantle

Next (inc) rnd P, inc 32 (36, 40) sts evenly spaced around—160 (180, 200) sts Break A. Change to B. Change to larger circular needle and cont in St st on all sts as foll:

Beg chart pat
Rnd 1 Work 20-st pat rep 8 (9, 10) times.
Cont to foll chart in this manner through rnd 20, then rep rnds 1-20 twice more, then rnd 1 once. Break yarns. Change to smaller needles and C.
Next (dec) rnd K, dec 32 (36, 40) sts evenly spaced around—128 (144, 160) sts.
Next 5 rnds Beg with a p rnd, work in garter st for 5 rnds. Do not break C.

Flap
Next rnd Slip last 8 sts on RH needle back to LH needle, bind off these 8 sts, then bind off next 64 (72, 80) sts—56 (64, 72) sts. Break C. Change to B. You will now be working back and forth in garter st and stripe pat as foll:
Work 6 rows each in B, D, A, B, C and B.
Bind off all sts loosely knitwise. ■

No-Fear Felting

Place sleeve in a zippered pillowcase. Set the water level on your washing machine to low, and the temperature to hot. Put in a little clear laundry detergent, an old towel or two (or a pair of old jeans, or a couple of rubber balls or flip flops) to help with agitation. Set your washer for a heavy load and check the felting progress every 5 or 10 minutes. Do not let the sleeve go through the spin cycle, as this may cause creasing. You may have to repeat this felting process one or more times to adequately felt the sleeve and reach finished measurements. If so, drain the water from the washing machine each time and start again. You may also add some boiling water to the machine. When the sleeve is felted, rinse it in cold water, and roll it in a towel to squeeze out the excess water. Hand-block to measurements. Place sleeve on a flat surface. Stuff lightly with newspaper to wick away water and help it dry. Let air-dry flat for one to two days. Sew on snaps for closure.

Getting Closure

I used snaps to close up this laptop cozy, but use your imagination to come up with other ideas. Pretty buttons, a zipper, elastic loops or hook-and-loop closures, felted ties and leather buckles would all be fun alternatives.

Southwest-Style Sleeved Wrap

My friend and publisher Trisha Malcolm suggested I design a garment that would be a combination of jacket and shawl. I thought back to the 1970s and 80s and the handweaving craze. Handweavers everywhere were making "ruanas"—large pieces of fabric with a split halfway up the piece worn as shawls or wraps. I thought I could update the idea to fit my crazy colorwork patterning.

Magic Multiple for Edging:
The center front opening could be trimmed in any edge treatments, such as bobbles or picot edging.
Colorwork Chart Multiple:
4, 5, 10 or 20 sts

SIZE
One size fits most.

FINISHED MEASUREMENTS
Bust: 60"/152.5cm
Length: 32"/81cm (excluding fringe)
Upper arm: 17"/43cm

YARN
Nashua Handknits *Julia* (wool/mohair/alpaca), 1¾oz/50g, 93yd/85m
A Magenta NHJ2083—2 skeins
B Blue Thyme NHJ4936—5 skeins
C Rock Henna NHJ2230—5 skeins
D Dried Wheat NHJ1028—2 skeins
E Anemone NHJ9235—5 skeins
F Lady's Mantle NHJ3961—2 skeins
G Espresso NHJ0118—5 skeins
H Geranium NHJ6085—4 skeins

NEEDLES
For jacket body
Size 5 and 7 (3.75 and 4.5mm) circular needles, 32"/81cm long *or size needed to obtain correct gauge*

For sleeves
One set (4) each sizes 5 and 7 (3.75 and 4.5mm) double-pointed needles (dpns) *or size needed to obtain correct gauge*

NOTIONS
◆ Scrap yarn
◆ Stitch markers
◆ Tapestry needle
◆ Matching sewing thread
◆ Sewing machine

GAUGE
20 sts and 22 rnds = 4"/10cm in St st over chart pats using larger circular needle.
Be sure to obtain the correct gauge.

Notes
1. The jacket is worked in the round forming a tube, with steek sts at beginning and end of rounds.
2. Cast-on and bind-off edges will become side seams and armhole openings.
3. After knitting is completed, the jacket is cut open and the steek sts are unraveled to form a fringe at bottom edge.
4. The front opening is made by using scrap yarn and knitting rows which will be removed later. When the scrap yarn stitches are removed, you will pick up the live sts and work a garter-stitch band to finish the front opening.
5. All one-color rnds are worked on smaller needle and all two-color rnds are worked on larger needle.

Abbreviations
M1 Make 1

BODY
With smaller circular needle and A, cast on 341 sts. Join taking care not to twist sts on needle, pm for beg of rnds.

Garter st ridges
Rnd 1 K10 (steek sts), pm, k to last 10 sts, pm, k10 (steek sts).
Rnd 2 K10, sl marker, p to next marker, sl marker, k10. Break A. Change to B.
Rnd 3 Knit.
Rnd 4 K10, sl marker, p to next marker, sl marker, k10. Break B. Change to larger needle and C.

First Panel—Beg chart I
Cont in St st as foll:
Rnd 1 Work first 10 steek sts, sl marker, work 20-st pat rep 16 times, then work st 1 once more, sl marker, work last 10 steek sts. Cont to foll charts in this manner through rnd 27. Break yarns. Change to smaller needle and E.

Garter st ridges
Rnd 1 Knit.
Rnd 2 K10, sl marker, p to next marker, sl marker, k10. Break E. Change to F.
Rnds 3 and 4 Rep rnds 1 and 2. Break F. Change to larger needle and C.

Second Panel—Beg chart II
Cont in St st as foll:
Rnd 1 Work first 10 steek sts, sl marker, work 20-st pat rep 16 times, then work st 1 once more, sl marker, work last 10 steek sts. Cont to foll charts in this manner through rnd 27. Break yarns. Change to smaller needle and A.

Garter st ridges
Rnd 1 Knit.
Rnd 2 K10, sl marker, p to next marker, sl marker, k10. Break A. Change to F.
Rnds 3 and 4 Rep rnds 1 and 2. Break F. Change to larger needle and H.

Third Panel—Beg chart III
Cont in St st as foll:
Rnd 1 Work first 10 steek sts, sl marker, work 20-st pat rep

Schematic diagram

64" (Bind-off Edge)

LEFT FRONT — 30"

BACK

60"

Front Opening

RIGHT FRONT — 30"

32" (Cast-On Edge) 32"

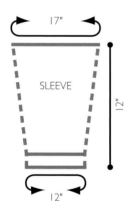

SLEEVE

17"

12"

12"

12"

Stitches

GARTER STITCH
Rnd 1 Knit.
Rnd 2 Purl.
Rep rnds 1 and 2 for garter st.

GARTER STITCH RIDGE
Rnd 1 Knit.
Rnd 2 Purl.
Work rnds 1 and 2 for garter st ridge.

GARTER STITCH
Knit every row.

STOCKINETTE STITCH
Knit every round.

---

16 times, then work st 1 once more, sl marker, work last 10 steek sts. Cont to foll charts in this manner through rnd 27. Break yarns. Change to smaller needle and F.

Garter st ridges and front opening
Rnd 1 Knit.
Rnd 2 K10, sl marker, p to next marker, sl marker, k10. Break F. Change to scrap yarn and work as foll:
K 10 steek sts, sl marker, k160, turn work, purl to end. Break scrap yarn. Change to C.
Rnds 3 and 4 Rep rnds 1 and 2. Break C. Change to larger needle and E.

Fourth Panel—Beg chart I
Cont in St st as foll:
Rnd 1 Work first 10 steek sts, sl marker, work 20-st pat rep 16 times, then work st 1 once more, sl marker, work last 10 steek sts. Cont to foll charts in this manner through rnd 27. Break yarns. Change to smaller needle and D.

Garter st ridges
Rnd 1 Knit.
Rnd 2 K10, sl marker, p to next marker, sl marker, k10. Break D. Change to G.
Rnds 3 and 4 Rep rnds 1 and 2. Break G. Change to larger needle and C.

Fifth Panel—Beg chart II
Cont in St st as foll:
Rnd 1 Work first 10 steek sts, sl marker, work 20-st pat rep 16 times, then work st 1 once more, sl marker, work last 10 steek sts. Cont to foll charts in this manner through rnd 27. Break yarns. Change to smaller needle and F.

Garter st ridges
Rnd 1 Knit.
Rnd 2 K10, sl marker, p to next marker, sl marker, k10. Break F. Change to G.
Rnds 3 and 4 Rep rnds 1 and 2. Break G. Change to larger needle and H.

Sixth Panel—Beg chart III
Cont in St st as foll:
Rnd 1 Work first 10 steek sts, sl marker, work 20-st pat rep 16 times, then work st 1 once more, sl marker, work last 10 steek sts. Cont to foll charts in this manner through rnd 27. Break yarns. Change to smaller needle and B.

Garter st ridges
Rnd 1 Knit.
Rnd 2 K10, sl marker, p to next marker, sl marker, k10. Break B. Change to C.
Rnd 3 and 4 Rep rnds 1 and 2. Bind off all sts knitwise.

LEFT SLEEVE
Cuff
With smaller dpn and H, cast on 60 sts. Divide sts evenly on 3 dpns. Join and pm taking care not to twist sts on needles. Purl next rnd. Break H. Change to D. Cont in garter st, working 2 rnds each in color sequence as foll: D, B, H and D. Break D. Change to B.

Next (inc) rnd K, inc 3 sts evenly spaced around—63 sts. Purl next rnd. Break B.

Beg chart IV
Change to A. Cont in St st on all sts as foll:

Rnd 1 K1 with G, pm, work 10-st pat rep 6 times, then work st 1 once more, pm, k1 with A.

Rnd 2 K1 with A, sl marker, work 10-st rep 6 times, then work st 1 once more, sl marker, k1 with G. Work chart through rnd 13, then rep rnds 1–13 to the end. AT THE SAME TIME, cont to alternate colors used for the 2 sts between st markers to create a checkerboard pat (faux "sleeve seam"). Work 2 rnds then begin sleeve increases.

Shape sleeve
Next (inc) rnd K1 with G, sl marker, M1 incorporating inc in chart pat, work chart to next maker, M1 incorporating inc in chart pat, sl marker, k1 with A. Cont to inc 1 st after first marker and 1 st before 2nd marker every 4th rnd 11 times more—87 sts. Work even until piece measures 12"/30.5 from beg. Bind off all sts knitwise.

RIGHT SLEEVE
Work cuff same as left sleeve. Cont to work same as left sleeve, working chart IV foll color key for right sleeve.

FINISHING
Cut the steek to form the fringe by cutting the jacket in the center ditch between the two groups of 10 steek sts; do not cut near the chart pat areas.

Fringe
Using a knitting needle or tapestry needle and beginning at the bound-off edge, carefully unravel 4 rnds of sts from the 10 steek sts at each end of the jacket. Tie each set of 4 unraveled ends in an overhand knot, positioning the knot against the chart pat section. Cont in this manner until all unraveled tails have been knotted. AT THE SAME TIME, when you reach the center, unravel the 2 rows of scrap yarn and keep them loose; you will deal with them after the fringing is completed.

Front opening trim
Using a knitting needle, unravel the 2 rows of scrap yarn, picking up the live sts (one side of front at a time) with smaller circular needle—320 sts. Join G. Working back and forth, work in garter st for 2 rows. Bind off all sts loosely.

A Knit Trick
This entire jacket is knit in the round in large horizontal bands of color. A steek is knit to form the fringe on the bottom, and the center front opening is made by knitting with scrap yarn, ripping it out when the knitting and fringing is complete and then picking up the open stitches for the garter stitch border.

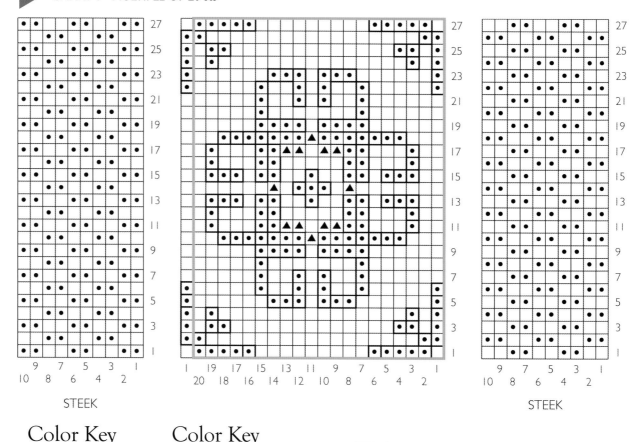

STEEK   STEEK

Color Key
for First Panel

☐ **C** Rock Henna

⊡ **D** Dried Wheat

▲ **C** Rock Henna then
duplicate stitch with
B Blue Thyme

Color Key
for Fourth Panel

☐ **E** Anemone

⊡ **G** Espresso

▲ **E** Anemone then
duplicate stitch with
D Dried Wheat

knitwise. Place markers 8½"/21.5cm down from shoulders on fronts and back. Sew side seams to markers. Sew sleeves into armholes. Weave in ends. Spritz jacket with water, especially the kinked strands of fringe. Trim fringe to to make even. Steam or block to even out colorwork.

Embroidery for first panel
Using tapestry needle and B, embroider duplicate stitches (see page 22) in center of each motif as shown on chart I. Using a double strand of A in tapestry needle, work a French knot (see page 171) in center of each motif.

Embroidery for second panel
Using tapestry needle and C, embroider 3 cross stitches (see page 171) along center of each motif as shown on chart II.

Embroidery for third panel
Using tapestry needle and B, embroider duplicate stitches in center of each motif as shown on chart III. Using a double strand of F in tapestry needle, work a French knot in center of each motif.

Embroidery for fourth panel
Using tapestry needle and D, embroider duplicate stitches in center of each motif as shown on chart I. Using a double strand of B in tapestry needle, work a French knot in center of each motif.

Embroidery for fifth panel
Using tapestry needle and D, embroider 3 cross stitches along center of each motif as shown on chart II.

Embroidery for sixth panel
Using tapestry needle and G, embroider duplicate stitches in center of each motif as shown on chart III. Using a double strand of E in tapestry needle, work a French knot in center of each motif. ■

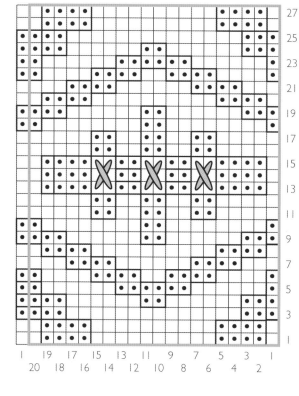

▶ CHART II   MULTIPLE OF 20 sts

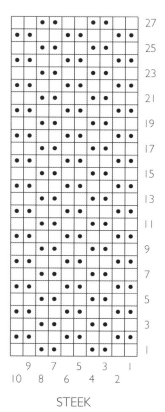

STEEK

STEEK

Color Key
for Second Panel

☐ **B** Blue Thyme

⊡ **G** Espresso

✕ Cross stitch with
H Geranium

Color Key
for Fifth Panel

☐ **C** Rock Henna

⊡ **B** Blue Thyme

✕ Cross stitch with
D Dried Wheat

My Inspiration
I have always been a fan of Native American rugs. I love their colors and bold motifs. For this wrap, I used these rugs as a launching point for the color choices.

CHART III   MULTIPLE OF 20 sts

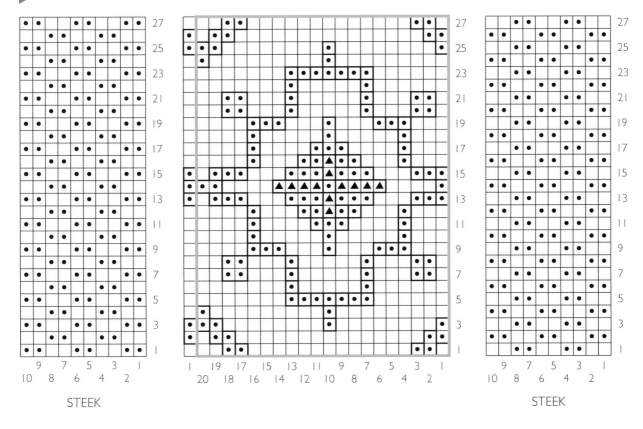

STEEK

STEEK

Color Key
for Third Panel

☐ **H** Geranium

⊡ **B** Blue Thyme

▲ **H** Geranium, then duplicate stitch with **G** Espresso

Color Key
for Sixth Panel

☐ **H** Geranium

⊡ **F** Lady's Mantle

▲ **H** Geranium, then duplicate stitch with **G** Espresso

CHART IV   MULTIPLE OF 10 sts

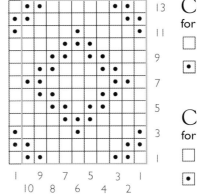

Color Key
for Right Sleeve

☐ **E** Anemone

⊡ **G** Espresso

Color Key
for Left Sleeve

☐ **A** Magenta

⊡ **G** Espresso

Pompom Bolster

Years ago, I saw a beautiful bolster at an Indian import store. It was sewn of silk sari fabric in a mishmash of patterns. I didn't buy it, but I did remember it, and it inspired this design. The main part is knit in the round into a long tube. The end is shaped like a hat. To close the opposite end, just knit a second "hat" without the tube!

Magic Multiple for Edging:
There are no edges in this project.
Colorwork Chart Multiple:
4, 6, 12 or 24 stitches

FINISHED MEASUREMENTS
Approx 18"/45.5cm long x 12"/30.5cm circumference (excluding pompoms)

YARN
Nashua Handknits *Julia* (wool/mohair/alpaca), 1¾oz/50g, 93yd/85m
A Geranium NHJ6085—1 skein
B Golden Honey NHJ2163—1 skein
C Velvet Moss NHJ6086—1 skein
D Magenta NHJ2083—1 skein
E Lady's Mantle NHJ3961—2 skeins
F Purple Basil NHJ3158—2 skeins

NEEDLES
For main section of bolster
Size 5 and 7 (3.75 and 4.5mm) circular needles, 16"/40cm long *or size to obtain correct gauge*

For first and second ends
One set (4) size 5 (3.75mm) double-pointed needles (dpns) *or size to obtain correct gauge*

NOTIONS
◆ Stitch marker
◆ Tapestry needle
◆ 8" x 20"/20.5cm x 51cm Firm Fill Bolster form (see Resources on page 169)

GAUGE
20 sts and 22 rnds = 4"/10cm in St st over chart pats using larger circular needle.
Be sure to obtain correct gauge.

Stitches
STOCKINETTE STITCH
Knit every round.

GARTER STITCH
Rnd 1 Knit.
Rnd 2 Purl.
Rep rnds 1 and 2 for garter st.

TWO-COLOR GARTER STITCH
(multiple of 4 sts)
Rnd 1 *K2 with D, k2 with B; rep from * around.
Rnd 2 *Bring D to front and p2, bring D to back, bring B to front and p2, bring B to back; rep from * around.
Work rnds 1 and 2 for two-color garter st.

REVERSE STOCKINETTE STITCH RIDGE
Rnd 1 Knit.
Rnds 2 and 3 Purl.
Work rnds 1–3 for rev St st ridge.

BOLSTER
Main section
With smaller circular needle and A, cast on 120 sts. Join taking care not to twist sts on needle, pm for beg of rnds.

Beg chart I
NOTE All one-color rnds are worked on smaller needle and all two-color rnds are worked on larger needle. Cont in St st on all sts as foll:
Rnd 1 Work 12-st pat rep 10 times. Cont to foll chart in this manner through rnd 13. Break yarns. Change to smaller needle and C.
Next 2 rnds Work rnds 1 and 2 for garter st ridge. Break C. Change to D.
Next 2 rnds Work rnds 1 and 2 for two-color garter st. Break yarns. Join C.
Next 2 rnds Work rnds 1 and 2 for garter st ridge. Break C. Change to F.

Beg chart II
NOTE All one-color rnds are worked on smaller needle and all two-color rnds are worked on larger needle. Cont in St st on all sts as foll:
Rnd 1 Work 24-st pat rep 5 times. Cont to foll chart in this manner through rnd 24, then rep rows 1–24 twice more. Break yarns. Change to smaller needle and C.
Next 2 rnds Work rnds 1 and 2 for garter st ridge. Break C. Change to D.
Next 2 rnds Work rnds 1 and 2 for two-color garter st using F instead of D. Break yarns. Join C.
Next 2 rnds Work rnds 1 and 2 for garter st ridge. Break C. Change to D.

Beg chart III
NOTE All one-color rnds are worked on smaller needle and all two-color rnds are worked on larger needle. Cont in St st on all sts as foll:
Rnd 1 Work 12-st pat rep 10 times. Cont to foll chart in this manner through rnd 12. Break yarns. Change to smaller needle and E.
Next (dec) rnd K, dec 3 sts evenly spaced around—117 sts.
Next 2 rnds Purl. Change to F.

Shape first end

NOTE Change to dpns when there are too few sts to work comfortably on circular needle.

Dec rnd 1 *K11, k2tog; rep from * around—108 sts.
Purl next 2 rnds. Break F. Change to A.
Dec rnd 2 *K10, k2tog; rep from * around—99 sts.
Purl next 2 rnds. Break A. Change to B.
Dec rnd 3 *K9, k2tog; rep from * around—90 sts.
Purl next 2 rnds. Break B. Change to D.
Dec rnd 4 *K8, k2tog; rep from * around—81 sts.
Purl next 2 rnds. Break D. Change to E.
Dec rnd 5 *K7, k2tog; rep from * around—72 sts.
Purl next 2 rnds. Break E. Change to C.
Dec rnd 6 *K6, k2tog; rep from * around—63 sts.
Purl next 2 rnds. Break C. Change to A.
Dec rnd 7 *K5, k2tog; rep from * around—54 sts.
Purl next 2 rnds. Break A. Change to B.
Dec rnd 8 *K4, k2tog; rep from * around—45 sts.
Purl next 2 rnds. Break B. Change to F.
Dec rnd 9 *K3, k2tog; rep from * around—36 sts.
Purl next 2 rnds. Break F. Change to E.
Dec rnd 10 *K2, k2tog; rep from * around—27 sts.
Purl next 2 rnds. Break E. Change to D.
Dec rnd 11 *K1, k2tog; rep from * around—18 sts.
Purl next 2 rnds.
Dec rnd 12 *K2tog; rep from * around—9 sts. Cut D leaving a 6"/15.5cm tail. Thread tail in tapestry needle, then thread through rem sts. Pull tog tightly and secure end.

SECOND END

With smaller circular needle and E, cast on 117 sts. Join taking care not to twist sts on needle, pm for beg of rnds.
Work rnds 1–3 for rev St st ridge. Purl next rnd. Shape second end same as first end.

FINISHING

Duplicate stitch embroidery

Using tapestry needle and C, embroider a duplicate stitch (see page 22) over B st in center of each cross on rnd 7 of chart I.

Straight stitch and cross stitch embroidery

Using tapestry needle and C, embroider a vertical straight stitch down center of each diamond motif (from rnd 4 to rnd 10 of chart III), then a horizontal straight stitch across (from st 4 to st 9). Using A, embroider a cross stitch (see page 171) over each intersection of straight stitches. Steam-block main section of bolster to even out colorwork.

Pompoms (make 2)

Make a 4½"/11.5cm diameter pompom using B, D and E (see page 170). Sew to center of first end. Make a 2nd pompom using C, D and E, then sew to center of second end. Sew second end to open end of bolster, leaving half of it unstitched. Insert bolster; sew opening closed. ∎

CHART I   MULTIPLE OF 12 sts

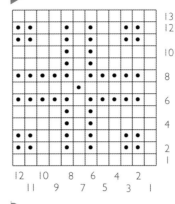

Color Key

☐ **A** Geranium
⊡ **B** Golden Honey

CHART II   MULTIPLE OF 24 sts

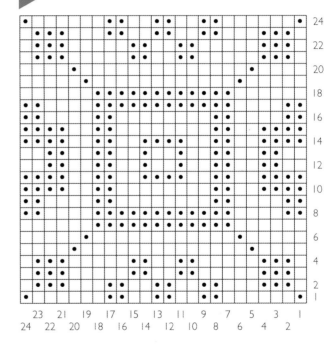

Color Key

☐ **E** Lady's Mantle
⊡ **F** Purple Basil

CHART III
MULTIPLE OF 12 sts

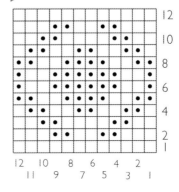

Color Key

☐ **D** Magenta
⊡ **B** Golden Honey

Extra-Long Scarf for Extra-Cold Days

Last October, my family and I took a trip to northern Vermont just when the leaves were beginning to change. As we drove around the countryside oohing and aahing at the changing colors, I designed this scarf to echo the autumn beauty. (I love to knit in the car.) With its double layer of fabric and extra-thick knitting, this scarf is the perfect protection from the winter winds.

Magic Multiple for Edging:
Substitute any of the cast-off edgings for the curly edging.
Color Chart Multiple: 5, 10 or 15 sts

FINISHED MEASUREMENTS
Approx 81"/205.5cm long x 6"/15cm wide (excluding fringe)

YARN
Nashua Handknits *Julia* (wool/mohair/alpaca), 1¾oz/50g, 93yd/85m
A Purple Basil NHJ3158—2 skeins
B Squash NHJ0120—2 skeins
C Deep Blue Sea NHJ6396—2 skeins
D Harvest Spice NHJ0178—2 skeins
E Golden Honey NHJ2163—2 skeins
F Lady's Mantle NHJ3961—2 skeins
G Coleus NHJ4345—2 skeins

NEEDLES
One set (4) each sizes 5 and 7 (3.75 and 4.5mm) double-pointed needles (dpns) *or size needed to obtain correct gauge*

NOTIONS
◆ Stitch marker
◆ Tapestry needle

GAUGE
20 sts and 22 rnds = 4"/10cm in St st over chart pats using larger dpns. *Be sure to obtain correct gauge.*

Stitches

STOCKINETTE STITCH
Knit every round.

REVERSE STOCKINETTE STITCH RIDGE
Rnd 1 Knit.
Rnds 2 and 3 Purl.
Work rnds 1–3 for rev St st ridge.

CURLY FRINGE
(multiple of 5 sts)
Rnd 1 (RS) With smaller dpns, pick up and k 1 st in each st around.
Rnd 2 *Bind off 5 sts purlwise, cast on 10 sts to RH needle using backward loop method, turn; bind off first 10 sts knitwise, turn, place last st from bind-off on LH needle; rep from * to end.
Work rnds 1 and 2 for curly fringe.

SCARF
With smaller dpns and A, cast on 60 sts. Divide sts evenly between 3 dpns. Join taking care not to twist sts on needle, pm for beg of rnds.

First section
***Reverse stockinette stitch ridge**
Rnds 1–3 Work rnds 1–3 of rev St st ridge. Break A. Change to B.

Beg chart I
NOTE All one-color rnds are worked on smaller dpns and all two-color rnds are worked on larger dpns.
Using B for first color and C for second color, cont in St st as foll:
Rnd 1 Work 5-st pat rep 12 times. Cont to foll chart in this manner through rnd 11. Break yarns. Change to smaller dpns and A.
Reverse stockinette stitch ridge
Rnds 1–3 Work rnds 1–3 of rev St st ridge. Break A. Change to D.

Beg chart II
NOTE All one-color rnds are worked on smaller dpns and all two-color rnds are worked on larger dpns. Using D for first color and E for second color, cont in St st as foll:
Rnd 1 Work 10-st pat rep 6 times. Cont to foll chart in this manner through rnd 13. Break yarns. Change to smaller dpns and A.
Reverse stockinette stitch ridge
Rnds 1–3 Work rnds 1–3 of rev St st ridge. Break A. Change to F.

Beg chart III
NOTE All one-color rnds are worked on smaller dpns and all two-color rnds are worked on larger dpns. Using F for first color and G for second color, cont in St st as foll:
Rnd 1 Work 5-st pat rep 12 times. Cont to foll chart in this manner through rnd 15. Break yarns. Change to smaller dpns and A.
Reverse stockinette stitch ridge
Rnds 1–3 Work rnds 1–3 of rev St st ridge. Break A. Change to B.

Beg chart IV

NOTE All one-color rnds are worked on smaller dpns and all two-color rnds are worked on larger dpns.

Using B for first color and C for second color, cont in St st as foll:

Rnd 1 Work 10-st pat rep 6 times. Cont to foll chart in this manner through rnd 11. Break yarns.

Change to smaller dpns and A.

Reverse stockinette stitch ridge

Rnds 1–3 Work rnds 1–3 of rev St st ridge. Break A. Change to D.

Beg chart V

NOTE All one-color rnds are worked on smaller dpns and all two-color rnds are worked on larger dpns.

Using D for first color and E for second color, cont in St st as foll:

Rnd 1 Work 5-st pat rep 12 times. Cont to foll chart in this manner through rnd 11. Break yarns. Change to smaller dpns and A.

Reverse stockinette stitch ridge

Rnds 1–3 Work rnds 1–3 of rev St st ridge. Break A. Change to F.

Beg chart VI

NOTE All one-color rnds are worked on smaller dpns and all two-color rnds are worked on larger dpns.

Using F for first color and G for second color, cont in St st as foll:

Rnd 1 Work 10-st pat rep 6 times. Cont to foll chart in this manner through rnd 13. Break yarns.

Change to smaller dpns and A.

Reverse stockinette stitch ridge

Rnds 1–3 Work rnds 1–3 of rev St st ridge. Break A. Change to B.

Beg chart VII

NOTE All one-color rnds are worked on smaller dpns and all two-color rnds are worked on larger dpns.

Using B for first color and C for second color, cont in St st as foll:

Rnd 1 Work 5-st pat rep 12 times. Cont to foll chart in this manner through rnd 9. Break yarns.

Change to smaller dpns and A.*

Second section

Rep from * to * of first section, working all rev St st ridges using A, and changing chart colors as foll:

Notes

1. For chart pats, all one-color rnds are worked on smaller dpns and all two-color rnds are worked on larger dpns.

2. All rev St st ridges are worked on smaller dpns.

 **CHART I**
MULTIPLE OF 5 sts

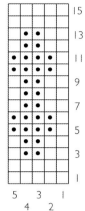

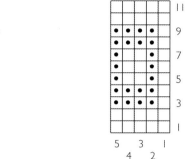 **CHART III**
MULTIPLE OF 5 sts

 CHART V
MULTIPLE OF 5 sts

 CHART VII
MULTIPLE OF 5 sts

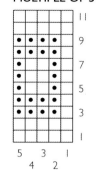

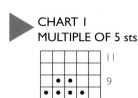 **CHART II**
MULTIPLE OF 10 sts

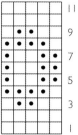

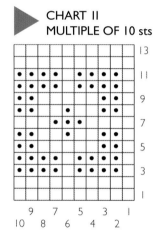

CHART IV
MULTIPLE OF 10 sts

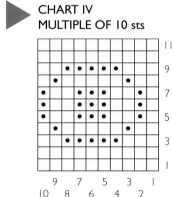

CHART VI
MULTIPLE OF 10 sts

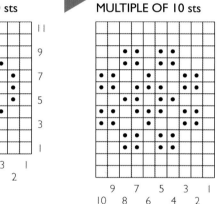

Color Key

☐ First Color
⊡ Second Color

CHART I: Use D for first color and E for second color.
CHART II: Use F for first color and G for second color.
CHART III: Use B for first color and C for second color.
CHART IV: Use D for first color and E for second color.
CHART V: Use F for first color and G for second color.
CHART VI: Use B for first color and C for second color.
CHART VII: Use D for first color and E for second color.

Third section
Rep from * to * of first section, working all rev St st ridges using A, and changing chart colors as foll:
CHART I: Use F for first color and G for second color.
CHART II: Use B for first color and C for second color.
CHART III: Use D for first color and E for second color.
CHART IV: Use F for first color and G for second color.
CHART V: Use B for first color and C for second color.
CHART VI: Use D for first color and E for second color.
CHART VII: Use F for first color and G for second color.

Fourth section
Rep first section.

Fifth section
Rep second section. Break yarns.
Change to smaller dpns and A.

Reverse stockinette stitch ridge
Rnds 1–3 Work rnds 1–3 of rev St st ridge.
Bind off all sts knitwise.

FINISHING
Steam-block to even out colorwork.

Curly fringe
With RS of cast-on edge facing, smaller dpns and F, work rnds 1 and 2 of curly fringe. Rep around bound-off edge. Sew top and bottom edges closed using F. ■

Mother-Daughter Mittens

The design of these mittens was inspired by the colors and motifs of an antique embroidered cloth I purchased at a flea market many years ago. I cherish this piece, which I found out later was probably made in Uzbekistan. I also wanted to honor the traditions of knitting and other needlecrafts that are so often passed down from mother to daughter. I truly feel I learned to knit and sew because of the generations of women in my family who all loved to work magic with a needle.

Magic Multiple for Edging: 6 sts
Colorwork Chart Multiple:
The colorwork for this design is stylized and worked over an odd number of sts that cannot be easily adapted to the charts in the glossary.

SIZES
Shown in size Child's Medium and Woman's Medium.

FINISHED MEASUREMENTS
Hand circumference: 6¾ (8½)"/17 (21.5)cm
Length of cuff: 4 (5)"/10 (12.5)cm

YARN
Nashua Handknits *Julia* (wool/mohair/alpaca), 1¾oz/50g, 93yd/85m
Child's mittens
A Pretty Pink NHJ8141—1 skein
B Velvet Moss NHJ6086—1 skein
C Spring Green NHJ5185—2 skeins
D Geranium NHJ6085—1 skein
Woman's mittens
A Golden Honey NHJ2163—1 skein
B Spring Green NHJ5185—1 skeins
C Midnight Blue NHJ6416—3 skeins
D Pretty Pink NHJ8141—1 skein

NEEDLES
One set (4) each sizes 5 and 7 (3.75 and 4.5mm) double-pointed needles (dpns) *or size needed to obtain correct gauge*

NOTIONS
◆ Stitch marker
◆ Stitch holders
◆ Tapestry needle

GAUGE
20 sts and 22 rnds = 4"/10cm in St st over chart pat using larger dpns. *Be sure to obtain correct gauge.*

Notes
1. Right and left mittens are made exactly the same.
2. All one-color rnds are worked on smaller dpns and all two-color rnds are worked on larger dpns.

Abbreviations
2-st RT Skip next st and knit the 2nd st, then knit the skipped st, sl both sts from needle tog.
M1 Make 1
k2tog Knit 2 stitches together

MITTENS (make 2)
Cuff
With smaller dpn and A, cast on 54 (66) sts. Divide sts evenly on 3 dpns. Join and pm, taking care not to twist sts on needles. Work rnd 1 of bobble edging. Purl next 2 rnds. Break A. Change to B. Work rnds 1–3 of rev St st ridge. Break B. Change to C. Work two-color twisted rib—36 (44) sts. Break yarns. Change to A. Work rnds 1–3 of rev St st ridge, dec 2 sts evenly spaced around last rnd—34 (42) sts. Break A. Change to C.

Hand
Change to larger dpns. Cont in St st as foll:

Beg chart I
Rnd 1 Work 17 (21) sts twice. Cont to foll chart I in this manner through rnd 3. Cont chart I and beg chart II as foll:
Shape thumb gusset
Rnd (inc) 4 K 17 (21), pm, M1 with C (st 1 of rnd 1 of chart II), pm, k 17 (21)—35 (43) sts.
Rnd 5 Work even (rnd 2 of chart II). Cont to work to top of chart I for hand, AT SAME TIME, cont to work rnd 3 of chart II as foll:
Rnd (inc) 6 K to first marker, sl marker, M1 with B, k 1 with C, M1 with B, sl marker, k to end—37 (45) sts.
Rnd 7 Work even (rnd 4 of chart II). Cont to inc for thumb gusset every other round (foll chart II) until there are 11 (13) sts between gusset markers—45 (55) sts.
Next rnd Work chart I to first marker, drop marker, place next 11 (13) sts on holder for thumb, drop next marker, work chart I to end—34 (42) sts. Cont to work chart I to rnd 32 (38). Break D. Change to smaller dpns. With C, cont to work even until hand measures 5½ (7)"/14 (17.5)cm from end of cuff.

Shape top
Next (dec) rnd *K2, k2tog; rep from * around, end k2—26 (32) sts. Knit next rnd.
Next (dec) rnd *K1, k2tog; rep from * around, end k2tog—17 (21) sts. Knit next rnd.

Stitches

BOBBLE EDGING
(multiple of 6 sts)
Rnd 1 (RS) *P3, work [k1, p1] twice in next st, turn; p4, turn; k4, turn; p4, turn; pass the 2nd st over the first, the 3rd st over the first, the 4th st over the first st (bobble made), sl this st to RH needle, p2; rep from * around.
Work rnd 1 for bobble edging.

REVERSE STOCKINETTE STITCH RIDGE
Rnd 1 Knit.
Rnds 2 and 3 Purl.
Work rnds 1–3 for rev St st ridge.

TWO-COLOR TWISTED RIB
(begs with a multiple of 6 sts)
Rnd 1 *K4 with C, k2 with D; rep from * around.
Rnd 2 *P4 with C, k2 with D; rep from * around.
Rnd 3 *P4 with C, 2-st RT with D; rep from * around.
Rep rnds 2 and 3 for 1 (1½)"/2.5 (4)cm, end with rnd 3.
Next (dec) rnd *P1, p2tog, p1 with C, k2 with D; rep from * around.
(now has a multiple of 5 sts)
Rnd 4 *P3 with C, 2-st RT with D; rep from * around.
Rnd 5 *P3 with C, k2 with D; rep from * around.
Rep rnds 4 and 5 for 1"/2.5cm, end with rnd 4.
Next (dec) rnd *P1, p2tog with C, k2 with D; rep from * around.
(now has a multiple of 4 sts)
Rnd 6 *P2 with C, 2-st RT with D; rep from * around.
Rnd 7 *P2 with C, k2 with D; rep from * around.
Rep rnds 6 and 7 for 1 (1¼)"/2.5 (3)cm, end with rnd 6.

STOCKINETTE STITCH
Knit every round.

Next (dec) rnd *K2tog; rep from * around, end k1—9 (11) sts.
Next (dec) rnd *K2tog; rep from * around, end k 1—5 (6) sts. Cut yarn leaving a 6"/15.5cm tail. Thread tail in tapestry needle, then thread through rem sts. Pull tog tightly and secure end on WS.

Thumb
Place sts from thumb gusset holder on 2 larger dpns. With RS facing, join color in progress at beg of thumb sts to cont in vertical stripe pat as established.
Next rnd K across thumb sts, then pick up and k 1 st at base of hand—12 (14) sts. Divide sts between 3 dpns, then pm for beg of rnds. Work even in vertical stripe pat until thumb measures 1½ (1¾)"/4 (4.5)cm. Break B. Change to smaller dpns. With C, cont in St st as foll:

Shape top
Next (dec) rnd *K2tog; rep from * around—6 (7) sts.
Next (dec) rnd *K2tog; rep from * around, end k 0 (1)—3 (4) sts. Cut yarn leaving a 6"/15.5cm tail. Thread tail in tapestry needle, then thread through rem sts. Pull tog tightly and secure end on WS.

FINISHING
Use yarn tail at base of thumb to close up gap between thumb and hand. Weave in ends.

Lazy daisy stitch embroidery
Referring to photo, using tapestry needle and A, embroider 3 (5) lazy daisy stitches (see page 171) in center top of floral motifs on back of right and left mittens as shown.

French knot embroidery
Referring to photo, using a double strand of A in tapestry needle, work 11 (12) French knots (see page 171) in center of floral motifs as shown.

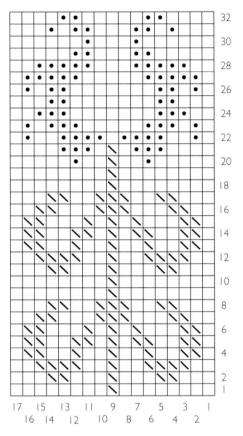

CHART 1 FOR CHILD'S MITTEN
MULTIPLE OF 17 sts

Color Key

☐ **C** Spring Green

◼ **B** Velvet Moss

⊡ **D** Geranium

▶ CHART I FOR WOMAN'S MITTEN
MULTIPLE OF 21 sts

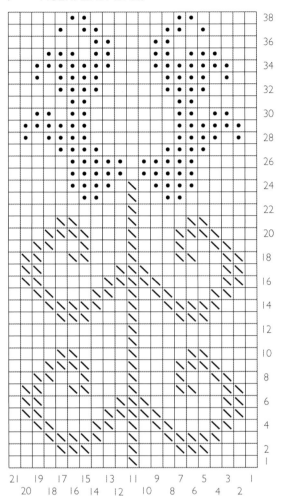

38
36
34
32
30
28
26
24
22
20
18
16
14
12
10
8
6
4
2
1

21 19 17 15 13 11 9 7 5 3 1
20 18 16 14 12 10 8 6 4 2

▶ CHART II FOR
THUMB GUSSET

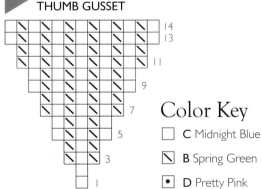

14
13
11
9
7
5
3
1

Color Key

☐ **C** Midnight Blue

◩ **B** Spring Green

⊡ **D** Pretty Pink

Custom-Design Your Own Floral Mittens

To design your own motif, start by making a chart the same size as the floral chart. Simply plot out a box on graph paper that is 17 (21) stitches wide by 32 (38) rows high, then draw your design in the center.

Hen Party Pullover

Chickens come in all different breeds and colors, and I tend to collect them like knitters collect yarn. One of my favorite times of day is when I go out and feed my girls their mash and scraps. This cheerful pullover is perfect to slip on on a chilly morning to feed the chickens.

Magic Multiple for Edging: 4 sts
Colorwork Chart Multiple:
5 or 10 sts

SIZES
X-Small (Small, Medium, Large, Extra Large). Shown in size Small.

FINISHED MEASUREMENTS
Bust: 36 (40, 44, 48, 52)"/91.5 (101.5, 111.5, 122, 132)cm
Length: 24 (24½, 25½, 26½, 27)"/61 (62, 64.5, 67.5, 68.5)cm
Upper arm: 15 (16, 17, 18, 19)"/38 (40.5, 43, 45.5, 48)cm

YARN
Nashua Handknits *Julia* (wool/mohair/alpaca), 1¾oz/50g, 93yd/85m
MC Persimmon NHJ0121—7 (8, 9, 10, 11) skeins
A Velvet Moss NHJ6086—2 skeins
B Golden Honey NHJ2163—2 skeins
C Magenta NHJ2083—2 skeins
D Spring Green NHJ5185—2 (2, 2, 3, 3) skeins

Notes
1. Body and sleeves are each made separately in the round to the yoke.
2. Yoke is worked in the round.
3. Use smaller circular needle or dpns for all one-color rnds and larger circular needle or dpns for all two-color rnds.

Abbreviations
M1 Make 1

NEEDLES
For sweater body
Size 5 and 7 (3.75 and 4.5mm) circular needles, 32"/81cm long *or size needed to obtain correct gauge*

For sleeves and collar
◆ Size 5 (3.75 and 4.5mm) circular needle, 16"/40cm long
◆ One set (4) each sizes 5 and 7 (3.75 and 4.5mm) double-pointed needles (dpns) *or size needed to obtain correct gauge*

NOTIONS
◆ Stitch markers
◆ Tapestry needle

GAUGE
20 sts and 22 rnds = 4"/10cm in St st over chart pats using larger circular needle.
Be sure to obtain correct gauge.

BODY
With longer, smaller circular needle and A, cast on 172 (188, 208, 228, 244) sts. Join taking care not to twist sts on needle, pm for beg of rnds. Purl next 2 rnds. Break A. Change to larger circular needle and B. Work rnds 1–4 of three-color garter st twice. Break yarns.
Change to smaller needle and A.
Next (inc) rnd K inc 8 (12, 12, 16) sts evenly spaced around—180 (200, 220, 240, 260) sts. Purl next 2 rnds. Break A. Change to MC.
Next rnd K 90 (100, 110, 120, 130) sts, pm for underarm, k to end. Cont in St st until piece measures 14 (14½, 15, 16, 16)"/35.5 (37, 38, 40.5, 40.5)cm from beg.
Next rnd *K to 6 (7, 8, 9, 9) sts before next marker, k 12 (14, 16, 18, 18) sts (dropping marker), place these sts on holder for underarm; rep from * once more. Leave rem 156 (172, 188, 204, 224) sts on needle for front and back.

SLEEVES
With smaller dpn and A, cast on 44 (44, 48, 48, 48) sts. Divide sts evenly on 3 dpns. Join and pm taking care not to twist sts on needles. Purl next 2 rnds. Break A. Change to larger dpns and B. Work rnds 1–4 of three-color garter st twice. Break yarns. Change to smaller dpns and A.
Next (inc) rnd K inc 6 (8, 6, 8, 8) sts evenly spaced around—50 (52, 54, 56, 56) sts. Purl next 2 rnds. Break A. Change to MC.

Shape sleeve
NOTE Change to shorter, smaller circular needle when there are too many sts to work comfortably on dpns.
Next (inc) rnd K1, M1, k to 1 st before marker, M1, k1. Rep last rnd every 4th rnd 17 (18, 19, 21, 24) times more—86 (90, 94, 100, 106) sts. Work even until piece measures 17 (17½, 18, 18½, 18½)"/43 (44.5, 45.5, 47, 47)cm from beg.
Next rnd K to 6 (7, 8, 9, 9) sts before marker, k 12 (14, 16, 18, 18) sts (dropping marker), place these sts on holder for underarm. Leave rem 74 (76, 78, 82, 88) sts on a spare circular needle.

YOKE
Next (joining) rnd With longer, smaller circular needle and MC, k 78 (86, 94, 102, 112) sts from body needle (front), pm, k 74 (76, 78, 82, 88) sts from a sleeve needle, pm, k 78 (86, 94, 102, 112) sts from body needle (back), pm, k 74 (76, 78,

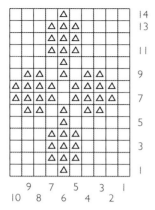

14
13
11
9
7
5
3
1

9 7 5 3 1
10 8 6 4 2

Color Key

◻ **D** Spring Green

△ **C** Magenta

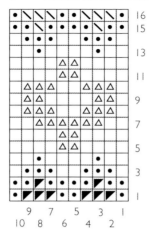

16
15
13
11
9
7
5
3
1

9 7 5 3 1
10 8 6 4 2

Color Key

◻ **D** Spring Green

△ **C** Magenta

◻ **B** Golden Honey

◤ **MC** Persimmon

• **A** Velvet Moss

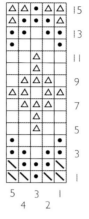

15
13
11
9
7
5
3
1

5 3 1
4 2

Color Key

◻ **D** Spring Green

△ **C** Magenta

◻ **B** Golden Honey

• **A** Velvet Moss

5
3
1

3 1
4 2

Color Key

△ **C** Magenta

◻ **B** Golden Honey

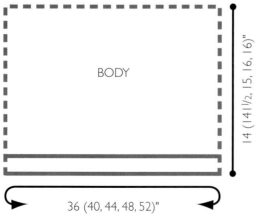

Easy Does It

Yoke sweaters are perfect projects for beginning Fair Isle knitters. Just be sure to keep the floats loose.

BODY

14 (14¹/2, 15, 16, 16)"

36 (40, 44, 48, 52)"

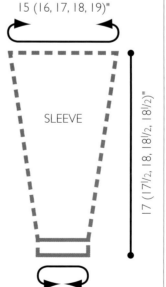

15 (16, 17, 18, 19)"

SLEEVE

17 (17¹/2, 18, 18¹/2, 18¹/2)"

8¹/2 (8¹/2, 9¹/2, 9¹/2, 9¹/2)"

Stitches

REVERSE STOCKINETTE STITCH RIDGE
Rnd 1 Knit.
Rnds 2 and 3 Purl.
Work rnds 1–3 for rev St st ridge

THREE-COLOR GARTER STITCH
(multiple of 4 sts)
Rnd 1 *K2 with B, k2 with C; rep from * around.
Rnd 2 *P2 with B, p2 with C; rep from * around.
Rnd 3 *K2 with C, k2 with D; rep from * around.
Rnd 4 *P2 with C, p2 with D; rep from * around.
Work rnds 1–4 for three-color garter st.

2 X 2 TWO-COLOR CORRUGATED RIB
(multiple of 4 sts)
Rnd 1 *K2 with MC, k2 with D; rep from * around.
Rnd 2 *K2 with MC, p2 with D; rep from * around.
Rep rnd 2 for corrugated rib.

STOCKINETTE STITCH
Knit every round.

82, 88) sts from rem sleeve needle, pm for beg of rnds—304 (324, 344, 368, 400) sts on the circular needle. Cont in St st, work even for 0 (0, 3, 3, 6) rnds.
Next rnd K dec 4 (dec 4, dec 4, inc 2, dec 0) sts evenly spaced around—300 (320, 340, 370, 400) sts. Break MC. Change to larger needle and A.

Beg chart I
NOTE All rnds are worked on larger needle. Cont in St st on all sts as foll:
Rnd 1 Work 10-st pat rep 30 (32, 34, 37, 40) times.
Cont to foll chart in this manner through rnd 16. Break B. Change to smaller needle and D. Knit next rnd.
Next (dec) rnd K dec 60 (60, 70, 90, 80) sts evenly spaced around—240 (260, 270, 290, 320) sts. Change to larger needle.

Beg chart II
NOTE All rnds are worked on larger needle. Cont in St st on all sts as foll:
Rnd 1 Work 10-st pat rep 24 (26, 27, 29, 30) times.
Cont to foll chart in this manner through rnd 14. Break C. Change to smaller needle and D. Knit next rnd.
Next (dec) rnd K dec 85 (90, 95, 100, 110) sts evenly spaced around—155 (170, 175, 190, 210) sts. Change to larger needle.

Beg chart III
NOTE All rnds are worked on larger needle. Cont in St st on all sts as foll:
Rnd 1 Work 5-st pat rep 31 (34, 35, 38, 42) times.
Cont to foll chart in this manner through rnd 15. Break A. Change to smaller needle and C. Knit next rnd.
Next (dec) rnd K dec 50 (62, 60, 70, 85) sts evenly spaced around—104 (108, 116, 120, 124) sts. Change to larger needle.

Beg chart IV
NOTE All rnds are worked on larger needle. Cont in St st on all sts as foll:
Rnd 1 Work 4-st pat rep 26 (27, 29, 30, 31) times.
Cont to foll chart in this manner through rnd 5. Break B. Change to smaller needle and C. Knit next rnd.
Next (dec) rnd K dec 8 (12, 16, 12, 16) sts evenly spaced around—96 (96 100, 108, 108) sts. Break C. Change to A.

Collar
Work rnds 1–3 of rev St st ridge. Break A. Change to MC. Work in corrugated rib for 2¼"/5.5cm. Break yarns. Change to A. Work in St st for 6 rnds. Bind off loosely knitwise.

FINISHING
Sew underarm seams. Weave in ends. Steam or block to even out colorwork.

French knot embroidery
Refer to photo. Using a double strand of B in tapestry needle, work 2 French knots (see page 171) in center of each motif of chart II.

Duplicate stitch embroidery
Refer to photo. Using tapestry needle and D, embroider a duplicate stitch (see page 22) in center of each diamond motif of chart III. ■

Marrakesh Market Pillows

I often imagine what it would have been like to live in the early part of the 20th century and travel to the markets of Istanbul and Morocco to purchase rugs and bedspreads made by traveling nomads. The hand-dyed, handwoven fabrics with their handstitched details and imperfections are so appealing to me. The colors and patterns of this quartet of pillows, each named for a knitting friend (and one for me!), are inspired by these fabulous textiles.

Magic Multiple for Edging:
Varies by pillow; see page 142 to learn how to use any edging.
Colorwork Chart Multiple:
The 4 different pillows use different multiples
- Peggy's Pillow: 4, 6, 8, 12 or 24 sts
- Kristin's Pillow: 5, 6, 10, 15, or 30 sts
- Clara's Pillow: 5, 6, 10, 15 or 30 sts
- Therese's Pillow: 4, 6, 8, 12 or 24 sts

FINISHED MEASUREMENTS
Peggy's Pillow (middle right)
18" × 18"/45.5cm × 45.5cm
Kristin's Pillow (top left)
14" × 14"/35.5cm × 35.5cm
Clara's Pillow (middle left)
22" × 22"/56cm × 56cm
Therese's Pillow (bottom)
18" × 18"/45.5cm × 45.5cm

YARN
Nashua Handknits *Julia*
(wool/mohair/alpaca), 1¾oz/50g, 93yd/85m
Peggy's pillow (middle right)
A Golden Honey NHJ2163—1 skein
B Anemone NHJ9235—1 skein
C Spring Green NHJ5185—1 skein
D Harvest Spice NHJ0178—1 skein
E Velvet Moss NHJ6086 —1 skein

Kristin's pillow (top left)
A Blue Thyme NHJ4936—2 skeins
B Rock Henna NHJ2230—2 skeins
C Golden Honey NHJ2163—1 skein
D Pretty Pink NHJ8141—1 skein
E Lady's Mantle NHJ3961—1 skein
F Squash NHJ0120—1 skein

Clara's pillow (middle left)
A Lupine NHJ5178—1 skein
B Espresso NHJ0118—2 skeins
C Magenta NHJ2083—1 skein
D Spring Green NHJ5185—1 skein
E Squash NHJ0120—1 skein
F Blue Thyme NHJ4936—1 skein
Therese's pillow (bottom)
A Magenta NHJ2083—1 skein
B Espresso NHJ0118—1 skein
C Spring Green NHJ5185—1 skein
D Geranium NHJ6085—2 skeins
E Golden Honey NHJ2163—2 skeins

NEEDLES
Size 5 and 7 (3.75 and 4.5mm) circular needles *or size to obtain correct gauge*
(See individual instructions for lengths needed)

NOTIONS
- Stitch markers
- Tapestry needle
- Matching sewing thread
- Sewing machine
(See individual instructions for additional notions)

GAUGE
20 sts and 22 rnds = 4"/10cm in St st over chart pats using larger circular needle.
20 sts and 40 rnds = 4"/10cm in rev St st ridge using smaller circular needle.
Be sure to obtain correct gauge.

PEGGY'S PILLOW
Needles and additional notions
- Size 7 (4.5mm) circular needle, 16"/40cm long
- Size 5 (3.75mm) circular needles, 16"/40cm and 24"/60cm long
- ⅝yd/.5m of 45"/114.5cm-wide medium-weight backing fabric
- 18"/45.5cm knife-edge down pillow form

Pillow top
With shorter, smaller circular needle and A, cast on 82 sts. Join taking care not to twist sts on needle, pm for beg of rnds. Cont in St st on all sts as foll:
Beg chart I
NOTE All one-color rnds are worked on shorter, smaller needle and all two-color rnds are worked on larger needle. Cont in St st on all sts as foll:
Rnd I Work first 3 steek sts, pm, work 5-st pat rep 15 times, then work st 1 once more, pm, work last 3 steek sts. Cont to foll chart in this manner (slipping markers) through rnd 11. Break yarns. Change to shorter, smaller needle and C.
Reverse stockinette stitch ridge
Rnds 1–3 Keeping 3 steek sts at beg and end of rnds in St st, work rnds 1–3 of rev St st ridge over rem sts, dec 3 sts evenly spaced around last rnd—79 sts. Break C. Change to larger needle and E.

Beg chart II
Rnd I Work first 3 steek sts, sl marker, work 24-st pat rep 3 times, then work st 1 once more, sl marker, work last 3 steek sts. Cont to foll chart in this manner through rnd 21, then rep rnds 1–21 once more, then rnds 1 and 2. Break yarns. Change to shorter, smaller needle and C.

REVERSE STOCKINETTE STITCH RIDGE
Rnds 1–3 Keeping 3 steek sts at beg and end of rnds in St st, work rnds 1–3 of rev St st ridge over rem sts, inc 3 sts evenly spaced around first rnd—82 sts. Break C. Change to A.

Beg chart III
NOTE All one-color rnds are worked on shorter, smaller

So Comfy!

Pillows are perfect projects for summertime knitting. They aren't too big or heavy, and by winter you'll have a pile of colorful cushions for your couch or armchair.

Notes

1. Pillows are worked in the round forming a tube, with steek sts at beginning and end of rounds.
2. During finishing, the steeks are secured with machine stitching, then cut open forming a flat piece. See page 21 for securing a steek.
3. All one-color rnds are worked on smaller needle and all two-color rnds are worked on larger needle.

Peggy's pillow features autumn harvest colors.

needle and all two-color rnds are worked on larger needle. Cont in St st on all sts as foll:

Rnd 1 Work first 3 steek sts, slip marker, work 5-st pat rep 15 times, then work st 1 once more, sl marker, work last 3 steek sts. Cont to foll chart in this manner through rnd 11. Break B. Bind off knitwise using A.

FINISHING

Securing and cutting steek

See page 21 before you begin. It is important to keep the knit fabric flat and neat while stitching. Do not pull on it as you sew or it will distort and ripple. Set sewing machine to straight stitch. On each side of steek section, sew between the steek st and the chart pat st; this is called "stitching in the ditch." Now, set sewing machine to a medium zigzag stitch. Stitch the two center steek sts as foll: locate the 3rd steek st and sew a row of sts on top of the knit sts, then rep along top of the 4th steek st. Using sharp scissors, cut through the center of the two zigzag rows of stitching, taking care not to snip the sewing machine stitches.

Mitered border

Rnd 1 (RS) With RS facing, longer, smaller circular needle and E, pick up and k 76 sts evenly spaced across cast-on edge, pm, pick up and k 1 st in corner, pm, pick up and k 58 sts evenly spaced across first steek edge, pm, pick up and k 1 st in corner, pm, pick up and k 76 sts evenly spaced across bound-off edge, pm, pick up and k 1 st in corner, pm, pick up and k 58 sts evenly spaced across 2nd steek edge, pm, pick up and k 1 st in corner, pm for beg of rnds—272 sts.

Rnd (inc) 2 *P to next marker, inc 1 using backward loop method, sl marker, k1, sl marker, inc 1; rep from * 3 times more—8 sts increased.

Rnd 3 *P to next marker, sl marker, k1, sl marker; rep from * 3 times more. Break E. Change to D.

Rnd (inc) 4 *K to next marker, inc 1 using backward loop method, sl marker, k1, sl marker, inc 1; rep from * 3 times more—8 sts increased.

Rnd 5 *P to next marker, sl marker, k1, sl marker; rep from * 3 times more.

Rnd (inc) 6 *P to next marker, inc 1 using backward loop method, sl marker, k1, sl marker, inc 1; rep from * 3 times more—8 sts increased. Break D. Change to C.

Rnd 7 *K to next marker, sl marker, k1, sl marker; rep from * 3 times more.

Rnds 8 and 9 Rep rnds 6 and 5. Break C. Change to B.

Rnds 10–12 Rep rnds 4-6. Break B. Change to A.

Rnds 13–15 Rep rnds 7, 2 and 3. Break A. Change to E.

Rnds 16–18 Rep rnds 4-6. Bind off all sts loosely knitwise.

CHART I FOR PEGGY'S PILLOW
MULTIPLE OF 5 sts

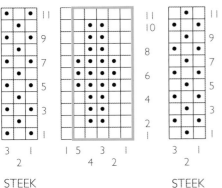

STEEK   STEEK

CHART III FOR PEGGY'S PILLOW
MULTIPLE OF 5 sts

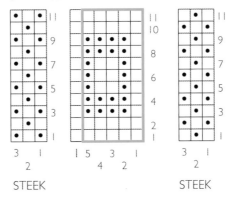

STEEK   STEEK

Color Key
For Charts 1 and 3

- ☐ **A** Golden Honey
- ⊡ **B** Anemone

CHART II FOR PEGGY'S PILLOW
MULTIPLE OF 24 sts

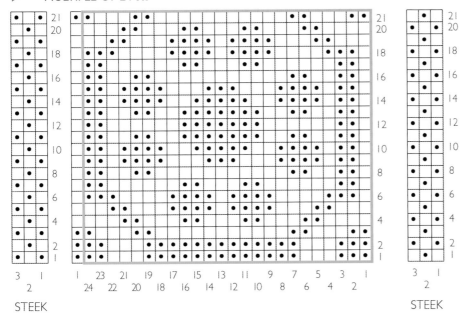

STEEK   STEEK

Stitches
STOCKINETTE STITCH
Knit every round.

**REVERSE STOCKINETTE
STITCH RIDGE**
Rnd 1 Knit.
Rnds 2 and 3 Purl.
Work rnds 1–3 for rev St st
ridge.

Color Key

- ☐ **D** Harvest Spice
- ⊡ **E** Velvet Moss

Cross stitch and straight stitch embroidery

Using tapestry needle and C, embroider a cross stitch (see page 171) in center of each cross motif of chart I; see photo. Using D, embroider a short vertical straight stitch over the intersection of the cross stitch, then embroider a short horizontal stitch over the intersection and vertical straight stitch. Working in cross stitch, using tapestry needle and D, embroider a cross stitch in center of each rectangle motif of chart III. Using C, embroider straight stitches same as for cross motifs.

Blocking

Using a spray bottle, thoroughly mist the pillow top with warm water. With your hands, work the water into the knitted fabric. Using large t-pins, pin out the fabric on flat padded surface (like an unused bed). Using a steam iron and holding the iron 2" away from the fabric, steam lightly. Avoid touching the pillow with the iron or the fabric may become flattened or scorched. Leave to dry. Alternately, handwash pillow top in cold water with a cold rinse and lay flat to dry.

Assembling pillow

Cut a piece of backing fabric 1"/2.5cm larger all around than pillow top. Turn each edge ½"/1.3cm over to WS and press in place. Hand-stitch pillow top to backing around three sides. Insert pillow form; sew opening closed. ∎

My pillow started as a large swatch to which I added an edging.

KRISTIN'S PILLOW
Needles and additional notions
◆ Size 7 (4.5mm) circular needle, 16"/40cm long
◆ Size 5 (3.75mm) circular needle, 24"/60cm long
◆ ½yd/.5m of 45"/114.5cm-wide medium-weight backing fabric
◆ 16"/40.5cm knife-edge down pillow form

Pillow top
With larger circular needle and A, cast on 67 sts. Join taking care not to twist sts on needle, pm for beg of rnds. Cont in St st on all sts as foll:
Beg chart pat
Rnd 1 Work first 3 steek sts, pm, work 30-st pat rep twice, then work st 1 once more, pm, work last 3 steek sts. Cont to foll chart in this manner (slipping markers) through rnd 30,

then rep rnds 1–30 once more. Break B. Bind off all sts knitwise using A.

FINISHING
Securing and cutting steek
See Peggy's Pillow.

Mitered border
Rnd 1 (RS) With RS facing, smaller circular needle and C, pick up and k 61 sts evenly spaced across cast-on edge, pm, pick up and k 1 st in corner, pm, pick up and k 45 sts evenly spaced across first steek edge, pm, pick up and k 1 st in corner, pm, pick up and k 61 sts evenly spaced across bound-off edge, pm, pick up and k 1 st in corner, pm, pick up and k 45 sts evenly spaced across 2nd steek edge, pm, pick up and k 1 st in corner, pm for beg of rnds—216 sts.

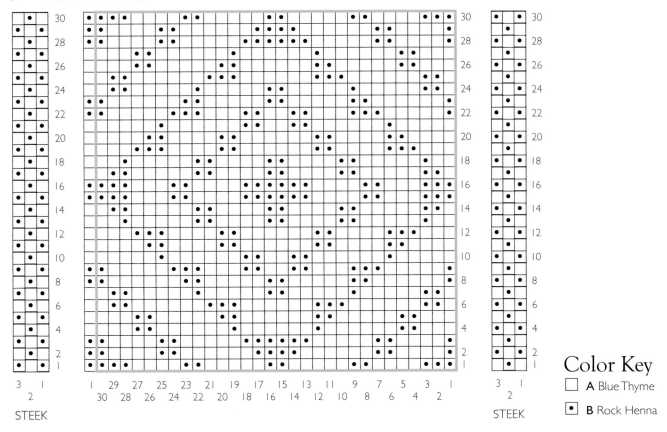

STEEK

STEEK

Color Key

☐ **A** Blue Thyme

⊡ **B** Rock Henna

Rnd (inc) 2 *P to next marker, inc 1 using backward loop method, sl marker, k1, sl marker, inc 1; rep from * 3 times more—8 sts increased.

Rnd 3 *P to next marker, sl marker, k1, sl marker; rep from * 3 times more. Break C. Change to D.

Rnd (inc) 4 *K to next marker, inc 1 using backward loop method, sl marker, k1, sl marker, inc 1; rep from * 3 times more—8 sts increased.

Rnd 5 *P to next marker, sl marker, k1, sl marker; rep from * 3 times more.

Rnd (inc) 6 *P to next marker, inc 1 using backward loop method, sl marker, k1, sl marker, inc 1; rep from * 3 times more—8 sts increased. Break D. Change to E.

Rnd 7 *K to next marker, sl marker, k1, sl marker; rep from * 3 times more.

Rnds 8 and 9 Rep rnds 6 and 5. Break E. Change to F.

Rnds 10–12 Rep rnds 4–6. Bind off all sts loosely knitwise.

Chain stitch embroidery
Working in chain stitch (see page 171), using tapestry needle

and C, outline RH edge of first bottom and top diamonds, then LH edge of last bottom and top diamonds; see photo. Using D, outline LH edge of first bottom and top diamonds, then RH edge of last bottom and top diamonds.

Running stitch embroidery
Using D, embroider running stitches (see page 171) over and under all C chain stitches. Using C, embroider running stitches over and under all D chain stitches.

French knot embroidery
Using a double strand of E in tapestry needle, work two French knots (see page 171) at each intersection where chain stitch lines meet.

Blocking
See Peggy's Pillow.

Assembling pillow
See Peggy's Pillow. ■

CHART III FOR CLARA'S PILLOW
MULTIPLE OF 30 sts

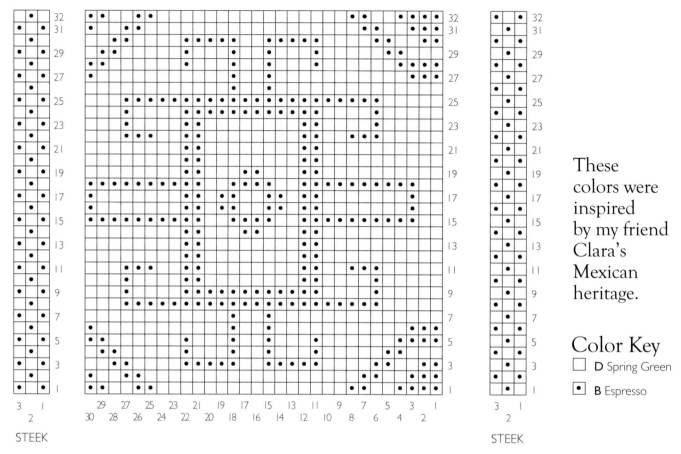

STEEK   STEEK

These colors were inspired by my friend Clara's Mexican heritage.

Color Key
☐ **D** Spring Green
⊡ **B** Espresso

CLARA'S PILLOW
Needles and additional notions
◆ Size 7 (4.5mm) circular needle, 16"/40cm long
◆ Size 5 (3.75mm) circular needles, 16"/40cm and 29"/74cm long
◆ ¾yd/.75m of 45"/114.5cm-wide medium-weight backing fabric
◆ 22"/56cm knife-edge down pillow form

Pillow top
With larger circular needle and A, cast on 97 sts. Join taking care not to twist sts on needle, pm for beg of rnds. Change to shorter, smaller needle and cont in St st on all sts as foll:

Beg chart I
NOTE All one-color rnds are worked on shorter, smaller needle and all two-color rnds are worked on larger needle. Cont in St st on all sts as foll:
Rnd 1 Work first 3 steek sts, pm, work 15-st pat rep 6 times, then work st 1 once more, pm, work last 3 steek sts.

Cont to foll chart in this manner (slipping markers) through rnd 21. Break yarns. Change to shorter, smaller needle and C.

Reverse stockinette stitch ridges
Rnds 1–3 Keeping 3 steek sts at beg and end of rnds in St st, work rnds 1–3 of rev St st ridge over rem sts. Break C. Change to D.
Rnds 4–6 Keeping 3 steek sts at beg and end of rnds in St st, work rnds 1–3 of rev St st ridge over rem sts. Break D. Change to E.

Beg chart II
NOTE All one-color rnds are worked on shorter, smaller needle and all two-color rnds are worked on larger needle. Cont in St st on all sts as foll:
Rnd 1 Work first 3 steek sts, sl marker, work 10-st pat rep 9 times, then work st 1 once more, sl marker, work last 3 steek sts. Cont to foll chart in this manner through rnd 12. Break yarns. Change to shorter, smaller needle and B.

Reverse stockinette stitch ridges
Rnds 1–3 Keeping 3 steek sts at beg and end of rnds in St st, work rnds 1–3 of rev St st ridge over rem sts. Break B. Change to C.
Rnds 4–6 Keeping 3 steek sts at beg and end of rnds in St st, work rnds 1–3 of rev St st ridge over rem sts. Break C. Change larger needle and B.

Beg chart III
NOTE All rnds are worked on larger needle. Cont in St st on all sts as foll:
Rnd 1 Work first 3 steek sts, sl marker, work 30-st pat rep 3 times, then work st 1 once more, sl marker, work last 3 steek sts. Cont to foll chart in this manner through rnd 32. Break yarns. Change to shorter, smaller needle and C.

Reverse stockinette stitch ridges
Rnds 1–3 Keeping 3 steek sts at beg and end of rnds in St st, work rnds 1–3 of rev St st ridge over rem sts. Break C. Change to A.

Rnds 4–6 Keeping 3 steek sts at beg and end of rnds in St st, work rnds 1–3 of rev St st ridge over rem sts. Break A. Change to E.

Beg chart IV
NOTE All one-color rnds are worked on shorter, smaller needle and all two-color rnds are worked on larger needle. Cont in St st on all sts as foll:
Rnd 1 Work first 3 steek sts, sl marker, work 10-st pat rep 9 times, then work st 1 once more, sl marker, work last 3 steek sts. Cont to foll chart in this manner through rnd 13. Break yarns. Change to shorter, smaller needle and B.

Reverse stockinette stitch ridges
Rnds 1–3 Keeping 3 steek sts at beg and end of rnds in St st, work rnds 1-3 of rev St st ridge over rem sts. Break B. Change to F.
Rnds 4–6 Keeping 3 steek sts at beg and end of rnds in St st, work rnds 1-3 of rev St st ridge over rem sts. Break F. Change to C.

Beg chart V
NOTE All one-color rnds are worked on shorter, smaller needle and all two-color rnds are worked on larger needle. Cont in St st on all sts as foll:
Rnd 1 Work first 3 steek sts, sl marker, work 15-st pat rep 6 times, then work st 1 once more, sl marker, work last 3 steek sts. Cont to foll chart in this manner through rnd 21. Break B. Bind off knitwise using C.

FINISHING
Securing and cutting steek
See Peggy's Pillow.

Mitered border
Rnd 1 (RS) With RS facing, longer, smaller circular needle and C, pick up and k 91 sts evenly spaced across cast-on edge, pm, pick up and k 1 st in corner, pm, pick up and k 83 sts evenly spaced across first steek edge, pm, pick up and k 1 st in corner, pm, pick up and k 91 sts evenly spaced across bound-off edge, pm, pick up and k 1 st in corner, pm, pick up and k 83 sts evenly spaced across 2nd steek edge, pm, pick up and k 1 st in corner, pm for beg of rnds—352 sts.
Rnd (inc) 2 *P to next marker, inc 1 using backward loop method, sl marker, k1, sl marker, inc 1; rep from * 3 times more—8 sts increased.
Rnd 3 *P to next marker, sl marker, k1, sl marker; rep from * 3 times more. Bind off all sts loosely purlwise.

Blocking
See Peggy's Pillow.

Assembling pillow
See Peggy's Pillow. ∎

CHART I FOR CLARA'S PILLOW
MULTIPLE OF 15 sts

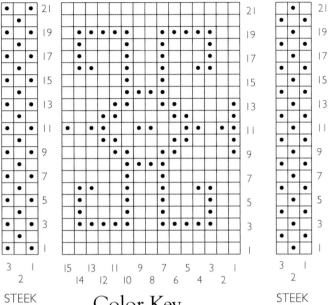

STEEK

CHART V FOR CLARA'S PILLOW
MULTIPLE OF 15 sts

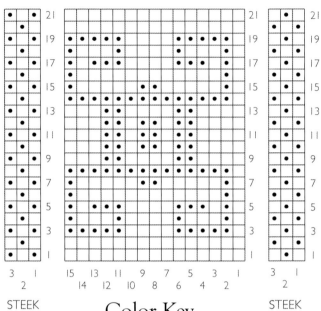

STEEK

Color Key

☐ **A** Lupine

☒ **B** Espresso

Color Key

☐ **C** Magenta

☒ **B** Espresso

CHART II FOR CLARA'S PILLOW
MULTIPLE OF 10 sts

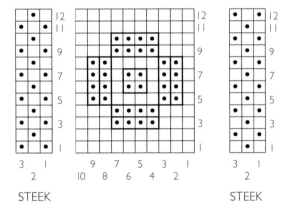

STEEK   STEEK

CHART IV FOR CLARA'S PILLOW
MULTIPLE OF 10 sts

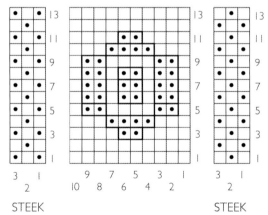

STEEK   STEEK

Color Key

☐ **E** Squash

☒ **F** Blue Thyme

Color Key

☐ **E** Squash

☒ **F** Blue Thyme

THERESE'S PILLOW

Needles and additional notions
◆ Size 7 (4.5mm) circular needle, 16"/40cm long
◆ Size 5 (3.75mm) circular needles, 16"/40cm and 29"/74cm long
◆ ⅝yd/.5m of 45"/114.5cm-wide medium-weight backing fabric
◆ 18"/45.5cm knife-edge down pillow form

Pillow top
With shorter, smaller circular needle and A, cast on 79 sts. Join taking care not to twist sts on needle, pm for beg of rnds. Cont in St st on all sts as foll:

Beg chart I
NOTE All one-color rnds are worked on shorter, smaller needle and all two-color rnds are worked on larger needle. Cont in St st on all sts as foll:
Rnd 1 Work first 3 steek sts, pm, work 24-st pat rep 3 times, then work st 1 once more, pm, work last 3 steek sts. Cont to foll chart in this manner (slipping markers) through rnd 12. Break yarns. Change to shorter, smaller needle and C.

Reverse stockinette stitch ridge
Rnds 1–3 Keeping 3 steek sts at beg and end of rnds in St st, work rnds 1–3 of rev St st ridge over rem sts. Break C. Change to larger needle and D.

Beg chart II
NOTE All two-color rnds are worked on larger needle. Cont in St st on all sts as foll:
Rnd 1 Work first 3 steek sts, sl marker, work 24-st pat rep 3 times, then work st 1 once more, sl marker, work last 3 steek sts. Cont to foll chart in this manner through rnd 24, then rep rnds 1–24 twice more, then rnd 1 once. Break yarns. Change to shorter, smaller needle and A.

Reverse stockinette stitch ridge
Rnds 1–3 Keeping 3 steek sts at beg and end of rnds in St st, work rnds 1–3 of rev St st ridge over rem sts. Break A. Change to C.

Beg chart III
NOTE All one-color rnds are worked on shorter, smaller needle and all two-color rnds are worked on larger needle. Cont in St st on all sts as foll:
Rnd 1 Work first 3 steek sts, pm, work 24-st pat rep 3 times, then work st 1 once more, pm, work last 3 steek sts. Cont to foll chart in this manner through rnd 12. Break B. Bind off knitwise using C.

I love the intricate pattern of Therese's pillow.

FINISHING
Securing and cutting steek
See Peggy's Pillow.

Mitered border
Rnd 1 (RS) With RS facing, longer, smaller circular needle and B, pick up and k 73 sts evenly spaced across cast-on edge, pm, pick up and k 1 st in corner, pm, pick up and k 80 sts evenly spaced across first steek edge, pm, pick up and k 1 st in corner, pm, pick up and k 73 sts evenly spaced across bound-off edge, pm, pick up and k 1 st in corner, pm, pick up and k 80 sts evenly spaced across 2nd steek edge, pm, pick up and k 1 st in corner, pm for beg of rnds—310 sts.
Rnd (inc) 2 *P to next marker, inc 1 using backward loop method, sl marker, k1, sl marker, inc 1; rep from * 3 times more—8 sts increased.
Rnd 3 *P to next marker, sl marker, k1, sl marker; rep from * 3 times more. Break C. Change to D.
Rnd (inc) 4 *K to next marker, inc 1 using backward loop method, sl marker, k1, sl marker, inc 1; rep from * 3 times more—8 sts increased.

CHART I FOR THERESE'S PILLOW
MULTIPLE OF 24 sts

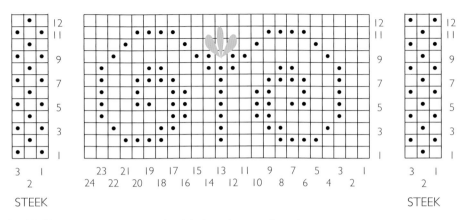

STEEK   STEEK

Color and Stitch Key

☐ **A** Magenta

⊡ **B** Espresso

E Lazy daisy stitches with Golden Honey

Rnd 5 *P to next marker, sl marker, k1, sl marker; rep from *
3 times more.

Rnd (inc) 6 *P to next marker, inc 1 using backward loop
method, sl marker, k1, sl marker, inc 1; rep from * 3 times
more. Break D. Change to C.

Rnd 7 *K to next marker, sl marker, k1, sl marker; rep from *
3 times more.

Rnds 8 and 9 Rep rnds 6 and 5. Bind off all sts loosely
knitwise.

Duplicate stitch embroidery
Using tapestry needle and B, embroider duplicate stitches
(see page 22) in center of motif as shown on chart IV.

French knot embroidery
Using a double strand of C in tapestry needle, work a French
knot (see page 171) in center of each motif as shown on
chart IV and photo.

Straight stitch and cross stitch embroidery
Using tapestry needle and B, embroider a vertical straight
stitch down center of each square motif, then a horizontal
straight stitch across; see photo. Using C, embroider a cross
stitch (see page 171) over each intersection of straight
stitches.

Lazy daisy stitch embroidery
Using tapestry needle and E, embroider three lazy daisy
stitches (see page 171) in center of each motif as shown on
chart I. Using D, embroider three lazy daisy stitches in center
of each motif as shown on chart III.

Blocking
See Peggy's Pillow.

Assembling pillow
See Peggy's Pillow. ■

CHART IV FOR THERESE'S PILLOW
MULTIPLE OF 24 sts

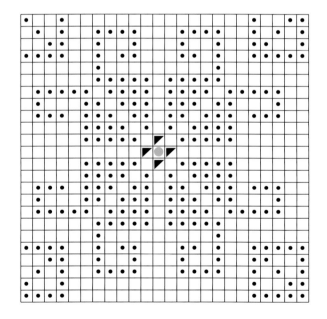

Color and Stitch Key

◪ **B** Duplicate stitch with Espresso

● **C** French knots with Spring Green

► CHART II FOR THERESE'S PILLOW
MULTIPLE OF 24 sts

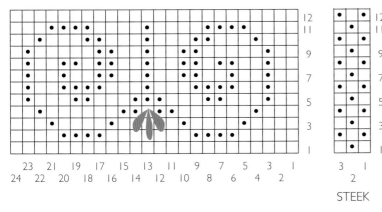

STEEK

STEEK

Color Key

☐ E Golden Honey

⊡ D Geranium

At the Farmhouse

As you can see by my hand-painted walls, plaid chair and these colorful pillows, I think you can never have too much pattern or color!

► CHART III FOR THERESE'S PILLOW
MULTIPLE OF 24 sts

STEEK

Color and Stitch Key

☐ C Spring Green

⊡ B Espresso

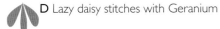 D Lazy daisy stitches with Geranium

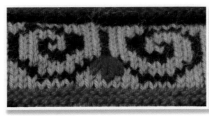

117

Last-Minute Mitts and Hat

I love deadlines because they make my creative juices flow. When I was in the planning stages for this book, my project list included "fingerless gloves." I knew they were small and rather easy to make and kept moving them to the bottom of the list. Suddenly I had less than a week to go before the shoot and the fingerless gloves still were nowhere near to being knit. Thank goodness for Susan, one of my fabulously talented knitting friends, who helped me out with the knitting and was even able to whip up a matching hat. With their floppy floral textured borders and colorful embroidery, they turned out even cuter than I expected.

Magic Multiple for Edging: 5 sts
(NOTE If you choose a different edging, cast on the number of sts needed after the floral edging is complete.)
Colorwork Chart Multiple: 5 sts

SIZES
Child's Medium (Woman's Small, Woman's Medium, Woman's Large). Shown in size Woman's Medium.

FINISHED MEASUREMENTS
Hat
Head circumference: 18 (19, 20, 22)"/45.5 (48, 51, 56)cm
Fingerless gloves
Hand circumference: 6½ (7¼, 8, 8¾)"/16.5 (18.5, 20.5, 22)cm
Length of cuff: 1¾"/4.5cm

YARN
Nashua Handknits *Julia* (wool/mohair/alpaca), 1¾oz/50g, 93yd/85m
A Blue Thyme NHJ4936—2 skeins
B Golden Honey NHJ2163—1 skein
C Purple Basil NHJ3158—1 skein
D Squash NHJ0120—1 skein
E Coleus NHJ4345—1 skein

NEEDLES
◆ Size 7 (4.5mm) circular needle, 16"/40cm long *or size needed to obtain correct gauge*
◆ Size 5 (3.75mm) circular needle, 16"/40cm and 24"/60cm long
◆ One set (4) each sizes 5 and 7 (3.75 and 4.5mm) double-pointed needles (dpns)

NOTIONS
◆ Stitch marker
◆ Stitch holders
◆ Tapestry needle

GAUGE
20 sts and 22 rnds = 4"/10cm in St st over chart pat using larger dpns. *Be sure to obtain correct gauge.*

Notes
1. Right and left fingerless gloves are made exactly the same.
2. All one-color rnds are worked on smaller dpns and all two-color rnds are worked on larger dpns.

Abbreviations
M1 Make 1
k2tog Knit 2 stitches together
k3tog Knit 3 stitches together

HAT
Brim
With longer, smaller needle and A, cast on 198 (209, 220, 242) sts. Join and pm taking care not to twist sts on needles. Work rnds 1–6 of floral edging (changing to shorter, smaller needle after rnd 5)—90 (95, 100, 110) sts. Break A. Change to B.
Cont in garter st, working 2 rnds each in color sequence as foll: B, C and B. Break yarns. Change to A.

Beg chart 1
NOTE All one-color rnds are worked on smaller needle and all two-color rnds are worked on larger needle.
Cont in St st on all sts as foll:
Rnd 1 Work 5-st pat rep 18 (19, 20, 21) times.
Cont to foll chart in this manner through rnd 22. Break E. Change to smaller needle and B.
Next rnd K dec 0 (inc 1, inc 2, dec 2) sts evenly spaced around—90 (96, 102, 108) sts. Purl next rnd. Break B. Change to A.

Shape crown
NOTE Change to smaller dpns when there are too few sts to work comfortably on circular needle.
Next (dec) rnd *K 13 (14, 15, 16), k2tog; rep from * around—84 (90, 96, 102) sts. Knit next rnd.
Next (dec) rnd *K 12 (13, 14, 15), k2tog; rep from * around—78 (84, 90, 96) sts. Knit next rnd.
Next (dec) rnd *K 11 (12, 13, 14), k2tog; rep from * around—72 (78, 84, 90) sts. Knit next rnd.
Next (dec) rnd *K 10 (11, 12, 13), k2tog; rep from * around—66 (72, 78, 84) sts. Knit next rnd. Cont to dec in this manner, dec 6 sts every other rnd until 6 sts rem. Cut yarn, leaving a 6"/15.5cm tail. Thread tail in tapestry needle, then thread through rem sts. Pull tog tightly and secure end on WS.

FINISHING
Weave in ends.

French knot embroidery
Referring to photo, using a double strand of E in tapestry needle, embroider a French knot (see page 171) in center of each circle motif of chart I.

Chain stitch embroidery
Using tapestry needle and D, embroider a line of chain stitches (see page 171) along rnd 8 of chart I.

Running stitch embroidery
Using E in tapestry needle, embroider running stitches (see page 171) over and under all D chain stitches around hat. Using A, embroider a line of running stitches (going under and over every other st) on rnd 15 of chart I.

Cross stitch embroidery
Using tapestry needle and A, embroider a cross stitch (see page 171) in center of each square motif of chart I.

FINGERLESS GLOVES
Cuff
With shorter, smaller circular needle and A, cast on 66 (77, 88, 99) sts. Join and pm taking care not to twist sts on needles.
Work rnds 1–6 of floral edging (changing to smaller dpns after rnd 5)—30 (35, 40, 45) sts. Break A. Change to B. Cont in garter st, working 2 rnds each in color sequence as foll: B, C and B. Break yarns.

Hand
Change to A.

Beg chart I
NOTE All one-color rnds are worked on smaller dpns and all two-color rnds are worked on larger dpns.
Cont in St st on all sts as foll:
Rnd 1 Work 5-st pat rep 6 (7, 8, 9) times. Cont to foll chart in this manner through rnd 6. Cont chart I and beg chart II as foll:

Shape thumb gusset
Rnd (inc) 7 K 15 (18, 20, 23), pm, M1 with A (st 1 of rnd 1 of chart II), pm, k 15 (17, 20, 22)—31 (36, 41, 46) sts.
Rnd 8 Work even (rnd 2 of chart II).
Rnd (inc) 9 K to first marker, sl marker, M1 with C, k 1 with C, M1 with C, sl marker, k to end—33 (38, 43, 48) sts.
Rnd 10 Work even (rnd 4 of chart II). Cont to inc for thumb gusset every other round (foll chart II) until there are 9 (11, 15, 17) sts between gusset markers—39 (46, 55, 62) sts.
Next rnd Work chart I to first marker, drop marker, place next 9 (11, 15, 17) sts on holder for thumb, drop next marker, work chart I to end—30 (35, 40, 45) sts. When rnd 22 of chart I is completed, rep chart beg on rnd 1. AT THE SAME TIME, work even until hand measures 3½ (4, 4½, 5)"/

CHART I

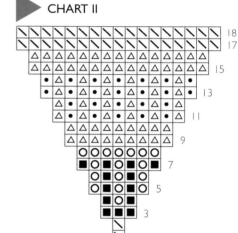

Color Key

△	E Coleus
⊙	D Squash
■	C Purple Basil
•	B Golden Honey
◺	A Blue Thyme

CHART II

9 (10, 11.5, 12.5)cm from end of cuff. Break yarns. Change to smaller dpns and D. Work 2 rnds in garter st. Break D. Change to C. Knit next rnd. Bind off all sts purlwise.

Thumb
Place sts from thumb gusset holder on 2 smaller dpns. With RS facing, join same color as was used for last rnd worked.
Next rnd K across thumb sts, then pick up and k 1 st at base of hand—10 (12, 16, 18) sts. Divide sts between 3 smaller dpns, then pm for beg of rnds. Break yarn. Change to B. Work 2 rnds in garter st. Break B. Change to A. Knit next rnd. Bind off all sts purlwise.

FINISHING
Weave in ends. Embellish fingerless gloves with embroidery same as hat. ■

Stitches

FLORAL EDGING
(multiple of 11 sts; decs to a multiple of 5 sts)

Rnd 1 *P 4, k3 , work [k1, p1] twice in next st, turn; p4, turn; k4, turn; p4, turn; pass the 2nd st over the first, the 3rd st over the first, the 4th st over the first st (bobble made), sl this st to RH needle, k3; rep from * around.

Rnds 2–4 *P4, k7; rep from * around.

Rnd 5 *P4, slip next 3 sts knitwise to RH needle, sl sts back to LH needle, k3tog, k1, k3tog; rep from * around.

Rnd 6 *P4, [bring yarn to front, sl next 3 sts to RH needle, bring yarn to back, sl 3 sts back to LH needle] twice wrapping sts tightly, knit the 3 wrapped sts tog; rep from * around.
Work rnds 1–6 for floral edging.

GARTER STITCH
Rnd 1 Knit.
Rnd 2 Purl.

STOCKINETTE STITCH
Knit every round.

Your Choice
If you're not a fan of fingerless gloves, refer to the Mad for Plaid Mittens (page 61) and lengthen the fingerless gloves/half mittens into full mittens.

Op Art Ottoman

I've had an idea for a knitted ottoman ever since I purchased an ottoman covered with an antique kilim several years ago. I chose bold circle, square and diamond motifs, reminiscent of the 1960s, then colored the piece in my favorite Middle Eastern shades.

Magic Multiple for Edging:
Choose a cast-off edging with a multiple of 5 or 10 sts
Colorwork Chart Multiple: 5, 10, 15 or 30 sts

FINISHED MEASUREMENTS

Top
Approx 18¼"/46.5cm wide × 26¼"/66.5cm long

Skirt
Approx 6½"/16.5cm high

YARN

Nashua Handknits *Julia* (wool/mohair/alpaca), 1¾oz/50g, 93yd/85m
A Lady's Mantle NHJ3961—2 skeins
B Deep Blue Sea NHJ6396—1 skein
C Anemone NHJ9235—2 skeins
D Golden Honey NHJ2163—1 skein
E Espresso NHJ0118—4 skeins
F Pretty Pink NHJ8141—1 skein
G Harvest Spice NHJ0178—3 skeins

NEEDLES

For top
Size 5 and 7 (3.75 and 4.5mm) circular needles, 16"/40cm long *or size to obtain correct gauge*

For skirt
Three each size 5 and 7 (3.75 and 4.5mm) circular needles, 32"/81cm long

NOTIONS

◆ Stitch markers
◆ Tapestry needle
◆ Matching sewing thread
◆ Sewing machine

SUPPLIES

◆ 6"/15cm-thick firm foam (see Resources on page 169)
◆ ½"/13mm-thick plywood
◆ Four 5" × 3⅞"/12.5cm × 10cm spiral bun feet, style 41050P (see Resources), plus tools for installation
◆ #120 and #220 sandpapers
◆ Tack cloth
◆ Two 1"/2.5cm flat brushes
◆ White latex primer
◆ Latex semi-gloss paint in desired color
◆ White craft glue
◆ Staple gun with ½"/13mm staples
◆ Safety glasses

GAUGE

20 sts and 22 rnds = 4"/10cm in St st over chart pats using larger circular needle.
Be sure to obtain correct gauge.

Notes

1. Ottoman cover is worked in two sections: top and skirt.
2. Top is worked in the round forming a tube, with steek sts at beginning and end of rounds.
3. During finishing, the steeks are secured with machine stitching, then cut open forming a flat piece. See page 21 for securing a steek.
4. The skirt is picked up around the edge of the top and worked in the round.
5. All one-color rnds are worked on smaller needle and all two-color rnds are worked on larger needle.

OTTOMAN COVER

Top

With shorter, smaller circular needle and A, cast on 99 sts. Join taking care not to twist sts on needle, pm for beg of rnds. Cont in St st on all sts as foll:

*Beg chart I
NOTE All one-color rnds are worked on smaller needle and all two-color rnds are worked on larger needle. Cont in St st on all sts as foll:
Rnd 1 Work first 3 steek sts, pm, beg 2 sts before st 1, then work 30-st pat rep 3 times, end chart 1 st after st 30, pm, work last 3 steek sts. Cont to foll chart in this manner (slipping markers) through rnd 34. Break yarns. Change to smaller needle and C.

GARTER ST RIDGES

Rnds 1 and 2 Keeping 3 steek sts at beg and end of rnds in St st, work rnds 1 and 2 of garter st over rem sts. Break C. Change to D.
Rnds 3 and 4 Keeping 3 steek sts at beg and end of rnds in St st, work rnds 1 and 2 of garter st over rem sts. Break D. Change to E.

BEG CHART II

NOTE All one-color rnds are worked on smaller needle and all two-color rnds are worked on larger needle. Cont in St st on all sts as foll:
Rnd 1 Work first 3 steek sts, pm, beg 2 sts before st 1, then work 30-st pat rep 3 times, end chart 1 st after st 30, pm, work last 3 steek sts. Cont to foll chart in this manner (slipping markers) through rnd 34.* Break yarns. Change to smaller needle and D.

GARTER ST RIDGES

Rnds 1 and 2 Keeping 3 steek sts at beg and end of rnds in St st, work rnds 1 and 2 of garter st over rem sts. Break D. Change to C.
Rnds 3 and 4 Keeping 3 steek sts at beg and end of rnds in St st, work rnds 1 and 2 of garter st over rem sts. Break C. Change to A. Rep from * to * once more. Bind off loosely knitwise using E.

FINISHING

Securing and cutting steek
See page 21 before you begin. It is important to keep the knit fabric flat and neat while stitching. Do not pull on it as

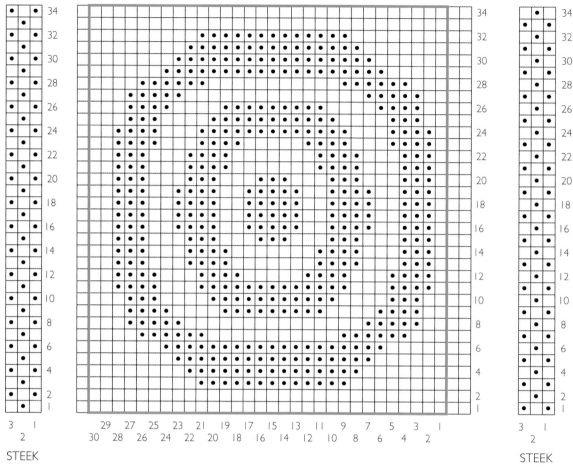

CHART I
MULTIPLE OF 30 sts

STEEK

STEEK

Color Key

☐ **A** Lady's Mantle

⊡ **B** Deep Blue Sea

you sew or it will distort and ripple. Set sewing machine to straight stitch. On each side of steek section, sew between the steek st and the chart pat st; this is called "stitching in the ditch." Now, set sewing machine to a medium zigzag stitch. Stitch the two center steek sts as foll: locate the 3rd steek st and sew a row of sts on top of the knit sts, then rep along top of the 4th steek st. Using sharp scissors, cut through the center of the two zigzag rows of stitching, taking care not to snip the sewing machine stitches.

Skirt

Rnd I (RS) With RS facing, a longer, smaller circular needle and C, pick up and k 90 sts evenly spaced across cast-on edge, then 150 sts evenly spaced across first steek edge; with another circular needle, pick up and k 90 sts evenly spaced across bound-off edge, then 150 sts evenly spaced across 2nd steek edge I st in corner, pm for beg of rnds—480 sts. Work in the rnd using third needle. Purl next rnd. Break C. Change to D. Work around in garter st for 2 rnds. Break D. Change to G and larger needles.

Beg chart III

Rnd I Work 30-st pat rep 16 times. Cont to foll chart in this manner through rnd 30. Break yarns. Change to C and smaller needles. Work around in garter st for 6 rnds. Bind off all sts loosely knitwise. Steam-block to even out colorwork. ■

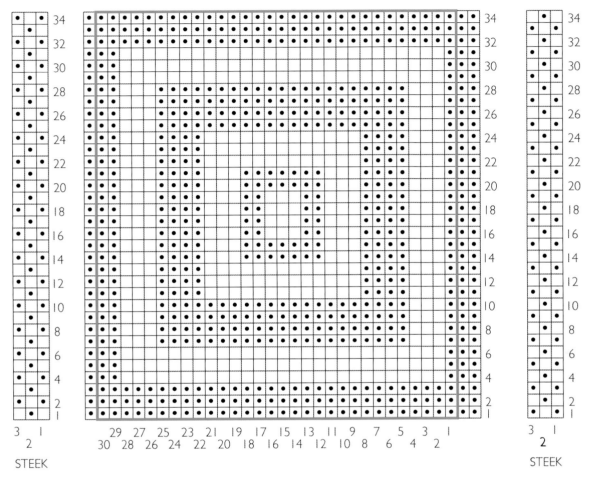

► CHART II
MULTIPLE OF 30 sts

STEEK   STEEK

Color Key

☐ **F** Pretty Pink

⊡ **E** Espresso

Stitches
STOCKINETTE STITCH
Knit every round.

GARTER STITCH
Rnd 1 Knit.
Rnd 2 Purl.
Rep rnds 1 and 2 for garter st.

At the Farmhouse

This cheerful bench is now our favorite spot to sit when we're putting on our boots in the morning.

▶ **CHART III**
MULTIPLE OF 30 sts

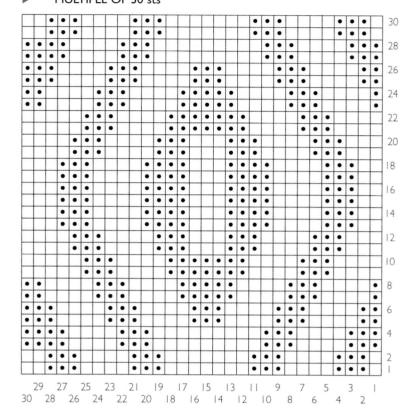

Row numbers (right side): 30, 28, 26, 24, 22, 20, 18, 16, 14, 12, 10, 8, 6, 4, 2, 1

Column numbers (bottom): 29 27 25 23 21 19 17 15 13 11 9 7 5 3 1 / 30 28 26 24 22 20 18 16 14 12 10 8 6 4 2

Color Key

☐ **G** Harvest Spice
⊡ **E** Espresso

◤ DIY Ottoman

This sturdy ottoman is quick and easy to build.

Purchasing foam and plywood
Measure the width and length of your cover. Purchase foam cut to your measurements and plywood cut to same size as foam.

Preparing plywood and feet
Sand all surfaces with #120, then #220 sandpapers; wipe with tack cloth.

Assembling ottoman base
Attach feet to plywood following manufacturer's directions.

Painting
Apply one coat of primer and two coats of color, allowing drying between each coat. Refer to label directions for drying times.

Gluing foam
Brush a thick coat of white glue on top of ottoman base. Place foam on top, then press to adhere. Let dry overnight.

Assembling ottoman
Cover base with ottoman cover. Wearing safety glasses, staple skirt to side edges of base, hiding staples between garter st ridges. ■

Lazy Daisy Teapot Cozy

While not worked in a pattern, this cozy by no means lacks color. The bobble edging and multi-colored ridges at the top frame the solid-colored cozy. Embroidered flowers add a touch of whimsy.

Magic Multiple for Edging: 10 sts
Colorwork Chart Multiple:
This is a solid-colored project.

SIZES
Small (Medium, Large).
Shown in size Large.
◆ To determine what size to make, use a tape measure to measure around the outside of your pot (including the handle and spout). Pick the circumference closest to your measurement, keeping in mind that it's best to have the cozy be a bit roomy, rather than too snug. To determine height, measure from the bottom to the top, keeping the tape measure slack for the most accurate measurement. Adjust the height when knitting the sides if needed.

FINISHED MEASUREMENTS
Circumference 22 (24, 26)"/56 (61, 66)cm
Height 10 (10½, 11)"/25.5 (26.5, 28)cm (excluding knitted knob)

YARN
Nashua Handknits *Julia* (wool/mohair/alpaca), 1¾oz/50g, 93yd/85m
A Golden Honey NHJ2163—1 skein
B Harvest Spice NHJ0178—1 skein
C Bright Blue NHJ4037—2 skeins
D Spring Green NHJ5185—1 skein
E Persimmon NHJ0121—1 skein
F Gourd NHJ1784—1 skein

NEEDLES
For sides of cozy
Size 6 (4mm) circular needle, 16"/40cm long *or size needed to obtain correct gauge*
For top of cozy
One set (4) size 6 (4mm) double-pointed needles (dpns) *or size needed to obtain correct gauge*

NOTIONS
◆ Stitch marker
◆ Tapestry needle
◆ Polyester fiberfill

GAUGE
20 sts and 22 rnds = 4"/10cm in St st using size 6 (4mm) circular needle. *Be sure to obtain correct gauge.*

Abbreviations
dec 2 Slip 2 stitches knitwise to RH needle, k1, pass the 2 slipped stitches over the k1
k2tog Knit 2 stitches together

Stitches
BOBBLE EDGING
(multiple of 10 sts)
Rnd 1 (RS) *P9, work [k1, p1] twice in next st, turn; p4, turn; k4, turn; p4, turn; pass the 2nd st over the first, the 3rd st over the first, the 4th st over the first st (bobble made), sl this st to RH needle; rep from * around.
Work rnd 1 for bobble edging.

GARTER STITCH
Rnd 1 Knit.
Rnd 2 Purl.
Rep rnds 1 and 2 for garter st.

STOCKINETTE STITCH
Knit every round.

TEA COZY
Sides
With circular needle and A, cast on 110 (120, 130) sts. Join, taking care not to twist sts on needle, pm for beg of rnds. Work rnd 1 of bobble edging. Purl next 2 rnds. Break A, change to B. Work around in garter st for 6 rnds. Break B. Change to C. Cont in St st until piece measures 6½"/16.5cm from beg or desired length.
(NOTE Length of top of cozy is approx 3½ (4, 4½)"/9 (10, 11.5)cm. Subtract this number for size being made to determine whether you need to adjust length of sides.)
Next (dec) rnd K, dec 8 (6, 4) sts evenly spaced around— 102 (114, 126) sts. Break C. Change to A.

Top

NOTE Change to dpns when there are too few sts to work comfortably on circular needle.

Rnd 1 *K 7 (8, 9), dec 2, k 7 (8, 9); rep from * around—90 (102, 114) sts.
Rnds 2 and 3 Purl. Break A. Change to B.
Rnd 4 *K 6 (7, 8), dec 2, k 6 (7, 8); rep from * around—78 (90, 102) sts.
Rnds 5 and 6 Purl. Break B. Change to D.
Rnd 7 *K 5 (6, 7), dec 2, k 5 (6, 7); rep from * around—66 (78, 90) sts.
Rnds 8 and 9 Purl. Break D. Change to E.
Rnd 10 *K 4 (5, 6), dec 2, k 4 (5, 6); rep from * around—54 (66, 78) sts.
Rnds 11 and 12 Purl. Break E. Change to C.
Rnd 13 *K 3 (4, 5), dec 2, k 3 (4, 5); rep from * around—42 (54, 66) sts.
Rnds 14 and 15 Purl. Break C. Change to A.
Rnd 16 *K 2 (3, 4), dec 2, k 2 (3, 4); rep from * around—30 (42, 54) sts.
Rnds 17 and 18 Purl. Break A. Change to D.
Rnd 19 *K 1 (2, 3), dec 2, k 1 (2, 3); rep from * around—18 (30, 42) sts.
Rnds 20 and 21 Purl. Break D.

◆ For Small size only
Change to F.
Rnd 22 [Dec 2] 6 times—6 sts.
Rnds 23 and 24 Purl. Break yarn.

◆ For Medium and Large sizes only
Change to F.
Rnd 22 *K 1 (2), dec 2, k 1 (2); rep from * around—18 (30) sts.
Rnds 23 and 24 Purl. Break yarn.

◆ For Medium size only
Change to C.
Rnd 25 [Dec 2] 6 times—6 sts.
Rnds 26 and 27 Purl. Break yarn.

◆ For Large size only
Change to C.
Rnd 25 *K1, dec 2, k1; rep from * around—18 sts.
Rnds 26 and 27 Purl. Break C. Change to A.
Rnd 28 [Dec 2] 6 times—6 sts.
Rnds 29 and 30 Purl. Break yarn.

◆ For all sizes
Change to C (A, B).

Knitted knob
Rnds 1 and 2 Knit.
Rnd 3 [K into front and back of next st] 6 times—12 sts.
Rnd 4 Knit.
Rnd 5 [K into front and back of next st] 12 times—24 sts.
Rnds 6 and 7 Knit. Break yarn. Change to A (B, D).
Rnd 8 Purl.
Rnd 9 [K2tog] 12 times—12 sts.
Rnd 10 [K2tog] 6 times—6 sts.
Rnd 11 Knit. Cut yarn, leaving a 6"/15.5cm tail. Thread tail in tapestry needle, then thread through rem sts. Stuff knob firmly with fiberfill. Pull sts tog tightly and secure end.

FINISHING
Steam-block to even out stitches.

Applied bobbles (make 8)
With dpn and E, cast on 1 st.
Row 1 (WS) Work [k1, p1] twice in next st—4 sts.
Rows 2 and 4 Purl.
Row 3 Knit.
Row 5 Pass the 2nd st over the first, the 3rd st over the first, the 4th st over the first (bobble made). Cut yarn, leaving a 6"/15.5cm tail. Thread tail in tapestry needle, then thread through rem sts. Pull sts tog tightly, pushing purl side to RS; secure end. Weave tail into center of bobble to stuff and create nice rounded shape.

For flower centers, sew bobbles onto cozy, spacing them artfully around the solid-colored stockinette section (see photo on opposite page).

Woven bar leaves
Using tapestry needle and D, work two 1¼"/3cm-long woven bar leaves (see page 171) around each flower center (see photo on opposite page).

Petal Power
A few simple embroidery stitches add up to a garden's worth of colorful flowers.

Lazy daisy stitch embroidery
Using tapestry needle and either A or B, embroider seven to eight ⅝"/1.5cm to ⅞"/2cm-long lazy daisy stitch petals (see page 171) around each flower center. Alternate colors (see photo on opposite page).

French knot embroidery
Referring to photo on opposite page, and using a double strand of F in tapestry needle, work French knots (see page 171) in an overall pattern around flowers. ■

Cuffed Mittens and Socks

I like to design for all knitters – not just beginners and not just advanced knitters. When I am dreaming up projects, I think about what I can make that might be fun for all skill levels. These mittens and socks are it! Both of these projects begin in the exact same way—with a looped border and a Fair Isle floral cuff. After you finish the cuff, it is smooth sailing through the body of either the sock or the mitten.

Magic Multiple for Edging:
Begins with a multiple of 10 and finishes with a multiple of 5 or 10.
Color Chart Multiple:
Over a repeat of 14 sts. You can adapt the color charts in the back of the book by increasing a 12-stitch chart or decreasing a 15-stitch chart.

SIZES
Mittens
Woman's Small (Medium).
Shown in size Small.
Socks
Women's Small (Medium, Large).
Shown in size Medium.

FINISHED MEASUREMENTS
Mittens
Hand circumference
7 (8)"/17.5 (20.5)cm
Length of cuff 4½"/11.5cm
Socks
Length 8¼ (9½, 10¼)"/21 (24, 26)cm
Circumference around foot
7 (8, 9)"/17.5 (20.5, 23)cm

YARN
Nashua Handknits *Julia* (wool/mohair/alpaca), 1¾oz/50g, 93yd/85m
Mittens
A Lady's Mantle NHJ3961—1 skein
B Magenta NHJ2083—1 skein
C Steel Gray NHJ0122—2 skeins
D Squash NHJ0120—1 skein

Socks
A Lady's Mantle NHJ3961—1 skein
B Magenta NHJ2083—1 skein

C Steel Gray NHJ0122—2 skeins
D Squash NHJ0120—1 skein

NEEDLES
One set (4) each sizes 5 and 7 (3.75 and 4.5mm) dpns *or size needed to obtain correct gauge*
Size 7 (4.5mm) circular needle, 16"/40cm long

NOTIONS
◆ Stitch marker
◆ Stitch holders
◆ Tapestry needle

GAUGE
20 sts and 22 rnds = 4"/10cm in St st over chart pat using larger dpns.
20 sts and 24 = 4"/10cm in St st on smaller dpns.
Be sure to obtain correct gauge.

Notes
1. Right and left mittens are made exactly the same.
2. All one-color rnds are worked on smaller dpns and all two-color rnds are worked on larger dpns.

Abbreviations
M1 Make 1 (see page TK)
k2tog Knit 2 stitches together
p2tog Purl 2 stitches together
SKP Slip 1 stitch, knit 1 stitch, pass the slipped stitch over the knit st.
wyib With yarn in back.
wyif With yarn in front.

MITTENS (make 2)
Cuff
With circular needle and A, cast on 120 sts. Join and pm, taking care not to twist sts on needles. Work rnds 1 and 2 of loopy edging, changing to larger dpns on rnd 2—60 sts. Break A. Change to smaller dpns and B.
Next (dec) rnd K dec 4 sts—56 sts. Purl next 2 rnds. Break B. Change to larger dpns and C.
Beg chart
NOTE All one-color rnds are worked on smaller dpns and all two-color rnds are worked on larger dpns. Cont in St st on all sts as foll:
Rnd 1 Work 14-st pat rep 4 times. Cont to foll chart in this manner through rnd 17. Break C. Change to smaller dpns and B. Work rnds 1–3 of rev St st ridge. Break B. Change to A. Work rnds 1–3 of rev St st ridge. Break A. Turn cuff WS out. Change to C.

Hand
Next rnd K dec 16 sts evenly spaced around—40 sts. Purl next rnd. Knit next rnd. Cont in 2 x 2 rib for 4"/10cm, dec 5 (0) sts evenly spaced around last rnd—35 (40) sts. Break C. Change to B. Cont in stripe pat for 1¼ (1½)"/3 (4)cm.

Shape thumb gusset
Next (inc) rnd K18 (20), pm, M1, pm, k17 (20)—36 (41) sts. Knit next rnd.
Next (inc) rnd K to first marker, sl marker, M1, k to next marker, M1, sl marker, k to end—37 (43) sts. Knit next rnd. Rep last 2 rnds 5 (6) times more—48 (55) sts; 13 (15) sts between markers.
Next rnd K to first marker, drop marker, place next 13 (15) sts on holder for thumb, drop next marker, k to end—35 (40) sts. Work even in stripe pat until hand measures 3½ (4)"/9 (10)cm from end of thumb gusset.

Shape top
Next (dec) rnd [K2, k2tog] 8 (10) times, k 3 (0)—27 (30) sts. Knit next rnd.
Next (dec) rnd [K1, k2tog] 9 (10) times—18 (20) sts. Knit next rnd.
Next (dec) rnd [K2tog] 9 (10) times—9 (10) sts.

CHART FOR CUFFED SOCKS AND MITTENS
MULTIPLE OF 14 sts

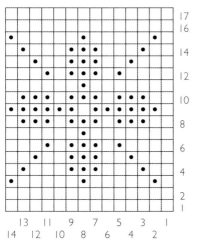

Color Key

☐ **C** Steel Gray

⊡ **D** Squash

► ### CHART FOR DUPLICATE STITCH

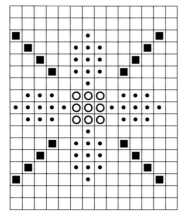

Color Key

◼ **A** Lady's Mantle

◎ **B** Magenta

Stitches

LOOPY EDGING
(multiple of 10 sts; decs to a multiple of 5 sts)
Rnd 1 Purl.
Rnd 2 *K5, pm, bind off next 5 sts using st before marker to beg the bind-off (there will now be 4 sts and a gap of the bind-off and 1 st on RH needle); rep from * around.
Work rnds 1 and 2 for loopy edging.

REVERSE STOCKINETTE STITCH RIDGE
Rnd 1 Knit.
Rnds 2 and 3 Purl.
Work rnds 1–3 for rev St st ridge.

STOCKINETTE STITCH
Knit every round.

2 X 2 RIB
(multiple of 4 sts)
Rnd 1 *K2, p2; rep from * around.
Rep rnd 1 for 2 x 2 rib.

STRIPE PATTERN
Working in St st, work *2 rnds B, 2 rnds A, 2 rnds D, 2 rnds C; rep from * (8 rnds) for stripe pat.

Next (dec) rnd [K2tog] 4 (5) times, k 1 (0)—5 sts. Cut yarn leaving a 6"/15.5cm tail. Thread tail in tapestry needle, then thread through rem sts. Pull tog tightly and secure end on WS.

Thumb
Place sts from thumb gusset holder on 2 smaller dpns. With RS facing, join color in progress at beg of thumb sts to cont in stripe pat as established.
Next rnd K across thumb sts, then pick up and k 1 st at base of hand—14 (16) sts. Divide sts between 3 dpns, then pm for beg of rnds. Work even in stripe pat until thumb measures 1¼ (1¾)"/3 (4.5)cm.

Shape top
Next (dec) rnd [K2tog, k2] 3 (4) times, k 2 (0)—11 (12) sts.
Next (dec) rnd [K2tog, k1] 3 (4) times, k 2 (0)—8 sts.
Next (dec) rnd [K2tog] 4 times—4 sts. Cut yarn leaving a 6"/15.5cm tail. Thread tail in tapestry needle, then thread through rem sts. Pull tog tightly and secure end on WS.

FINISHING
Use yarn tail at base of thumb to close up gap between thumb and hand. Weave in ends. Block or steam to even out colorwork.
Duplicate stitch embroidery
Using tapestry needle, embroider duplicate stitches (see page 22) foll chart for duplicate stitch embroidery.

SOCKS (make 2)
Cuff
Work same as mitten—56 sts.

Leg
Next rnd K dec 20 (16, 12) sts evenly spaced around—36 (40, 44) sts. Purl next rnd. Knit next rnd. Cont in 2 x 2 rib for 6"/15cm. Break C. Change to B.

Heel flap
Next (set up) rnd K 18 (20, 22) sts onto one needle for heel flap. Divide rem sts evenly on 2 needles for instep.
Heel flap is worked back and forth. Turn needle with heel sts so WS is facing. Cont as foll:
Row 1 (WS) K1, p to last st, k1.
Row 2 (RS) K1, *k1, wyib sl 1 st as if to purl; rep from * to last st, end k1. Rep these 2 rows for 2 (2, 2¼)"/5 (5, 5.5)cm, end with row 2.
Turn the heel
Row 1 (WS) P 11 (12, 13) sts, p2tog, p1, turn.
Row 2 (RS) Wyib sl first st as if to purl, k5, SKP, k1, turn.
Row 3 Wyif sl first st as if to purl, p6, p2tog, p1, turn.
Row 4 Wyib sl first st as if to purl, k7, SKP, k1, turn.
Row 5 Wyif, sl first st as if to purl, p8, p2tog, p1, turn.
Row 6 Wyib sl first st as if to purl, k9, SKP, k1,

turn—12 (14, 16) sts.

◆ **For Medium and Large sizes only**
Row 7 Wyif, sl first st as if to purl, p10, p2tog, p1, turn.
Row 8 Wyib sl first st as if to purl, k11, SKP, k1,
turn—12 (14) sts.

◆ **For Large size only**
Row 9 Wyif, sl first st as if to purl, p10, p2tog, p1, turn.
Row 10 Wyib sl first st as if to purl, k9, SKP, k1, turn—12 sts.

◆ **For all sizes**
Form gusset
Break B. Place all instep sts on one needle. Change to C.
With RS facing and using the needle holding the heel sts, pick
up and k 12 (12, 13) sts along selvage edge of heel flap; with
2nd needle, k 18 (20, 22) sts across instep sts; with 3rd
needle, pick up and k 12 (12, 13) sts along opposite selvage
edge of heel flap; then k first 6 sts from heel needle onto the
end of 3rd—54 (56, 60) sts. Pm at center back heel for beg
of rnds. Sts are now distributed as foll:
Needle #1—18 (18, 19) sts
Needle #2—18 (20, 22) sts
Needle #3—18 (18, 19) sts
Next (dec) rnd Needle #1: K to last 3 sts, k2tog, k1; Needle
#2: Knit; Needle #3 K1, SKP, k to end—2 sts dec (1 st each
from Needles #1 and #3). Knit next rnd. Rep last 2 rnds 8
(7, 7) times more—36 (40, 44) sts.

Foot
Cont in St st until foot measures 6¼ (7½, 8¼)"/16 (19, 21)cm
from back of heel. Break C. Change to A. Knit next 2 rnds.
Break A. Change to D.

Shape toe
Next (dec) rnd First needle—K to last 3 sts k2tog, k1; 2nd
needle—K1, SKP, k to last 3 sts, k2 tog, k1;
3rd needle—K1, SKP, k to end—4 sts dec. Knit next rnd. Rep
last 2 rnds 5 (6, 6) times more—12 (12, 16) sts. Place sts
from needles 1 and 3 on one needle for bottom of toe—6
(6, 8) sts on each needle. Cut D leaving a 12"/30.5cm tail.
Graft toe sts tog using Kitchener st.

FINISHING
Weave in ends. Block or steam to even out colorwork.

Duplicate stitch embroidery
Using tapestry needle, embroider duplicate stitches (see page
22) foll chart for duplicate stitch embroidery. ■

Norwegian Dreams Pullover

I've always loved the intricate Fair Isle sweaters of the Nordic countries. I first saw them on stylish skiers in the pages of sporting magazines. This design is very similar to the Norwegian designs I lusted after many years ago.

Magic Multiple for Edging: 7 sts
Colorwork Chart Multiple:
Smaller Border over multiple of 4 or 8 sts. Main part of body over 4, 5, 10 or 20 sts.

SIZES
X-Small (Small, Medium, Large, Extra Large). Shown in size Medium.

FINISHED MEASUREMENTS
Bust: 36 (40, 44, 48, 52)"/91.5 (101.5, 111.5, 122, 132)cm
Length: 22½ (23, 24, 24½, 25)"/ 57 (58.5, 61, 62, 63.5)cm
Upper arm: 15 (16, 17, 18, 19)"/38 (40.5, 43, 45.5, 48)cm

YARN
Nashua Handknits *Julia* (wool/mohair/alpaca), 1¾oz/50g, 93yd/85m
A Deep Blue Sea NHJ6396—1 (2, 2, 2, 2) skein
B Rock Henna NHJ2230—2 (2, 3, 3, 3) skeins
C Sage NHJ0115—6 (6, 7, 8, 9) skeins
D Dusk NHJ1505—2 (2, 2, 2, 3) skeins
E Purple Basil NHJ3158—5 (6, 6, 7, 8) skeins

NEEDLES
For sweater body
Size 5 and 7 (3.75 and 4.5mm) circular needles, 29"/75cm long *or size needed to obtain correct gauge*
For sleeves and collar
Size 5 (3.75 and 4.5mm) circular needle, 16"/40cm long
One set (4) each sizes 5 and 7 (3.75 and 4.5mm) double-pointed needles (dpns) *or size needed to obtain correct gauge*

NOTIONS
◆ Stitch markers
◆ Tapestry needle
◆ Matching sewing thread
◆ Sewing machine

GAUGE
20 sts and 22 rnds = 4"/10cm in St st over chart pats using larger circular needle.
Be sure to obtain correct gauge.

Abbreviations
p2sso Pass 2 slipped stitches over the k1
k2tog Knit 2 stitches together
ssk Slip, slip, knit these 2 stitches together
M1 Make 1

Stitches

POINTED EDGING
(multiple of 11 sts; decs to
a multiple of 7 sts)
Rnd 1 Purl.
Rnd 2 *K4, sl2, k1, p2sso,
k4; rep from * around.
Rnd 3 *P3, sl2 with yarn in
back, p1, p2sso, p3;
rep from * around.
Rnd 4 Purl.
Work rnds 1–4 for
pointed edging.

GARTER STITCH
Rnd 1 Knit.
Rnd 2 Purl.
Rep rnds 1 and 2 for
garter st.

STOCKINETTE STITCH
Knit every round.

K3, P3 RIB
(multiple of 6 sts)
Rnd 1 *K3, p3; rep from *
around.
Rep rnd 1 for k3, p3 rib.

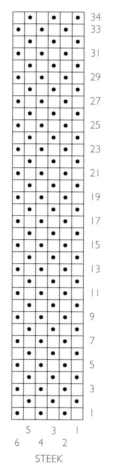

▶ CHART I
MULTIPLE
OF 8 sts

Color Key

☐ **B** Rock Henna

⊡ **D** Dusk

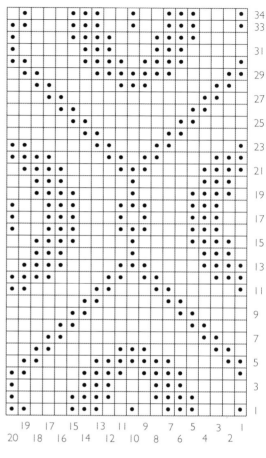

▶ CHART II
MULTIPLE OF 20 sts

STEEK

Color Key

⊡ **E** Purple Basil

☐ **C** Sage

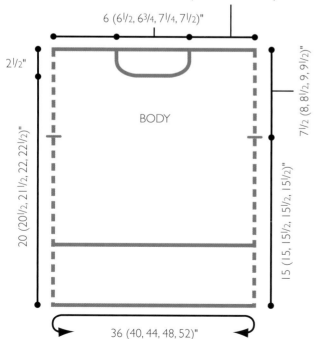

6 (6³/4, 7¹/2, 8¹/4, 9¹/4)"

6 (6¹/2, 6³/4, 7¹/4, 7¹/2)"

2¹/2"

BODY

20 (20¹/2, 21¹/2, 22, 22¹/2)"

7¹/2 (8, 8¹/2, 9, 9¹/2)"

15 (15, 15¹/2, 15¹/2, 15¹/2)"

36 (40, 44, 48, 52)"

15 (16, 17, 18, 19)"

SLEEVE

18 (18, 18¹/2, 18¹/2, 19)"

9¹/2 (9¹/2, 11¹/4, 12³/4, 12³/4)"

Notes
1. The body of the sweater is worked in the round to the shoulders with steeked sections for the armholes and front neck. During finishing, the steeks are secured with machine stitching, then cut open. See page 21 for securing a steek.
2. You will have to shape the sleeves by increasing at the underarm. See page 19 for an explanation of how to do this.
3. Each sleeve is worked in the round, then sewn into the cut armhole openings.
4. Use smaller circular needle or dpns for garter st rnds.
5. When working chart pats, use smaller circular needle or dpns for all one-color rnds and larger circular needle or dpns for all two-color rnds.

BODY
With longer, smaller circular needle and A, cast on 275 (308, 341, 374, 407) sts. Join taking care not to twist sts on needle, pm for beg of rnds. Work rnds 1–4 of pointed edging—175 (196, 217, 238, 259) sts. Cont in garter st, working 2 rnds each in color sequence as foll: B, C and A.

Next rnd K inc 1 (inc 4, dec 1, inc 2, dec 3) sts evenly spaced around—176 (200, 216, 240, 256) sts.

Next rnd Purl. Break A. Change to B.

Beg chart I
NOTE All one-color rnds are worked on smaller needle and all two-color rnds are worked on larger needle. Cont in St st on all sts as foll:

Rnd 1 Work 8-st pat rep 22 (25, 27, 30, 32) times. Cont to foll chart in this manner through rnd 9, then rep rnds 2-9 once more, then rnd 1 once. Break yarns. Change to smaller needle and A. Cont in garter st, working 2 rnds each in color sequence as foll: A and D. Break D. Change B.

Next (inc) rnd K inc 4 (0, 4, 0, 4) sts evenly spaced around—180 (200, 220, 240, 260) sts.

Next rnd P 90 (100, 110, 120, 130) sts, pm (for armhole steek placement), p to end. Break B. Change to E.

Beg chart II
NOTE All rnds are worked on larger needle. Cont in St st on all sts as foll:

Rnd 1 Work 20-st pat rep 9 (10, 11, 12, 13) times. Cont to foll chart in this manner through rnd 34, then rep rnds 1–34 to the end. AT THE SAME TIME, when piece measures 15 (15, 15½, 15½, 15½)"/38 (38, 39.5, 39.5, 39.5)cm from beg, establish steek sts each side for armhole openings as foll:

Establish armhole steeks
Next rnd Work chart II as established to next marker, sl marker, using the backward loop cast-on method, cast on 6 sts as foll: [1 st with C, 1 st with E] 3 times, pm; work chart II as established to next marker, sl marker, using the backward loop cast-on method cast on 6 sts as foll: [1 st with C, 1 st with E] 3 times, pm for new beg of rnd—192 (212, 232, 252, 272) sts. You will now be working chart II on 90 (100, 110, 120, 130) sts on front and back, and working steek chart (beg on rnd 2) on 6 sts each side of body. Work even until armhole steek section measures 5 (5½, 6, 6½, 7)"/12.5 (14, 15, 16.5, 17.5)cm from beg.

Shape front neck
Next rnd Work chart II as established across first 34 (38, 42, 46, 50) sts, bind off center 22 (24, 26, 28, 30) sts, work as established to end of rnd—34 (38, 42, 46, 50) sts each side of front neck bound-off sts, 90 (100, 110, 120, 130) sts on back and 6-st steek sections each side.

Establish front neck steek
Next rnd Work chart II as established across first 34 (38, 42, 46, 50) sts, pm, using the backward loop cast-on method, cast on 6 sts as foll: [1 st with C, 1 st with E] 3 times, pm, work as established to end of rnd—176 (194, 212, 230, 248) sts.

Next (dec) rnd Work chart II as established to 2 sts before next marker, k2tog, sl marker, work 6-st steek section at center front neck beg on rnd 2 of steek chart, sl marker, ssk, work as established to end of rnd—1 st dec from each side of front neck. Work next rnd even. Rep last 2 rnds 3 times more—30 (34, 38, 42, 46) sts each side of front neck bound-off sts. Work even in established pats until armhole steek section measures 7½ (8, 8½, 9, 9½)"/19 (20.5, 21.5, 23, 24)cm. Bind off all sts knitwise.

SLEEVES
With shorter, smaller circular needle and A, cast on 77 (77, 88, 99, 99) sts. Join, pm for beg of rnds. Work rnds 1–4 of pointed edging (changing to smaller dpns after rnd 2)—49 (49, 56, 63, 63) sts. Cont in garter st, working 2 rnds each in color sequence as foll: B, C and A.

Next rnd K dec 1 (dec 1, dec 0, inc 1, inc 1) st evenly spaced around—48 (48, 56, 64, 64) sts.

Next rnd Purl. Break A. Change to B.

Beg chart I
NOTE All one-color rnds are worked on smaller dpns and all two-color rnds are worked on larger dpns. Cont in St st on all sts as foll:

Rnd 1 Work 8-st pat rep 6 (6, 7, 8, 8) times. Cont to foll chart in this manner through rnd 9, then rep rnds 2–9 twice more, then rnd 1 once. Break yarns. Change to smaller dpns and A. Cont in garter st, working 2 rnds each in color sequence as foll: A and D. Break D. Change B.

Next (inc) rnd K inc 0 (0, 6, 2, 2) sts evenly spaced around—48 (48, 62, 66, 66) sts.

Next rnd Purl, dropping marker at end of rnd.

Beg chart II

NOTE All rnds are worked on larger dpns.

Cont in St st on all sts as foll:

◆ **For X-Small and Small sizes only**

Rnd 1 K1 with E, pm, work sts 18–20, work 20-st rep twice, work sts 1–3, pm, k1 with C.

Rnd 2 K1 with C, sl marker, work sts 18–20, work 20-st rep twice, work sts 1–3, sl marker, k1 with E.

◆ **For Medium size only**

Rnd 1 K1 with E, pm, work 20-st rep 3 times, pm, K1 with C.

Rnd 2 K1 with C, sl marker, work 20-st rep 3 times, sl marker, K1 with E.

◆ **For Large and X-Large sizes only**

Rnd 1 K1 with E, pm, work st 20, work 20-st rep 3 times, work st 1, pm, K1 with C.

Rnd 2 K1 with C, sl marker, work st 20, work 20-st rep 3 times, work st 1, sl marker, K1 with E.

◆ **For all sizes**

Cont to foll chart in this manner through rnd 34, then rep rnds 1–34 to the end. AT THE SAME TIME, alternate colors used for the 2 sts between st markers to create a checkerboard pat (faux "sleeve seam"). Work 2 rnds more.

Shape sleeve

NOTE Change to shorter, smaller circular needle when there are too many sts to work comfortably on dpns.

Next (inc) rnd K1 with E, sl marker, M1 incorporating inc in chart pat, work chart II to next markers, M1 incorporating inc in chart pat, sl marker, k1 with C. Cont to inc 1 st after first marker and 1 st before 2nd marker every 5th rnd 13

(15, 11, 11, 14) times more—76 (80, 86, 90, 96) sts. Work even until piece measures 18 (18, 18½, 18½, 19)"/45.5 (45.5, 47, 47, 48)cm from beg. Bind off all sts knitwise.

FINISHING

Securing and cutting the steeks

See page 21 before you begin. It is important to keep the knit fabric flat and neat while stitching. Do not pull on it as you sew or it will distort and ripple. Set sewing machine to straight stitch. On each side of an armhole steek section, sew between the steek st and the chart pat st; this is called "stitching in the ditch." Now, set sewing machine to a medium zigzag stitch. Stitch the two center steek sts as foll: locate the 3rd steek st and sew a row of machine sts on top of the knit sts, then rep along top of the 4th steek st. Using sharp scissors, cut through the center of the two zigzag rows of stitching from the bound-off edge to the beg of the steek section, taking care not to snip the sewing machine stitches. Rep for second armhole. Secure and cut front neck steek in the same manner. Sew shoulder seams.

Neckband

With RS facing, shorter, smaller needle, A, and beg at left shoulder seam, pick up and k 72 (72, 78, 84, 84) sts evenly spaced around neck edge. Join and pm for beg of rnds. Purl next rnd. Break A. Change to C. Work 2 rnds in garter st. Break C. Change to B. Knit next rnd. Cont in k3, p3 rib for 1½"/4cm. Break B. Change to C. Work 2 rnds in garter st. Break C. Change to A. Knit next rnd. Bind off all sts loosely purlwise. Sew sleeves into armholes. Weave in ends. Steam or block to even out colorwork. ■

Keep It Simple

When I am knitting colorwork charts, I don't like to fool with a lot of fancy shaping. I like to get into the rhythm of the chart and watch it grow into a beautiful piece of patterned, knit fabric. It's enough for me to make sure I don't make a mistake without thinking about shaping. That's why I find the square-shaped pullover the best vehicle for playing out my colorwork obsessions. I can knit it in the round all the way to the armholes. Then I add two steeks for each sleeve seam and continue on until the neck shaping. I add a steek at the center front of the neck and then only shape the slope of the side of the neck for a few rounds. I've been making sweaters like this for years and they stand the test of time. They might not always be in fashion, but they always look classic, smart and beautiful in an old-fashioned kind of way.

Designer
Sourcebook

Custom Edgings

An edging is a bit of decoration that doesn't take a lot of effort but really makes a knitted project something special. Sometimes edgings are a bit fiddly, but since most of them have only a few active fiddly knitting rows, they are well worth the effort. Adding a clever colorful edge to a simple garment can easily put it over the top.

Because edgings come at the beginning or end of the knitting and are somewhat separate from the garment as a whole, they're fairly interchangeable. That's why I set these edgings apart into their own section. Putting them all in one place makes it easier for you to reference and design with them when you're feeling adventurous. Take some time to try out all the edges included here. You'll understand exactly how to make them and feel confident you can mix them up.

Do you want to make the fun Cuffed Mittens and Socks (page 130) but you don't like the loopy edging? That's okay—everyone is entitled to their own knitting opinion. Are you crazy about the pointed edging in the Norwegian Dreams Pullover (page 134) but don't want to knit an entire sweater? Then swap the two and make a pair of mittens with the pointed edging. Remember—you're the boss of your knitting. No one is telling you what to do. Take the techniques in this chapter and start mixing them up.

SWAP IT

The edgings I have included fall into two major categories: those that can be worked using any amount of stitches and those that have a Magic Multiple. Edgings such as garter stitch stripes and reverse stockinette stitch ridges fit into the first category. There's no math involved, so you can swap these edgings freely without doing any calculations. Those that have a Magic Multiple are split into two subcategories: those that have a single-number Magic Multiple (such as 4 stitches) and those that have two numbers (the cast-on multiple that decreases to a Magic Multiple). Now don't be alarmed; it will all be explained as you read along.

MAGIC MULTIPLES

Let's first discuss the single-number Magic Multiple. With few exceptions, a pattern stitch is created by combining knit and purl stitches. The number of stitches that are combined to form a pattern that gets repeated is the multiple of stitches. In order for an edging to work out perfectly, the number of stitches that are to be cast on must be evenly divisible by the Magic Multiple. For instance, the Magic Multiple of the Two-Color Garter Stitch is 4 stitches. So, your cast-on number of stitches should be able to be divided by 4, such as 28, 40, 88 and so on.

If you have your heart set on swapping an edge treatment that isn't the same multiple, all is not lost. All you have to do is determine a number stitches close to the original cast-on number, by doing a little simple math. Here's how to do it:

Perhaps you want to knit the Bloomsbury Gauntlets (page 36) and want to replace the Sculpted Edging, which has a Magic Multiple of 7 stitches, with a Bobble Edging, which has a Magic Multiple of 6 stitches. You'll find that the stated cast-on number of 49 stitches cannot be evenly divided by 6, but by subtracting one stitch to 48 stitches, the math now works. To proceed, you would cast on 48 stitches, knit the edging, then increase one stitch as you work the last round of the edging to get yourself back to the original number.

To increase or decrease, that is the question. If it's only one or two stitches, it really doesn't matter, but if you are getting near a half-inch's worth of stitches, it's better to increase from the stated cast-on amount, then decrease to the original cast-on amount after the edging is completed.

Now, let's talk about substituting an edging with one that decreases over the course of the edge. These edgings are all located at the end of this chapter and include Loopy Edging, which I'll use as an example.

◆ LOOPY EDGING (worked in the round)

Cast-on multiple of 10 sts that decreases to the Magic Multiple—5 sts

Rnd 1 Purl.

Rnd 2 *K5, pm, bind off next 5 sts using st before marker to beg the bind-off (there will now be 4 sts and a gap of the bind-off and 1 st on RH needle); rep from * around.

Work rnds 1 and 2 for loopy edging.

To figure out how to use this edging, you have to work backwards. While you need to cast on a multiple of 10 stitches, you have to consider that you will end up with a multiple of 5 stitches. So 5 is the Magic Multiple to shoot for. Say your project directions state to cast on 102 stitches. Divide 102 by 5 (Magic Multiple of Loopy Edging when finished). You get 20, with 2 stitches remaining, which means you should use 20 as the repeat for figuring out the number of cast-on stitches. Multiply 20 x 10 (the cast-on multiple of the Loopy Edging) to get 200. That is the number of stitches you should cast on. After you work rounds 1 and 2, you will have 100 stitches left. You can then increase the number of stitches by 2 to give you the original number of stitches (102) needed for your original pattern. Carry on with the original instructions as given. If you are still a little iffy about how to do the math for an edging that has different numbers, you'll be happy to know that each edging pattern has a refresher course on how to figure the numbers for that particular stitch. ■

Versatile Garter Stitch Edgings, Borders and Accents

Add rich texture and color with these super pattern stitches. They are easy to swap with other trims because they will work with any number of stitches

GARTER STITCH
(worked in the round)
Magic Multiple—any number
Rnd 1 Knit.
Rnd 2 Purl.
Rep rnds 1 and 2 for garter st.

GARTER STITCH
(worked back and forth)
Magic Multiple—any number
Knit every row.

TWO-COLOR GARTER STITCH STRIPES
(worked in the round)
Magic Multiple—any number
Rnd 1 With A, knit.
Rnd 2 With A, purl.
Rnd 3 With B, knit.
Rnd 4 With B, purl.
Rep rnds 1–4 for two-color garter st stripes.

TWO-COLOR GARTER STITCH STRIPES
(worked back and forth)
Magic Multiple—any number
Rows 1 and 2 With A, knit.
Rows 3 and 4 With B, knit.
Rep rows 1–4 for two-color garter st stripes.

Two-Color Stripes

Three-Color Stripes

Color Tip
You can continue to add as many colors as you like. Just make sure to add each new color on an odd number round or row.

THREE-COLOR GARTER STITCH STRIPES
(worked in the round)
Magic Multiple—any number
Rnd 1 With A, knit.
Rnd 2 With A, purl.
Rnd 3 With B, knit.
Rnd 4 With B, purl.
Rnd 5 With C, knit.
Rnd 6 With C, purl.
Rep rnds 1–6 for three-color garter st stripes.

THREE-COLOR GARTER STITCH STRIPES
(worked back and forth)
Magic Multiple—any number
Rows 1 and 2 With A, knit.
Rows 3 and 4 With B, knit.
Rows 5 and 6 With C, knit.
Rep rows 1–6 for three-color garter st stripes.

GARTER STITCH RIDGE
(worked in the rnd)
◆ Add an extra splash of contrasting color with a single garter stitch ridge.
Magic Multiple—any number
Rnd 1 Knit.
Rnd 2 Purl.
Work rnds 1 and 2 for garter st ridge.

GARTER STITCH RIDGE
(worked back and forth)
Magic Multiple—any number
Rows 1 and 2 Knit.
Work rows 1 and 2 for garter st ridge.

TWO-COLOR GARTER STITCH
(worked in the round)
◆ Garter is usually thought of as a very simple stitch to be worked in solid or striped colors. But, by knitting it in two alternating colors in a round, it creates a fabulous checkerboard design. I must admit it's a bit tricky to do the first time, but after a few rounds, you'll get the hang of it. You'll find this edging used as a detail stripe for the Child's Zip-Up Cardigan (page 53) and the Pompom Bolster (page 90).
Magic Multiple—4 sts.
Rnd 1 *K2 with A, k2 with B; rep from * around.
Rnd 2 *Bring A to front and p2, bring A to back, bring B to front and p2, bring B to back;

Two-Color Garter Stitch

rep from * around.
Rnd 3 *K2 with B, k2 with A; rep from * around.
Rnd 4 *Bring B to front and p2, bring B to back, bring A to front and p2, bring A to back; rep from * around.
Work rnds 1–4 for two-color garter st.

Three-Color Garter Stitch

THREE-COLOR GARTER STITCH
(worked in the round)
◆ You can further mystify your friends and family by adding more colors to the checked garter stitch. This version uses 3 colors but you could also add 4, 5 or 6 colors depending on your desire. You can find Three-Color Garter Stitch featured on the Hen Party Pullover (see page 102).
Magic Multiple—4 sts.
Rnd 1 *K2 with A, k2 with B; rep from * around.
Rnd 2 *Bring A to front and p2, bring A to back, bring B to front and p2, bring B to back; rep from * around.
Rnd 3 *K2 with B, k2 with C; rep from * around.
Rnd 4 *Bring B to front and p2, bring B to back, bring C to front and p2, bring C to back; rep from * around.
Work rnds 1–4 for three-color garter st.

Ridges That Rock

Reverse stockinette stitch ridges are thicker than garter ridges. The first round (or row) sinks into the fabric and is where you establish the color change to avoid funny bumps on the right side of the work. Rounds (or rows) 2 and 3 show on the right side of the work. The purl bumps pop to the right side, making a neat-looking ridge. You can make reverse stockinette stitch ridges deeper (and thicker) by adding more reverse stockinette stitch rounds (or rows).

REVERSE STOCKINETTE STITCH RIDGE
(worked in the round)
Magic Multiple—any number
Rnd 1 Knit.
Rnds 2 and 3 Purl.
Work rnds 1–3 for rev St st ridge.

REVERSE STOCKINETTE STITCH RIDGE
(worked back and forth)
Magic Multiple—any number
Row 1 (RS) Knit.
Row 2 Knit.
Row 3 Purl.
Work rows 1–3 for rev St st ridge. If you are going to work a rev St st ridge beg on a WS row, work as foll:
Row 1 (WS) Purl.
Row 2 Purl.
Row 3 Knit.

Reverse St st Ridge

Using Garter Stitch and Reverse Stockinette Stitch Ridges

Both garter stitch ridge and reverse stockinette ridge tend to stretch out horizontally. To adjust for this, I work my ridge patterns on needles that are one or two sizes smaller than the colorwork sections. You may even find it necessary to work yours on needles 3 sizes smaller. To play it safe, work a circular gauge swatch of garter and reverse stockinette stitch ridges to determine the needle size you need to use.

Take a Ribbing

Corrugated ribbing is found on many traditional Fair Isle knits. It makes a thick fabric and is not as stretchy as your basic one-color 2 x 2 ribbing. I used it around the neckline of the Hen Party Pullover (page 102).

2 X 2 TWO-COLOR CORRUGATED RIB
(worked in the round)
Magic Multiple—4 sts.
Rnd 1 *K2 with A, k2 with B; rep from * around.
Rnd 2 *K2 with A, p2 with B; rep from * around.
Rep rnd 2 for 2 x 2 corrugated rib.

Corrugated Rib

2 X 2 TWO-COLOR CORRUGATED CHECKED RIB
(worked in the round)
◆ By using the same technique as 2 x 2 Corrugated Rib, but alternating the colors over the first 6 rounds, a checked effect is created. It is used for the Mad for Plaid Mittens (page 61).
Magic Multiple—4 sts.
Rnd 1 *K2 with A, k2 with B; rep from * around.
Rnds 2 and 3 *K2 with A, p2 with B; rep from * around.
Rnd 4 *K2 with B, k2 with A; rep from * around.
Rnds 5 and 6 *P2 with B, k2 with A; rep from * around.
Rep rnds 1–6 for 2 x 2 two-color corrugated checked rib. (To make this swatch, repeat rounds 1–3 for remainder of rib.)

Checked Rib

TWO-COLOR TWISTED RIB
(worked in the round)
◆ By taking the same basic concept of 2 x 2 Corrugated Rib, but this time twisting the stitches in the stockinette column, tiny cables are created. A variation of this rib was used for the Mother-Daughter Mittens (page 98). For this pattern stitch you will need to know this special abbreviation:
2-st RT Skip next st and knit the 2nd st, then knit the skipped st, sl both sts from needle tog
Magic Multiple—4 sts
Rnd 1 *K4 with A, k2 with B; rep from * around.
Rnd 2 *P4 with A, k2 with B; rep from * around.
Rnd 3 *P4 with A, 2-st RT with B; rep from * around.
Rep rnds 2 and 3 for two-color twisted rib.

Twisted Rib

Fringe Benefits

The curly fringe edging is applied after knitting is completed. It is made by picking up stitches along the edge, then binding off the edge while at the same time casting on and binding off stitches for the fringe. The fringes twist back upon themselves and curl. Experiment with casting on different numbers of stitches. This treatment was used on the Extra-Long Scarf for Extra-Cold Days (see page 94).

CURLY FRINGE

Magic Multiple—5 sts
Rnd 1 (RS) Pick up and k 1 st in each st around.
Rnd 2 *Bind off 5 sts purlwise, cast on 10 sts to RH needle using backward loop method, turn; bind off first 10 sts knitwise, turn, place last st from bind-off on LH needle; rep from * to end. Work rnds 1 and 2 for curly fringe.
NOTE To work this edging back and forth, pick up sts along edge from the RS, then turn and work rnd 2 from the WS.

Going Loopy

The loopy edging is worked as a cast-on treatment. By casting on twice as many stitches than needed, then binding off in groups of 5 stitches, decorative hanging loops are formed. Depending on the project, you may need to use a long circular needle to accommodate the large number of cast-on stitches. This edging is used on the Cuffed Mittens and Socks (see page 130).

LOOPY EDGING (worked in the round)

◆ To figure out how to use this edging, you have to work backwards. While you need to cast on a multiple of 10 stitches, you have to consider that you will end up with a multiple of 5 stitches. So 5 is the Magic Multiple to shoot for. Say your project directions state to cast on 100 stitches. Simply divide 100 by 5 = 20, then multiply 20 by 10 = 200. Therefore, cast on 200 stitches. After you work rnds 1 and 2, you will have 100 stitches left.

Cast-on multiple of 10 sts that decreases to the Magic Multiple—5 sts
Rnd 1 Purl.
Rnd 2 *K5, pm, bind off next 5 sts using st before marker to beg the bind-off (there will now be 4 sts and a gap of the bind-off and 1 st on RH needle); rep from * around.
Work rnds 1 and 2 for loopy edging.

Do the Wave

These easy yet intriguing edgings are made by working groups of cast-on stitches several times in the first row. The "pile-up" of garter stitches forms soft, sculpted edges. You can find Sculpted Edging on the Bloomsbury Gauntlets (see page 36).

SCULPTED EDGING

Magic Multiple—7 sts
Row 1 (WS) *K4, [k3, turn] 4 times, k3; rep from * to end.
Work row 1 for sculpted edging.
NOTES 1. The sculpted edging works for both back and forth knitting and working in the round.
2. To make this edging a bit wider, knit 2 more rows.

UNDULATING EDGE STITCH
(worked in the round)

Here's a similar wavy edging to consider. It's featured along the top edge of the On-the-Go Knitter's Tote (see page 64).
Magic Multiple—8 sts
Rnds 1, 3 and 5 *K8; turn work; k4; turn work; k 4; rep from * around.
Rnds 2, 4 and 6 Purl.
Work rnds 1–6 for undulating edge st.

Bubbly Bobbles

What could be cuter than a garment trimmed with perky knitted bobbles that dangle from the edge? You can change the spacing on the bobbles, making them further apart or closer together by increasing or decreasing the number of stitches between them. You'll find bobble edgings with various spacings (5, 6 or 10 stitches apart) featured on the Over-the-Top Shawl (see page 40), the Mother-Daughter Mittens (see page 98), and the Lazy Daisy Teapot Cozy (see page 127).

BOBBLE EDGING (worked in the round)
Magic Multiple—5, 6, or 10 sts.
Instructions are for a multiple of 5 sts. Changes for a multiple of 6 and 10 sts are in parentheses.
Rnd 1 (RS) *P 4 (5, 9), work [k1, p1] twice in next st, turn; p4, turn; k4, turn; p4, turn; pass the 2nd st over the first, the 3rd st over the first, the 4th st over the first st (bobble made), sl this st to RH needle; rep from * around. Work rnd 1 for bobble edging.

SEW ON BOBBLES
Traditionally bobbles are used with Aran (cabled) stitches to create extra texture. If knitted separately, they can be sewn onto an edging to create bits of bright colors and added interest. To make an individual bobble, work as follows: Cast on 1 st, leaving a long tail for sewing. Work [k1, p1] twice in st, turn; p4, turn; k4, turn; p4, turn; pass the 2nd st over the first, the 3rd st over the first, the 4th st over the first st. Cut yarn, leaving a 6"/15cm tail, then fasten off last st.

Get to the Point

The subtle shaped edge of the pointed cast-on is made by working decreases over two rounds. To make it more pronounced, after blocking, lay the project flat, pull the points out and hold with T-pins. Spritz the fabric with water, let the piece dry and the edge will stay pointy.

POINTED EDGING
(worked in the round)
◆ For Pointed Edging and Pointed Bobble Edging that follows, you again have to work backwards in order to figure out how many stitches to cast on. If the instructions say to cast on 110 stitches, divide 110 by 7 to get 15, with 5 stitches left over. Adjust 110 to 112 stitches, which is divisible by 7—the Magic Multiple you need. Divide 112 by 7 to get 16 repeats. To determine the number of stitches to cast on, multiply 16 by 11 = 176 stitches. After the decreases have been worked, you will have 112 stitches. Decrease by 2 stitches in the next round to give you the 110 stitches you need..
NOTE For this stitch and the one that follows, you need to know this special abbreviation: **p2sso** Pass 2 slipped stitches over the k1.
Cast-on multiple of 11 sts that decreases to the Magic Multiple—7 sts
Rnd 1 Purl.
Rnd 2 *K4, sl2, k1, p2sso, k4; rep from * around.
Rnd 3 *P3, sl2 with yarn in back, p1, p2sso, p3; rep from * around.
Rnd 4 Purl.
Work rnds 1–4 for pointed edging.

POINTED BOBBLE EDGING
(worked in the round)
◆ By adding bobbles to the pointy edges, I created a more exaggerated look. It is used on Julia's Sweater (see page 71).
Cast-on multiple of 11 sts that decreases to the Magic Multiple—7 sts

Rnd 1 *P5, work [k1, p1] twice in next st, turn; p4, turn; k4, turn; p4, turn; pass the 2nd st over the first, the 3rd st over the first, the 4th st over the first st (bobble made), sl this st to RH needle, p5; rep from * around.
Rnd 2 *P4, sl2, k1, p2sso, p4; rep from * around.
Rnd 3 *K3, sl2, k1, p2sso, k3; rep from * around.
Rnd 4 Purl.
Work rnds 1–4 for pointed bobble edging.

Pretty Posies

This clever edge is quite easy to knit and makes a striking floral border. It features bobbles on the edge and fuchsia-shaped flowers that are formed with a wrapping technique coupled with a k3tog decrease. It is used on the Last-Minute Mitts and Hat (see page 118). This edging would look very sweet on the bottom border of a little girl's sweater.

.FLORAL EDGING (worked in the round)

◆ Just like Loopy Edging, you have to work backwards in order to figure out how to swap this edging for another. While you need to cast on a multiple of 11 stitches, you have to consider that you will end up with the Magic Multiple of 5 stitches. If the instructions say to cast on 220 stitches, divide 220 by 5 = 44, then multiply 44 by 11 = 484. Therefore, cast on 484 stitches. After you work rnds 1 and 2, you will have 220 stitches left.

Cast-on multiple of 11 sts that decreases to the Magic Multiple—5 sts

Rnd 1 *P 4, k3 , work [k1, p1] twice in next st, turn; p4, turn; k4, turn; p4, turn; pass the 2nd st over the first, the 3rd st over the first, the 4th st over the first st (bobble made), sl this st to RH needle, k3; rep from * around.
Rnds 2–4 *P4, k7; rep from * around.
Rnd 5 *P4, slip next 3 sts knitwise to RH needle, sl sts back to LH needle, k3tog, k1, k3tog; rep from * around.
Rnd 6 *P4, [bring yarn to front, sl next 3 sts to RH needle, bring yarn to back, sl 3 sts back to LH needle] twice wrapping sts tightly, knit the 3 wrapped sts tog; rep from * around.
Work rnds 1–6 for floral edging.

Perky Picots

Picots add a delicate, lacy edge similar to those worked with a crochet hook. You'll find them at the bottom edges of the Child's Zip-Up Cardigan (see page 53). Picots also make a subtle edging treatment on small projects such as hats, mittens and gloves.

PICOT EDGING

◆ As before, you have to work in reverse to determine how many stitches to cast on so you will end up with the Magic Multiple of 5 stitches. If the instructions say to cast on 150 stitches, divide 150 by 5 = 30, then multiply 30 by 8 = 240. So, cast on 240 stitches. After you work row 1, you will have 150 stitches remaining.

Cast-on multiple of 8 sts that decreases to the Magic Multiple—5 sts

Row 1 (WS) *K2, (k2, sl 2nd st on RH needle over first st to bind off 1 st, [k1, bind off 1 st] twice), k2; rep from * to end.
Work row 1 for picot edging.

PICOT EDGING BIND-OFF

You can also add picots to an edge after a piece is completed.
Magic Multiple—5 sts
With RS facing, pick up a multiple of 5 sts across edge. Turn.
Next row (WS) Bind off 3 sts knitwise, *[sl st on RH needle back to LH needle and knit it again, then return the same st to LH needle] twice (stitch will end up on RH needle), bind off next 5 sts knitwise; rep from * until 2 sts rem (1 st on each needle); sl the st on RH needle back to LH needle and knit it again, then return the same st to LH needle and knit it once more; bind off last 2 sts.

Colorwork Chart Glossary

Once you feel comfortable with Fair Isle knitting, you'll realize that it is easy to customize a pattern by substituting different charts.

Each pattern in this book has a "Colorwork Chart Multiple" at the beginning of the instructions. For instance, for the Norwegian Dreams Pullover (page 134), the main part of the body has a Colorwork Chart Multiple of 4, 5, 10 or 20 sts, because the chart used has a 20-stitch multiple. This means that you can substitute any chart that has a stitch multiple of 4, 5, 10 or 20 sts, because they all divide evenly into 20.

The Colorwork Chart Glossary contains many different charts to choose from and is organized by stitch repeat number. When you find a chart in the glossary that you want to substitute into a pattern, swatch it. Depending on the chart and the usage (border or overall pattern repeat), you may want to skip a row or repeat a row on the chart. And if the stitch multiple is smaller than the original, you will have to repeat it. For example, if you substitute a chart with a 5-stitch multiple for a chart with a 20-stitch multiple, you would knit it 4 times. If you are pleased with the way the new chart worked out in color and stitch pattern, then substitute it into the base pattern provided. The main part of the instructions will remain the same.

When you feel even more adventurous, try designing your own charts by following the instructions in "Designing Fair Isle Knits" on page 28.

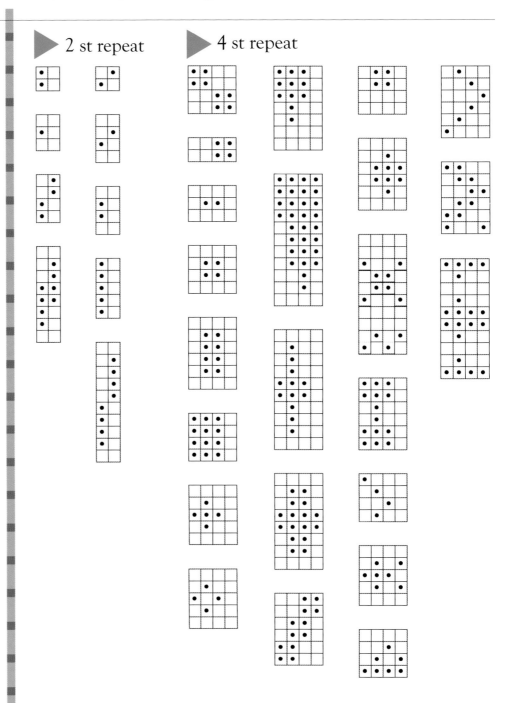

▶ 2 st repeat ▶ 4 st repeat

▶ 5 st repeat

▶ 6 st repeat

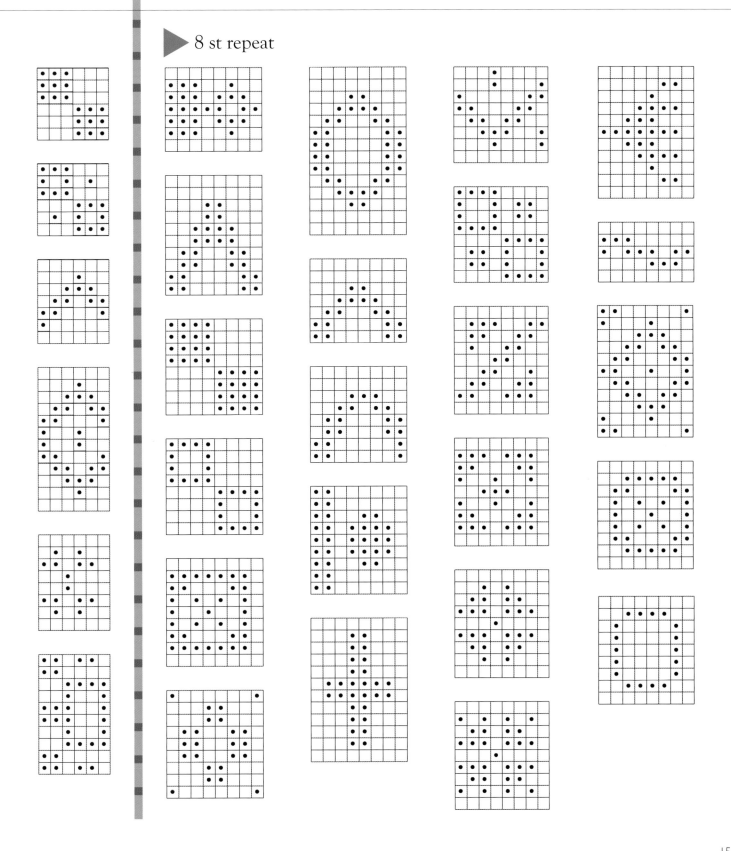

8 st repeat

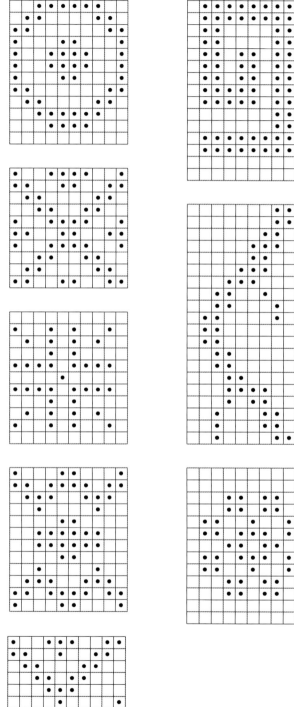

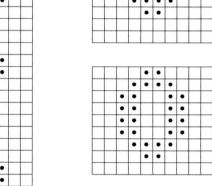

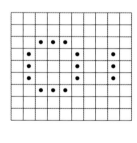

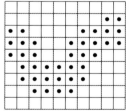

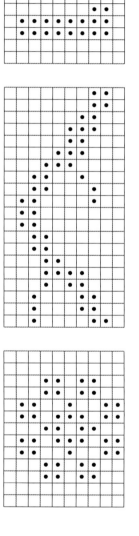

10 st repeat

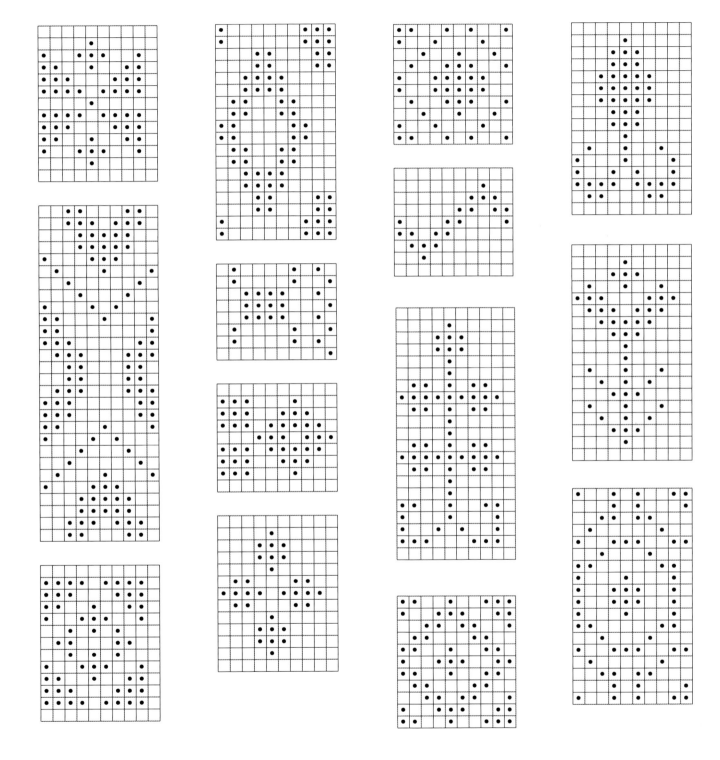

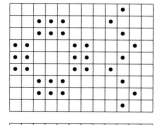

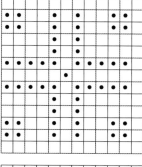

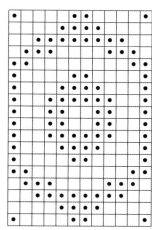

12 st repeat

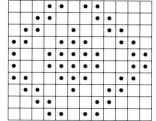

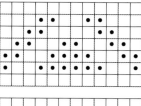

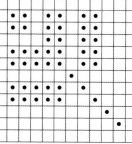

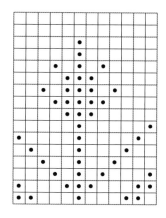

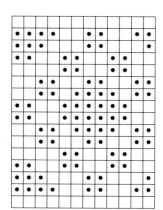

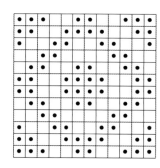

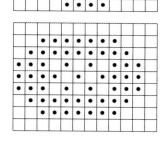

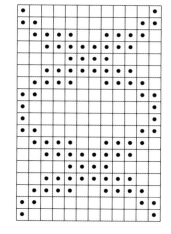

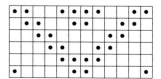

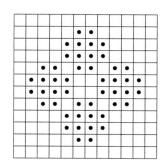

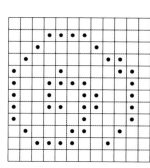

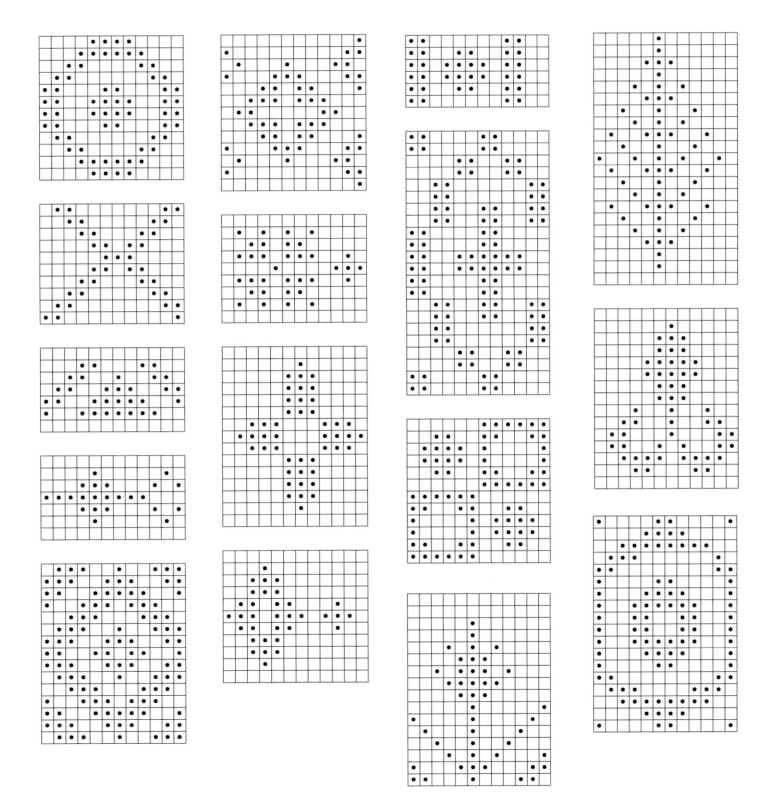

▶ 15 st repeat

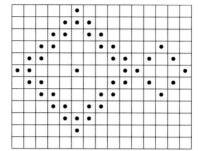

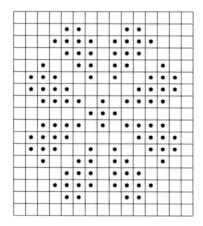

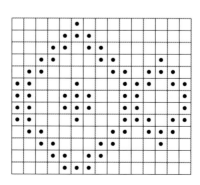

▶ 16 st repeat

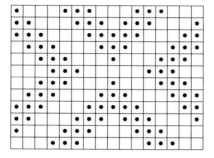

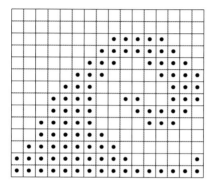

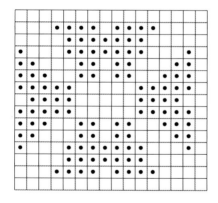

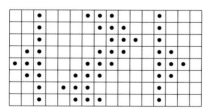

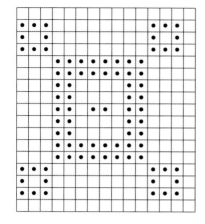

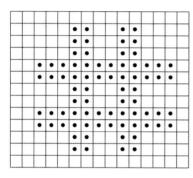

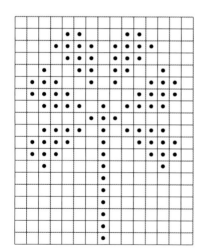

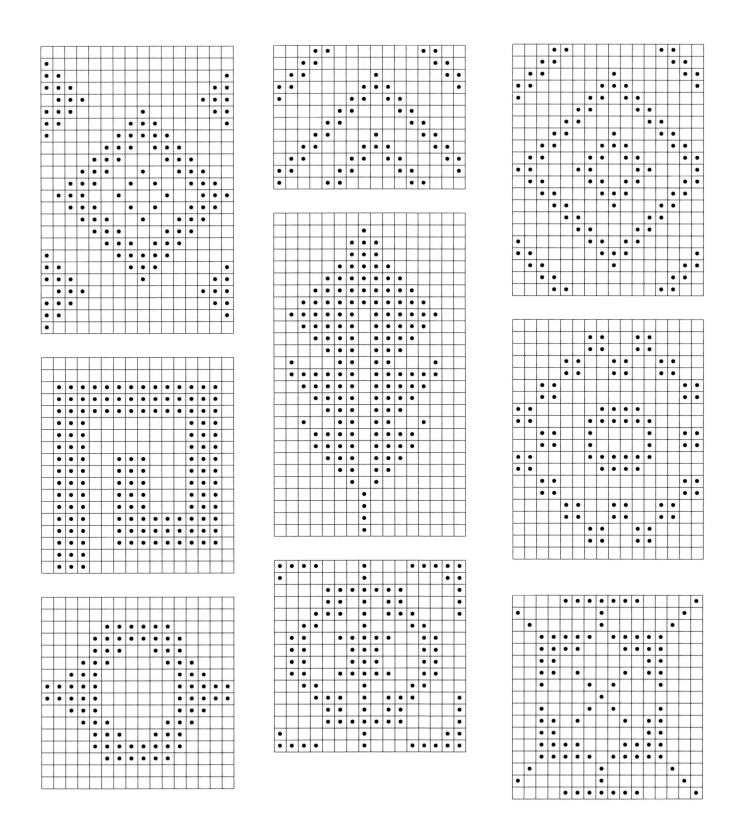

▶ 20 st repeat

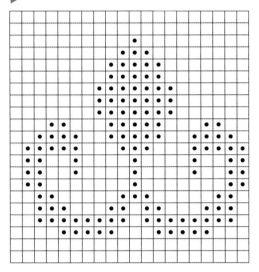

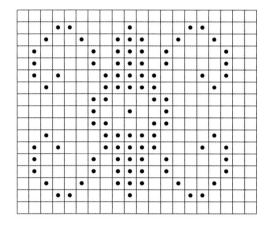

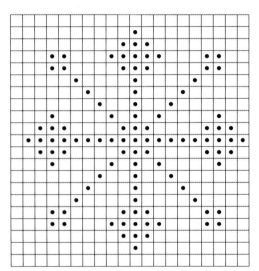

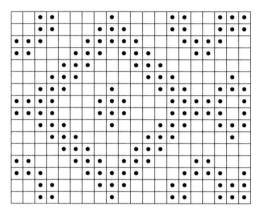

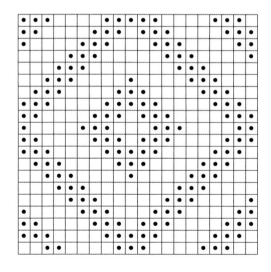

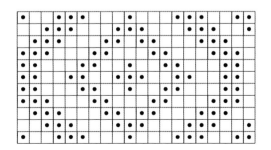

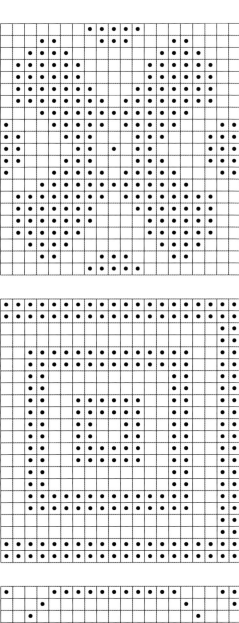

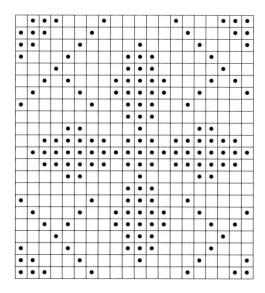

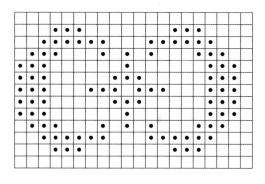

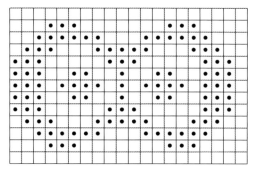

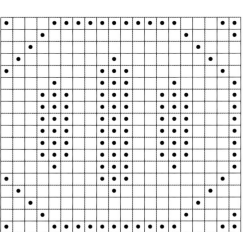

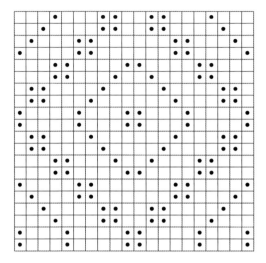

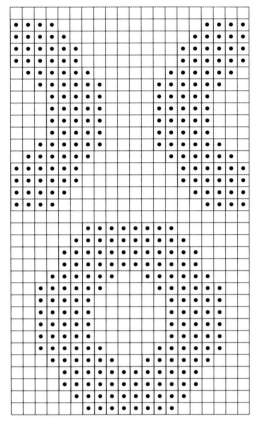

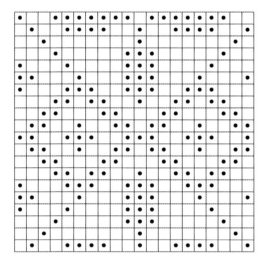

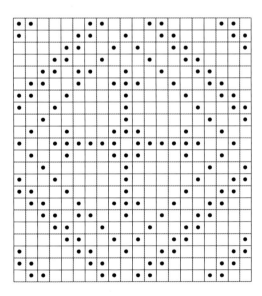

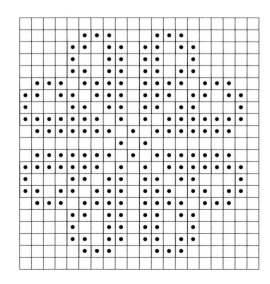

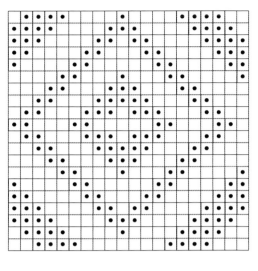

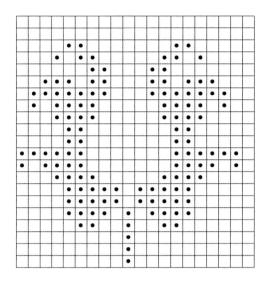

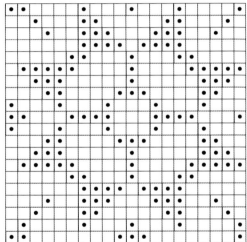

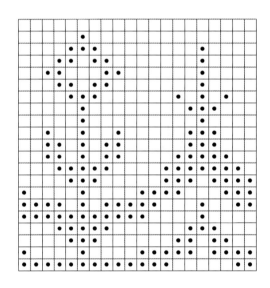

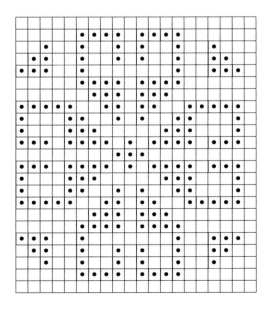

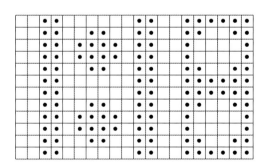

20 st repeat

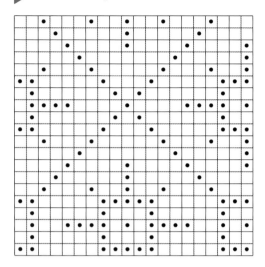

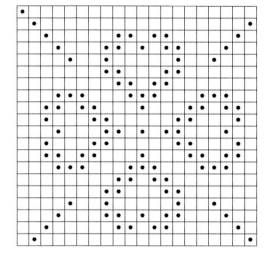

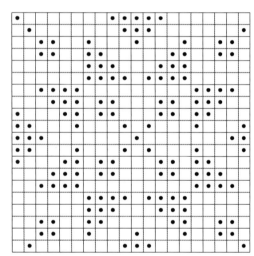

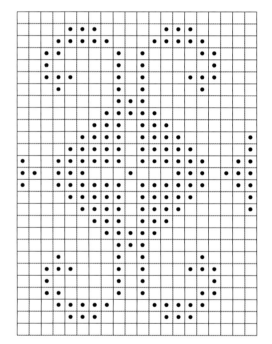

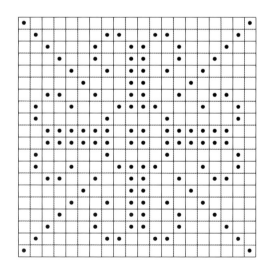

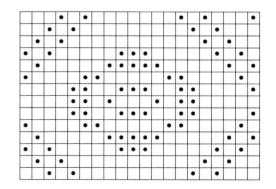

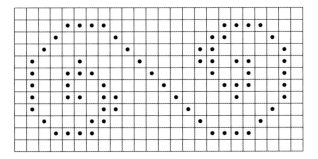

24 st repeat

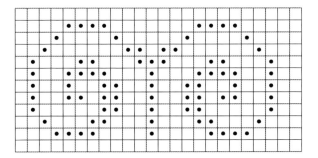

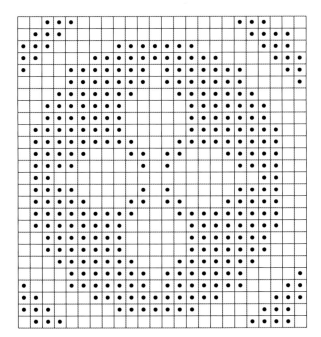

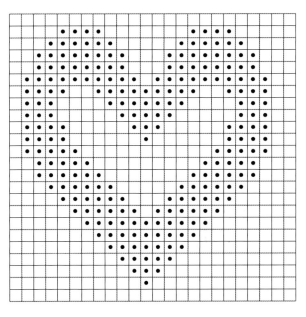

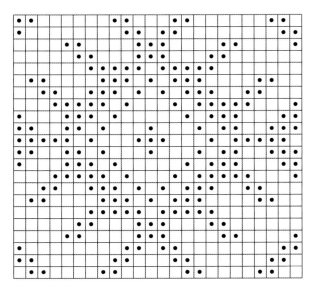

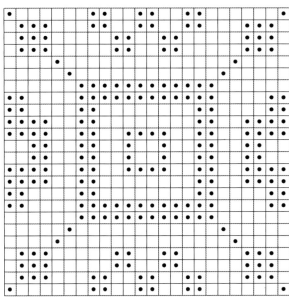

24 st repeat

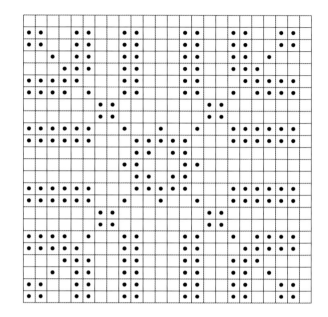

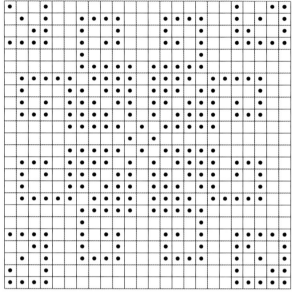

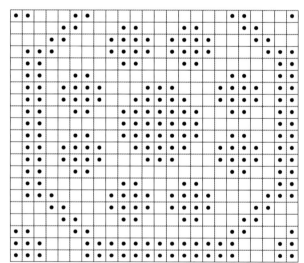

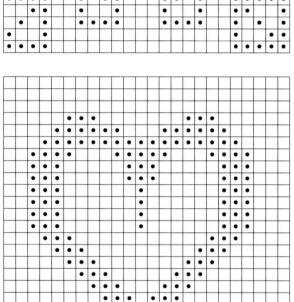

▶ 30 st repeat

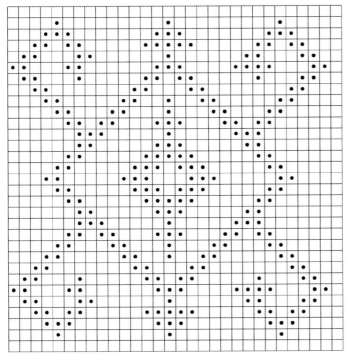

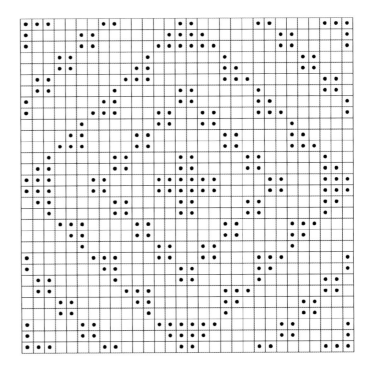

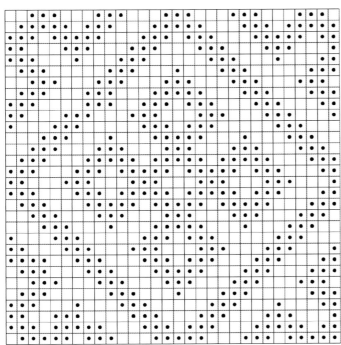

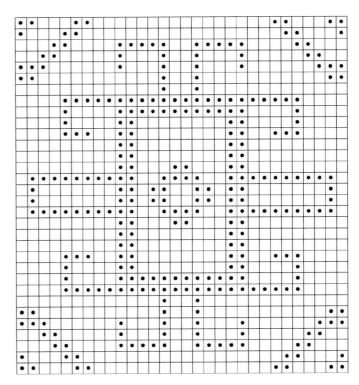

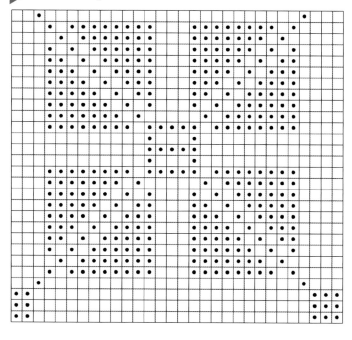

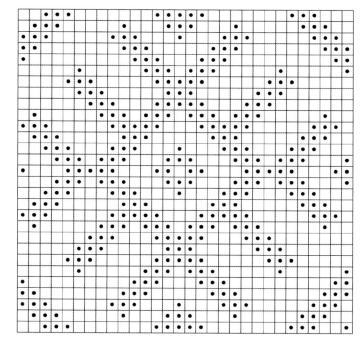

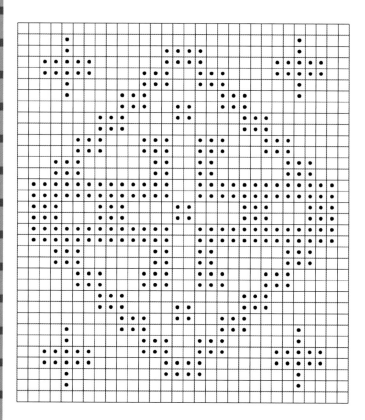

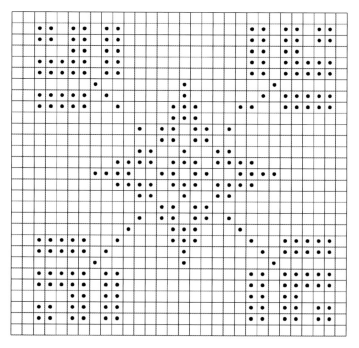

Abbreviations & Techniques

Abbreviations

approx	approximately
beg	begin(ning)
CC	contrasting color
ch	chain
cm	centimeter(s)
cn	cable needle
cont	continu(e)(ing)
dec	decreas(e)(ing)
dpn	double-pointed needle(s)
foll	follow(s)(ing)
g	gram(s)
inc	increas(e)(ing)
k	knit
LH	left-hand
lp(s)	loop(s)
m	meter(s)
mm	millimeter(s)
MC	main color
M1	make one
M1 p-st	make 1 purl stitch
oz	ounce(s)
p	purl
pat(s)	pattern(s)
pm	place marker
psso	pass slip stitch(es) over
rem	remain(s)(ing)
rep	repeat

RH	right-hand
RS	right side(s)
rnd(s)	round(s)
SKP	slip 1, knit 1, pass slip stitch over—one stitch has been decreased
SK2P	slip 1, knit 2 together, pass slip stitch over the knit 2 together—two stitches have been decreased
S2KP	slip 2 stitches together, knit 1, pass 2 slip stitches over knit 1
sl	slip
sl st	slip stitch
ssk	slip, slip, knit
sssk	slip, slip, slip, knit
st(s)	stitch(es)
St st	stockinette stitch
tbl	through back loop(s)
tog	together
WS	wrong side(s)
wyib	with yarn in back
wyif	with yarn in front
yd	yard(s)
yo	yarn over needle
*	repeat directions following * as many times as indicated
[ ]	repeat directions inside brackets as many times as indicated

Resources

Nashua Handknits *Julia* **Yarn**
Westminster Fibers
8 Shelter Drive
Greer, SC 29650
www.nashuaknits.com
info@nashuaknits.com

Bag Handles
Homestead Heirlooms LLC
Pewaukee, WI
262-352-8738
www.homesteadheirlooms.com

Bolster Insert
Company Store
La Crosse, WI
800-323-8000
www.thecompanystore.com

Foam
Buy Foam
866-672-3626
www.buyfoam.com

Spiral Bun Feet
Osborne Wood Products
4618 Highway 123N
Toccoa, GA 30577
800-849-8876
www.osbornewood.com

Zippers
Stan's Sewing Supplies
www.stanssewingsupplies.com

Contact Kristin
getting-stitched-on-the-farm.blogspot.com

Joining Seams

KITCHENER STITCH

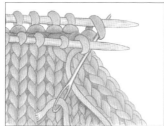

1. Insert tapestry needle purlwise (as shown) through first stitch on front needle. Pull yarn through, leaving that stitch on knitting needle.

2. Insert tapestry needle knitwise (as shown) through first stitch on back needle. Pull yarn through, leaving stitch on knitting needle.

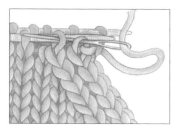

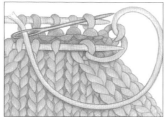

3. Insert tapestry needle knitwise through first stitch on front needle, slip stitch off needle and insert tapestry needle purlwise (as shown) through next stitch on front needle. Pull yarn through, leaving this stitch on needle.

4. Insert tapestry needle purlwise through first stitch on back needle. Slip stitch off needle and insert tapestry needle knitwise (as shown) through next stitch on back needle. Pull yarn through, leaving this stitch on needle.

Repeat steps 3 and 4 until all stitches on both front and back needles have been grafted. Fasten off and weave in end.

HOW TO MAKE A POMPOM

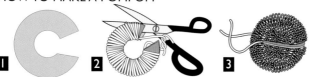

1. Cut two circular pieces of cardboard the width of the desired pompom, with a center hole in each. Then cut a pie-shaped wedge out of each circle. **2.** Hold the two circles together and wrap the yarn tightly around the cardboard. Then carefully cut around the cardboard. **3.** Tie a piece of yarn tightly between the two circles. Remove the cardboard and trim the pompom.

MATTRESS STITCH

1. To begin seaming
If you have left a long tail from your cast-on row, you can use this strand to begin sewing. To make a neat join at the lower edge with no gap, use the technique shown here.

Thread the strand into a yarn needle. With right sides of both pieces facing you, insert the yarn needle from back to front into the corner stitch of the piece without the tail. Making a figure eight with the yarn, insert the needle from back to front into the stitch with the cast-on tail. Tighten to close the gap.

2. Vertical seam
The vertical seam is worked from the right side and is used to join two edges row by row. It hides the uneven stitches at the edge of a row and creates an invisible seam, making it appear that the knitting is continuous.

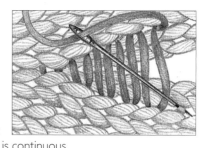

Insert the yarn needle under the horizontal bar between the first and second stitches. Insert the needle into the corresponding bar on the other piece. Continue alternating from side to side.

3. Horizontal seam
This seam is used to join two bound-off edges, and is worked stitch by stitch. You must have the same number of stitches on each piece so that the finished seam will resemble a continuous row of knit stitches. Be sure to pull the yarn tight enough to hide the bound-off edges.

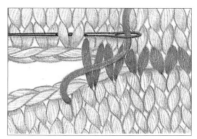

With the bound-off edges together, lined up stitch for stitch, insert the yarn needle under a stitch inside the bound-off edge of one side and then under the corresponding stitch on the other side. Repeat all the way across the join.

Embroidery Stitches

Running Stitch

Spider Web Stitch

You can use any number of "spokes" to start your web, as long as it is an odd number.

Instant Stitch Sampler

The Bloomsbury Gauntlets (page 36) use several of these embroidery stitches.

Lazy Daisy Stitch

Fern Stitch

French Knots

Woven Bar Stitch

Chain Stitch

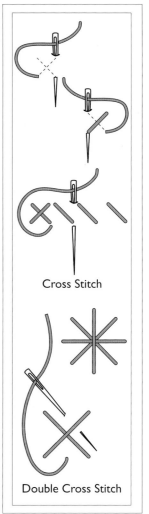

Cross Stitch

Double Cross Stitch

Acknowledgments

It takes a whole lot of people to make a book.
I have been fortunate to work with the talented staff at Sixth&Spring Books,
including my publisher Trisha Malcolm, stylist Julie Hines, managing editor Wendy Williams,
senior editor Michelle Bredeson, editor Erin Slonaker, technical editor Carla Scott,
creative director Joe Vior and especially art director Diane Lamphron, who directed the
photo shoot and designed this lovely book. Thanks to photographer John Gruen, whose eye
for light, beautiful backdrops and detail give the location photos their very special feeling.
Thanks to the beautiful models who happen to be my friends, too—Margaret Breeden,
Shalee Pratt, Bridget and Matthew Kenney and my daughter, Julia. I thank all of you for
bringing my vision to print in such a pretty and colorful way.

◆

Without a dedicated and talented group of knitters,
I would never be able to pull off such a large project. Millie Bankert, Robin Howard,
Therese Inverso, Margaret Maney, Jeanne Moran, Peggy Shuler and Noelle Wise
all contributed their knitting skills to this project.
A very special thanks to knitter and friend Susan Miles who has knit me out of so
many jams I'm afraid to count—including many of the projects on these pages.
Thank you all for your stunning work. Thanks to
Pat Harste for her technical editing skills and for making
sure every pattern is just right.

◆

A special thanks to my friends at Nashua Handknits who supplied all of the yarn for this
book and market my *Julia* yarn to yarn stores in the United States and Canada.
My friend Linda Pratt continues to be my greatest cheerleader, supporting me during every
step of my knitwear career. Susan Mills and Judi Gioioso constantly
step in to help out along my way.

◆

Thank you to my mom, Nancy K. Nicholas, who taught me that salmon is different from
cantaloupe, orange, persimmon or peach and that every color is beautiful.

◆

To all the knitters out there who have embraced and encouraged me along the way by
buying my books, knitting my designs, using my yarn, sending me letters and reading my blog
"Getting Stitched on the Farm," I thank you. May you enjoy this book full of colorful projects
as much as I have enjoyed putting it together for you.

◆

And, finally, to my fellow farmers in life—my husband, Mark Duprey, and our
daughter, Julia Nicholas Duprey—thank you for grounding me in reality and for putting up
with the lack of normality that comes with a project of this size. Life's a journey
and I'm so fortunate to have you two to share it with.

172